AQA Sociology

GCSE

Grahame Coates
Terry Gilpin
Rosie Owens
Ian Woodfield

Nelson Thornes

Published in 2009 by:
Nelson Thornes Ltd
Delta Place
27 Bath Road
CHELTENHAM
GL53 7TH
United Kingdom

10 11 12 13 / 10 9 8 7 6 5 4 3

A catalogue record for this book is available from the British Library

ISBN 978 1 4085 0270 9

Cover photograph by Jack Hollingsworth / Getty
Illustrations by Rupert Besley
Page make-up by AMR Design Ltd (www.amrdesign.com)

Printed and bound in China by 1010 Printing International Ltd

Contents

Introduction   5

UNIT ONE

1   Studying society   8

1.1   What is sociology?   8

1.2   How do we understand the language that sociologists use?   12

1.3   What is a social structure?   16

1.4   What is a social process?   20

1.5   What is a social issue?   24

1.6   What is quantitative research?   28

1.7   What is qualitative research?   34

1.8   Exam questions for Studying society   38

2   Education   42

2.1   Why do we have schools?   42

2.2   How do we measure educational success and failure?   44

2.3   What is the hidden curriculum?   48

2.4   What influences educational success beyond school?   52

2.5   Why is education a political issue?   58

2.6   What does social research tell us about education in contemporary Britain?   62

2.7   Exam questions for Education   66

3   Families   70

3.1   What is a family?   70

3.2   What is the conventional nuclear family?   74

3.3   Is marriage in decline?   78

3.4   What are role relationships in the family and how have they changed over time?   82

3.5   What are the alternatives to the family?   86

3.6   What does social research tell us about families in contemporary Britain?   88

3.7   Exam questions for Families   92

UNIT TWO

4   Crime and deviance   96

4.1   What is crime and deviance?   96

4.2   How do we measure the amount of criminal behaviour in society?   98

4.3   How do we explain criminal and deviant behaviour?   102

4.4   How do we attempt to control anti-social behaviour?   106

4.5   Who commits crime?   110

4.6   What does social research tell us about crime and deviance in contemporary Britain?   116

4.7   Exam questions for Crime and deviance   119

5   Mass media   122

5.1   What are the mass media?   122

5.2   Who owns the mass media?   126

5.3   What effect does the mass media have on society?   130

5.4   What are media stereotypes?   134

5.5   What is the impact of technological change?   138

5.6   What does social research tell us
about the mass media in Britain?   142

5.7   Exam questions for Mass media   145

6   Power   **148**

6.1   How democratic is Britain's political
system?   148

6.2   How involved are individual citizens
in the political process?   152

6.3   What is social reform?   156

6.4   Who has the power?   160

6.5   Who is in control?   164

6.6   What does social research tell us
about power in contemporary
Britain?   168

6.7   Exam questions for Power   171

7   Social inequality   **174**

7.1   What is social stratification?   174

7.2   What are life chances?   178

7.3   What barriers to achievement
exist?   182

7.4   How is wealth distributed in Britain
today?   186

7.5   What does it mean to be poor in
Britain today?   190

7.6   What does social research tell us
about social stratification in
contemporary Britain?   194

7.7   Exam questions for Social
inequality   196

Glossary   200

Index   208

Acknowledgements   212

Nelson Thornes has worked in partnership with AQA to make sure that this book offers you the best possible support for your GCSE course. All the content has been approved by the senior examining team at AQA, so you can be sure that it gives you just what you need when you are preparing for your exams.

How to use this book

This book covers everything you need for your course.

Learning Objectives

At the beginning of each section or topic you'll find a list of Learning Objectives based on the requirements of the specification, so you can make sure you are covering everything you need to know for the exam.

> **Objectives**
> **Objectives**
> **Objectives**
> **Objectives**
> First objective.
> Second objective.

AQA Examiner's Tips

Don't forget to look at the AQA Examiner's Tips throughout the book to help you with your study and prepare for your exam.

> **AQA Examiner's tip**
>
> Don't forget to look at the AQA Examiner's Tips throughout the book to help you with your study and prepare for your exam.

AQA Examination-style Questions

These offer opportunities to practise doing questions in the style that you can expect in your exam so that you can be fully prepared on the day.

AQA examination questions are reproduced by permission of the Assessment and Qualifications Alliance.

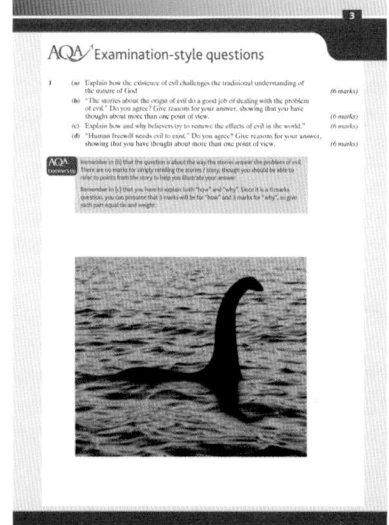

Visit **www.nelsonthornes.com/aqagcse** for more information.

What is sociology?

A key proposition for sociologists is that society exists and has a 'life of its own' which can be studied without reference to the particular individuals who live in it. We may each think we are unique but sociologists observe another reality: that our life with others is predictable and follows patterns. Studying sociology introduces students to the major patterns which constitute social life in 21st century Britain.

Whether sociology can or should be scientific like physics or biology has often been debated. There is no disagreement, however, about the need for sociological analysis to be based on evidence. From its beginnings, 'facts and figures' have been a cornerstone of sociology. Techniques for gathering data have been developed and refined. Today, researchers have available a range of methods which, when applied appropriately, produce results considered trustworthy.

■ AQA GCSE Sociology

AQA GCSE Sociology recognises the importance of research for a thorough understanding of the subject. Although you are no longer required to submit a piece of coursework, the examination continues to ask candidates how they would plan and conduct a sociological investigation. This textbook offers many opportunities for you to develop an understanding of research and its significance within sociology.

Students often ask their teachers: 'But what is the right answer?' 'There isn't one!' may seem a frustrating answer to those who prefer cut and dried answers. There have always been, and always will be, differing sociological approaches. The AQA GCSE Sociology specification expects you to be introduced to some of these, not in a 'so-and-so said this, and so-and-so said that' history of ideas way, but through reference to the discussions that differing viewpoints generate. Think about a woman taking her children to school. What do you see – an individual fulfilling her female destiny or an individual deprived by her gender of opportunities to be what she could have been? Think of mounted police charging pickets in the 1984 miners' strike. What do you see – brave public servants upholding law and order or agents of the coal bosses helping to exploit their workforce?

This book will help you to understand the ways in which such questions are discussed in sociology. It will point you in the direction of evidence, on the basis of which you can then judge the strengths and weaknesses of answers.

The specification

Content

The Studying Society section of Unit 1 is compulsory for those studying the Short Course and the Full Course. It invites you to learn about the kind of discipline that sociology is. What distinguishes sociology from other '-ologies'? With what sort of issues is it concerned? How does it study its subject matter? This section provides an appropriate context within which to develop an understanding of selected aspects of social life.

Some other areas of social activity are so fundamental to the existence of society that they need to be studied by anyone wishing to 'do sociology'. This is why Education and Families are also compulsory areas for both the Full Course and the Short Course.

- Education looks, for example, at why the social background of pupils influences their educational achievements.

- Families addresses such issues as how the changing nature of relationships between men and women influences the ways in which we live together.

Those studying the Full Course study a further four topics in Unit 2.

- Crime and Deviance raises questions about the accuracy of people's perceptions about the pattern of law-breaking behaviour in Britain.

- Mass Media looks at the influence that all forms of the mass media have on the way we see ourselves and others.

- Power looks, for example, at the extent to which the 'man and woman in the street' can influence political decisions.

- Social Inequality asks, among other things, why some live in luxury while others have little.

As a member of British society, you will be familiar in a general way with much of the content of these sections. This familiarity can offer a basis for knowledge. It can, on the other hand, create difficulties if you take your personal experience to be typical, rather than reflecting sociologically on these experiences. Undertaking the activities in the book will help you to develop your ability to be objective, which will help your performance in the exam.

Assessment

Each unit is assessed by means of an examination lasting 1 hour 30 minutes. For Unit 1 you must answer all three questions on the paper. For Unit 2 you must choose to answer three of the four questions on the paper. Each question covers a topic. Between them, the seven questions cover the whole of the content of the Full Course.

Questions are made up of a set of sub-questions, each requiring a different form of response. Sub-questions worth fewer marks can be answered successfully in single words, figures or sentences; those worth more marks require paragraphs or, for the final sub-question, a mini essay. To help to stimulate and guide your thinking on the topic, each question includes two sources, such as charts, extracts or photographs.

This textbook, and the accompanying online resources, offer guidance on how to answer exam questions successfully. They also give you the chance to practise answering questions yourself.

Features in this book

This book contains many features to help you learn and revise effectively.

Objectives

You will find these in the margin at the beginning of each topic within a chapter. They are based on the requirements of the specification, so you can make sure you are covering everything you need to know for the exam.

Check your understanding

You will find these questions at the end of each topic within a chapter. When you answer these questions you will immediately find out whether you have understood and can remember what you have read.

Activities

These occur on most pages and are aimed at helping you to learn actively. Many of them refer to textual and visual sources so they help you to develop your analytical skills.

Going further

Many of these activities encourage you to carry out further research on the topic, either in the classroom or at home. In some cases, suggestions are made about websites to use. These research activities will help to broaden your knowledge of the topic and develop useful examples to use when answering exam questions.

Did you know

These provide short sharp snippets of information.

Links

If there is relevant information in a different part of the book you will find a link to it in the margin.

Examiner's tips

The AQA Examiner's tips throughout the book will give you an insight into what examiners expect as well as pitfalls to avoid.

Exam questions

Guidance is given on how to answer exam questions effectively. Exemplar questions are also included at the end of every chapter. Try answering these so you are fully prepared.

1.1   What is sociology?

What is sociology?

Very few of us live our lives on our own – we are all in regular contact with other people and we interact with other people in groups and in various organisations.

We are all members of groups such as families, peer groups and friendship groups and we will come into contact with organisations such as the school, the workplace, the church, the legal system, the political system and the mass media.

Sociology is the study of the **society** in which we live and it examines how we are influenced and shaped through being members of groups and organisations. It concentrates on:

- the way we make society what it is
- the way society makes us what we are.

Activity

1   With you in the centre, draw a spider diagram to show all the groups and organisations to which you belong that help to shape you as a member of British society.

What does it mean to belong to a society?

> *There is no such thing as society. There are individual men and women, and there are families.*
>
> Margaret Thatcher, Prime Minister, 1987

If you are studying sociology you are likely to disagree strongly with this statement. Being a member of a society means that we all have something in common, and that common thread is our **culture**. We all share a way of life that is different from those who live in other cultures and this is defined by a set of laws, norms, roles and values.

Our everyday behaviour is shaped and guided by a set of formal written rules (**laws**) and informal, unwritten rules (**norms**) that are special to our particular culture. Breaking a law would lead to punishment whereas breaking a norm would be disapproved of.

We all perform a number of **roles** in our society. These are special patterns of behaviour expected of people in different situations. A teacher in front of a class will take on a completely different role from when she is interacting as a mother with her own children. A group of

Key terms

Society: a group of people who have common interests and a distinctive culture.

Culture: the whole way of life of a group of people passed from one generation to the next.

Law: a set of written rules regulating what may or may not be done by members of a society.

Norm: an informal rule that guides our behaviour in a particular situation.

Role: patterns of behaviour expected of people in different situations.

students will behave differently when they are in the classroom, out with their friends or at home with their parents.

To feel a part of the society in which we live there are likely to be a set of **values** that are shared by most members. We all have beliefs about what is right and wrong, what is good and bad, what is important and not important and these form the basis of our values.

A Varying norms

Activity

2 What is it that defines our culture? How has it changed over time and how is it different from other cultures?

Draw out the chart below and, in groups of three or four, try to think of at least one example for each of the 12 boxes.

	Give an example in Britain today	Give an example to show how they have changed in our society over the last 100 years	Give an example to show how they are different today in another culture
Laws			
Norms			
Roles			
Values			

Is it all just common sense?

Just because sociologists look at groups and organisations that we experience as part of our everyday life, it doesn't mean to say that we understand everything about how they work and how they influence our lives.

Sociologists try to look beneath the surface and are often quite critical of what they see. They also question and challenge things that perhaps we take for granted. Is the family the best 'breeding ground' for children? Is the family a marvellous institution for everyone in it? Is there a 'dark side' to family life? These are some of the themes that might be explored from a sociological perspective. As Peter Berger said, 'Things are not always what they seem.'

Sociologists try their best to be objective in the work they do. They develop theories, do practical research, collect and analyse data. In this way sociology is seen as a **social science**.

Sociology therefore focuses on the way individuals are influenced by groups and organisations. This differs from psychology, which looks at what makes individuals tick and particularly at the development of their personality and behaviour patterns.

Sociologists collect evidence, which can be assessed and checked by other sociologists. This differs from journalism, which presents a set of facts that are often seen as sensational or one-sided.

Why bother with social research at all?

The work that sociologists do helps to 'bring into the open' some of the serious social issues that are challenging our society at any particular time. They sometimes result in political discussions that lead to the development of **social policy** and sometimes to new laws that affect everyone. For example: debate, discussion and social research could consider the importance of good parenting. This might lead to changes in paid maternity and paternity leave or might lead to changes in the tax and benefits system for families with young children.

We can't change our society for the better until we know what needs to be improved and studying it from a sociological perspective helps us to focus on the big issues.

Activity

3 What does it mean to think sociologically? Why don't sociologists just accept everyday events without question?

List the skills that you think you will develop through your study of sociology that could help you move into one of the jobs mentioned in the Case study 'What job can I get?'.

Going further

The Joseph Rowntree Foundation (www.jrf.org.uk) is an organisation set up to try to 'overcome the causes of poverty, disadvantage and social evil'. Take a look at their website and have a look at some of the current programmes that use social research to bring about social change and a fairer society.

What job can I get?

Sociology graduates are found in a variety of jobs. Among the favourites are those in the social services, which, with a bit of extra study, could involve becoming a social worker. Alternatively, a job in education, the criminal justice system, in local and central government as a researcher or in the voluntary sector, perhaps working as a fundraiser, community development worker or counsellor, could be more your thing.

You will also have the skills to pursue a career in journalism, management or in academia.

Guardian Unlimited, 1 May 2008

B *Jobs that sociology students may get*

Check your understanding

1 What is the difference between a law and a norm? Give examples of both.

2 How is sociology different from psychology?

3 What do we mean when we say that sociology is a social science?

How do we understand the language that sociologists use?

What is a theoretical approach?

Although all sociologists look at the same picture of society, what they see depends on their **theoretical perspective**.

Some (structuralists) look at the big picture and show how society makes us what we are. They concentrate on the way that the structure of society has an influence on our everyday lives.

Others (interactionists) focus down on smaller groups and individuals – they concentrate on the way people behave within society, how they interact with others and how people live their daily lives which, in turn, makes society what it is.

Conflict or consensus theories

What is consensus?

Some sociologists say that society is held together because people share a set of key norms and values that are passed down from one generation to the next through the process we know as socialisation. They are very positive about the organisations and institutions in society and there is a general level of agreement on the way that society should develop. This is the basis of the **consensus** approach to sociology. Another word for consensus is agreement.

The main group of sociologists that follow these ideas are referred to as functionalists. Functionalists see all the different parts of society working together like the parts of a well-oiled machine. Each part has a role to play in making sure the machine works well – they all perform a function and they all need to work well in order for the machine to do its job properly.

Objectives

You will be able to:

- recognise that there are different theoretical approaches to studying society

- recognise the significance of different types of evidence in social research.

Key terms

Theoretical perspective: looking at a social issue through the eyes of one particular type of theorist.

⊂⊃links

Also see Topic 1.4 to find out more about socialisation.

Activity

1. The example used above is sometimes called the mechanical analogy as it compares society to a machine. The other example often used is called the organic analogy as it compares society to a living organism. Look in a biology textbook and choose the best example that shows parts of a plant or animal working together to make sure that the organism stays healthy.

A *All parts working smoothly*

What is conflict?

Some sociologists see society as being organised and structured so that some groups do better than others. This means that some people have control and the power to decide what others should do. A society organised in this way automatically involves disagreement and **conflict**.

Social classes have developed because wealth and power are not shared out equally in society. The group of sociologists who see social class as the main cause of conflict are referred to as Marxist sociologists. The differences that exist between the ruling class and the working class are the real reasons for disagreement and conflict. Workers are paid a wage but it is way below the value of the goods they produce as the capitalist class 'creams off' the rest of the money in the form of profits – they are seen to be exploiting their workers.

Some **feminist** sociologists identify conflict between men and women in society (gender conflict) as their main concern. Radical feminists see the root of the problem as male power or **patriarchy** and believe that this is seen in all institutions in society from the family through to the world of work.

Marxist feminists see the big problem springing from the fact that women 'look after' men who work in a **capitalist** system. If women do work, what they do is seen as less important than the work of men.

B *Wages for all workers?*

Did you know ??????

You can access information collected in large scale social research projects as much of the statistical data is available online.

Activity

2   Divide into two groups, one representing the Family and the other representing Schools. Then divide each of these groups into two and ask one to write down the key features as seen from a consensus perspective and the other from a conflict perspective. Arguments, or at least debate, should follow!

Going further

Why not look into the idea that not only women, but men also, can be feminists.

Feminist blogs might be a good starting point to examine the debate.

How do they present their data?

Later in this chapter you will look at the key features of both **quantitative** and **qualitative** data. Sociologists taking an interactionist approach would be likely to concentrate on qualitative data and be interested more in discussing the findings from observation and unstructured interviews. Their data would not, for example, be looking at graphs and percentages. Sociologists taking a more structural view would be more likely to look at social surveys. The data that structuralists collect allows them to compare responses between different groups in society.

The graphs and tables here are examples of quantitative data that might be generated from a social survey but the data doesn't speak for itself, it has to be analysed and evaluated. The activities suggested are examples of the questions you might look at if you had collected the data and wanted to make the meaning clear to others.

Key terms

Quantitative data: information that is presented as numbers which can be analysed using statistical methods.

Qualitative data: information in the form of text or images, that is rich in description and detail.

∞ links

Also see Topic 1.6 and Topic 1.7 if you want to find out more about the differences between quantitative and qualitative data.

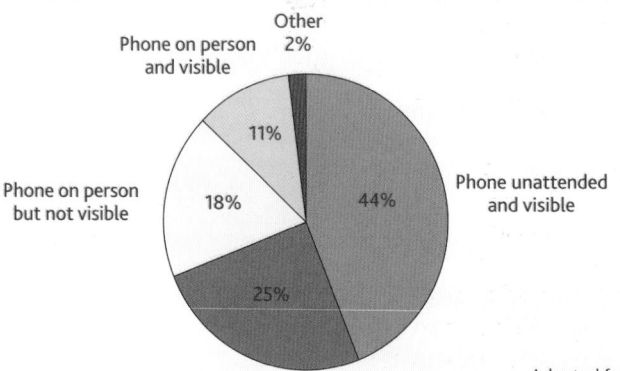

Mobile phone theft: by circumstance of how phone was stolen

Adapted from British Crime Survey (2008)

C *Mobile phone thefts*

Activity

3 Using pie chart **C**, answer these questions:

a What conclusions can you make based on the data in the pie chart above?

b What practical suggestions would you make to reduce the level of mobile phone theft?

Bar and column charts help people to see the relationships between one set of figures and another. In the one below, you would look for patterns and trends between offences and offenders.

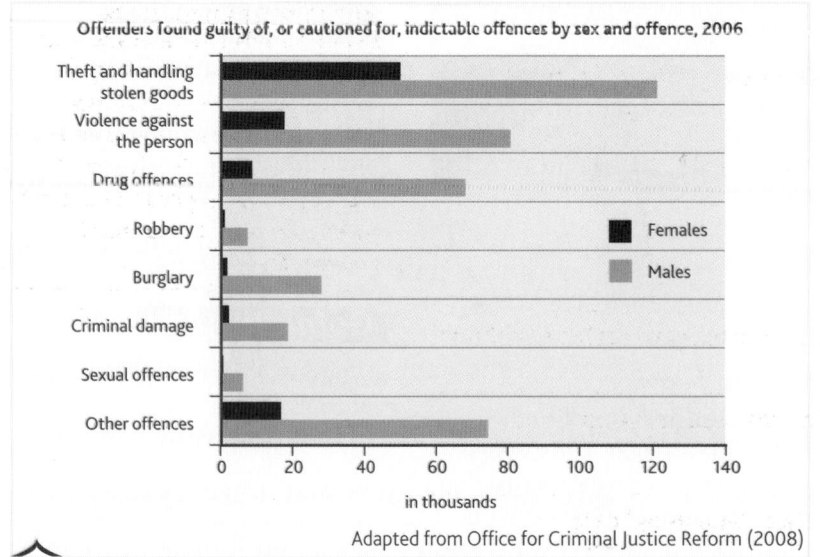

Offenders found guilty of, or cautioned for, indictable offences by sex and offence, 2006

in thousands

Adapted from Office for Criminal Justice Reform (2008)

D *Indictable offences*

Activity

4 Using bar chart **D**, answer these questions:

a What is the most striking trend in the data?

b What surprises you about the data?

c Do you understand the categories? What is the difference between burglary and robbery?

d Do you understand the title? What is an indictable offence?

e What 'other offences' can you think of that don't fit the main categories?

Case study

Choosing the best method

Sometimes sociologists simply choose the method they think will give them the best picture of events. Paul Willis, studying from a Marxist viewpoint, used observation – no graphs and charts here at all. You can probably see why when you look at the focus of his study.

Willis studied 12 working-class boys in a Midlands secondary school. He argued that these 'lads' (as they identified themselves) formed a distinctive 'counter-school sub-cultural grouping' characterised by opposition to the values and norms of the school. This group of disaffected boys felt superior to the more conformist pupils who they labelled as 'ear 'oles'. They showed little interest in academic work, preferring instead to amuse themselves as best they could through various forms of deviant behaviour in which 'having a laff' became the main objective of the school day. The lads also tried to identify with the adult, non-school world, by smoking, drinking and expressing strongly sexist and racist attitudes. Academic work had no value for these boys, who had little interest in gaining qualifications and saw manual work as superior to mental work.

Activities

5 Thinking of your own school or college, can you identify any sub-cultures similar to those described in the case study?

6 Suggest some reasons why sub-cultures form.

AQA **Examiner's tip**

Don't try too hard to make sociologists wear a particular theoretical label. Sometimes a piece of social research uses a variety of approaches and doesn't have a dominant theoretical framework.

Check your understanding

1 Why are interactionist sociologists more likely to gather qualitative data?

2 What problems do radical feminists see with patriarchy?

3 What is an analogy?

4 Explain what we mean when we talk of 'analysing' data.

Organisation and structure

We talk of structures in everyday life. A bridge has a structure to it, being made up of many different parts (cables, nuts, bolts, girders, etc.). All these parts work together to build the bridge and make it safe and secure.

All societies are built up of different parts and all are organised in some way. There are patterns of relationships and a set of organisations that act as the scaffolding that keeps society stable. All of the essential parts of society have a job to perform and they all fit with each other to hold society together.

Most societies have a system of **social stratification** as a basic element of their structure. Having different layers in a society highlights the differences between the groups but it also means that those in the same group have a feeling of togetherness. Sociologists see **social class** as a powerful form of stratification but other layers can be drawn depending on such features as age, **ethnicity**, **gender**, etc.

Placing people within these layers or **strata** means that some will be in higher or lower positions and some will have power, whereas others will be relatively powerless.

Social class in modern Britain

Social class can be measured in a number of ways but most social class scales use your occupation to decide where to place you. The scale introduced in 2001, which is now used in all official reports, is shown in Table **A**. It replaced a set of groupings known as the Registrar General's Classification that had been used since 1911. Some of the research you might come across could have used this classification and this can be seen in Table **B**. Market researchers and advertisers use the social grade classification shown in Table **C**.

Activities

1. Where do you place yourself on the scales in tables **A**, **B** and **C**? Why?

2. In a two-parent family where both parents work, whose job do you think should be used?

3. Why do you think there is no mention of 'upper' class in these scales?

4. In Table **A**, where do you draw the line between the middle class and working class?

Key terms

Social stratification: the way different groups in society are placed at different levels.

Social class: people having the same social status measured by such things as occupation and income.

Ethnicity: the classification of people into groups that share the same culture, history and identity.

Gender: the social and cultural differences between the sexes – between femininity and masculinity.

Strata: bands or layers showing particular characteristics which are different from those above and below.

Status: the honour or prestige attached to a person's position in society.

AQA Examiner's tip

Remember that each element of stratification can be considered on its own or in combination with others. You could look at the lower **status** of the working class but you might consider age, ethnicity and gender at the same time, for example, young, Afro-Caribbean, working-class males.

Did you know ???????

It is estimated that there are now over 425,000 millionaires in the UK, most of them based in London and the south-east of England.

A *National Statistics Socio-economic classification*

NS-SEC group	Examples of jobs	% of those employed
1.1 Employers and managers in larger organisations	company directors, senior company managers, senior civil servants, senior officers in police and armed forces	4.3
1.2 Higher professionals	doctors, lawyers, clergy, teachers and social workers	6.8
2 Lower managerial and professional occupations	nurses and midwives, journalists, actors, musicians, prison officers, lower ranks of police and armed forces	23.5
3 Intermediate occupations	clerks, secretaries, driving instructors, computer operators	14.0
4 Small employers and own account workers	publicans, farmers, taxi drivers, window cleaners, painters and decorators	9.9
5 Lower supervisory, craft and related occupations	printers, plumbers, television engineers, train drivers, butchers	9.8
6 Semi-routine occupations	shop assistants, hairdressers, bus drivers, cooks	18.6
7 Routine occupations	cleaners, labourers, waiters and refuse collectors	12.7
8 Never had paid work and the long term unemployed		

B *Registrar General's classification*

Class category	Class group	Examples of jobs	Middle/ Working Class
I	Professional occupations	accountant, doctor, university lecturer, dentist	MC
II	Managerial and technical	teacher, nurse, librarian, manager	MC
IIIN	Skilled occupations – non-manual	sales rep, shop assistant, secretary, policeman	MC
IIIM	Skilled occupations – manual	electrician, plumber, joiner, cook	WC
IV	Partly skilled occupations	postal worker, farm worker, bar worker, packer	WC
V	Unskilled occupations	labourer, cleaner, refuse collector, porter	WC

C *Social grade classification*

Class category	Class group	Explanation	% of population in each group
A	Upper middle class	very senior managers, top civil servants	3
B	Middle class	middle managers in large organisations, top managers in small organisations	20
C1	Lower middle class	junior managers and supervisors or clerical workers	28
C2	Skilled working class	skilled manual workers	21
D	Working class	semi and unskilled manual workers	18
E	Those at subsistence level	those who depend on the state for their income	10

Is social class still important?

To answer this question you need to look at whether there are still differences in the way that people in different social classes experience life. Is there inequality, for example, in lifestyle, health, educational qualifications? Some think that the inequalities that are seen between genders and ethnic groups are more important than those created by social class.

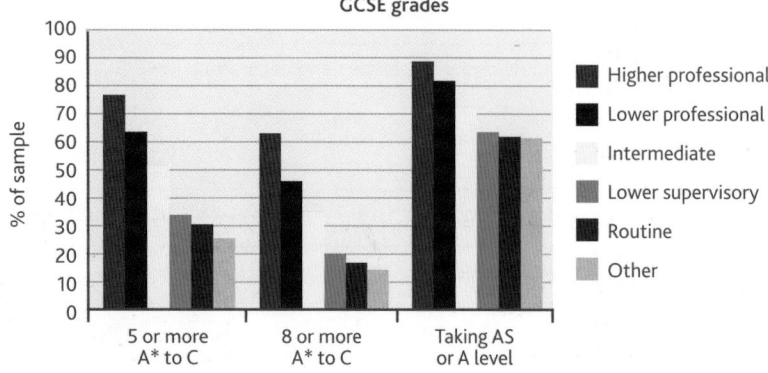

GCSE grades

Legend:
- Higher professional
- Lower professional
- Intermediate
- Lower supervisory
- Routine
- Other

y-axis: % of sample (0–100)

x-axis categories: 5 or more A* to C | 8 or more A* to C | Taking AS or A level

Adapted from ONS (2007)

D *GCSE grades*

Infant mortality rates

y-axis: Rate per 1000 live births (0–10)

x-axis: Class 1 and 2 | Class 3 | Class 4, 5, 6 and 7 | Class 8

NS–SEC

Adapted from ONS (2004)

E *Infant mortality*

Discussion activity

Do we live in a classless society?

In groups of two, look at Charts **D** and **E**.

One should look at the idea that class plays a vital part in our lives and the other should argue that class is no longer important (think of other types of difference that you could see as more important).

F *A classless society?*

What other social structures affect our everyday lives?

We all belong to groups and organisations that:

a are structures in themselves

b help to structure our everyday lives.

For example:

- Families. We all belong to a family of some form or another and, like it or not, families and the people within them, structure our lives. They mould and shape us into individuals who can take an active part in our society and they are responsible for teaching us the basic values and norms of our society. The structure of the family involves a complicated set of roles and relationships that are affected by such things as social class, **income**, age and gender. Living in families will be explored in greater detail in Chapter 3.

- Education. There are caring and educational structures that affect our lives from a very early age. Many babies have their days structured by care assistants in nurseries and crèches and we are all affected by schools, from the age of 4 or 5 through to 16. Most of you will choose to stay in full-time education until you are 18 and many will go on to higher education, leaving only when you reach 21 or 22 . Between one fifth and one quarter of your lives will be structured by the education process.

- Work. Many of you will have part-time jobs and most of you will find full-time employment after you gain skills and qualifications. For most people, work is a really structured and important part of their lives as it provides them with income, status, rivals and friends. It also organises most of our waking hours by deciding what time we should get up to get to work on time. Most people in full-time employment could be seen as working a 5:2 shift with weekends being their two days off work!

Key terms

Income: the money received by an individual in a period of time, for example, wages, interest on savings.

G *Schools affect many lives*

Going further

Try to find up-to-date information on the links between social class and other issues such as smoking, illness and incomes. A lot of statistical information can be found at: www.statistics.gov.uk/

Check your understanding

1 Which classification scale is now used to measure social class?

2 What forms of stratification, other than social class, are important in modern Britain?

3 Identify three important groups that influence and structure our daily lives.

What is a social process?

Things rarely just happen!

Our lives, from the day we are born all the way through to old age, are affected and influenced by:

- our contact with other people and
- our links with and membership of important organisations and groups.

We learn how to be responsible members of our society and we also learn that we can't do exactly what we want at all times – there are **constraints** on our behaviour. We gradually develop our own identity through a collection of important happenings, through a never-ending social process.

The process of learning to be a participating member of society is known as **socialisation** and the process of **social control** regulates our behaviour and brings about **conformity** to the norms and laws of society.

Socialisation as a social process

Within our own culture, for the most part we seem to understand each other and we all seem to be aware of what is regarded as appropriate or inappropriate behaviour. Would this be the case if we had not had contact with other people, some of whom have been very important in our lives? There have been a number of accounts of children who have grown up having had no contact with other people.

Case study

The monkey boy

John Ssabunnya, aged 14, was abandoned as a two-year-old in the dense jungle of Uganda to what seemed certain death. But a colony of African Green monkeys came across him and adopted the child as one of their own.

John learnt their mannerisms, became adept at climbing trees and lived on a diet of fruit, nuts and berries for the next three years.

In 1991 a tribeswoman saw him scavenging for food with the chimps and reported it to the people in her village. The naked boy was caught and taken to an orphanage, where he lived with the family of the orphanage manager. For the last eight years, he has learned human ways and has been taught to speak.

A *John now lives with people, but he still seems to be able to communicate with monkeys*

Activities

1   Think of five aspects of your behaviour as a five-year-old that John would know nothing about.

2   If John had joined your family at five-years-old what would have been the main barrier he would have faced in becoming 'one of us'.

Primary socialisation

This is the term used to describe the informal process through which you learn the norms, attitudes, values, and actions of your culture. It takes place in early childhood and the main shaping influence is usually the **family** and the home. The family is one of the most important agencies of socialisation.

It is here that you eventually learn such basic things as: how to communicate with others, how not to eat with your fingers, how and when to use a potty, the difference between right and wrong, and how to share with others. Many of these skills are copied and learned by watching what parents do. Good behaviour is praised whereas unacceptable behaviour is frowned upon.

It is in the family where you first develop your **gender** identity. This is where you learn what is seen as acceptable masculine and feminine behaviour. **Canalisation** results in girls and boys having different experiences in their early years. Although things are changing, there is still a pink/blue, female/male colour preference. Many girls use pink as an expression of their femininity and few parents would choose to dress their baby boy in pink. Many parents and most toy shops make distinctions between boys' toys and girls' toys.

There may be differences in the quality and emphasis of socialisation between families in different social classes and this might have an impact on children in later life, especially at school.

Key terms

Constraint: not being able to do what you want; being restricted or limited.

Socialisation: the lifelong process of learning the skills, customs, attitudes, norms and values of your culture.

Social control: the process by which people are persuaded to obey the rules and to conform.

Conformity: doing what is expected and behaving in a way that is in agreement with norms.

Family: a group of two or more persons associated by birth, cohabitation, marriage, or adoption.

Gender: the social and cultural differences between the sexes – between femininity and masculinity.

Canalisation: being channelled in a particular direction.

B *Learning through socialisation*

Secondary socialisation

There are other important agencies of socialisation that make sure you continue to learn the norms and values of your culture throughout the rest of your life. The relationships you have with individuals in this form of socialisation are far less personal and your links with people are much less emotional than with your family and close friends.

- School. This delivers knowledge and skills to prepare you for the big wide world through the **formal curriculum**. There is also another side to the socialisation process in schools through the **hidden curriculum**. You know that schools have rules. Most schools have a particular dress code or uniform (which is different for boys and girls). You are expected to be on time and respect the authority of your teacher in the classroom. You are expected to conform to the rules and you encounter problems if you don't.

- Peer group. Friends of a similar age have an important influence on your life. You expect your friends to behave in certain ways and they expect you to do the same. Peer groups can be a positive influence on your behaviour but they can also lead you in a deviant direction by expecting you to follow their lead. For example, many people say the reason they started smoking was because their friends encouraged them to do so. Peer group pressure can also play a big part in the development of your gender identity.

- Mass media. The media through television, films, the Internet, magazines, newspapers and books affect us all. They put us in touch with images and information that we would not receive through any other source. Much of our political socialisation, for example, comes through the media and our attitudes and emotions are affected by scenes we see in films and on the television.

- The workplace. As well as developing specific skills at work you also make friends with people you work with. You learn how to get on with some people and put up with others.

links

Also see Topic 2.3 for more information on the formal and hidden curriculum.

Activity

3 Think about gender socialisation. Take a look at the toy section of one of the major catalogue firms. What evidence do you see of particular toys being targeted at boys and girls?

Going further

The primary and secondary socialisation you receive will differ according to such factors as your social class, gender and ethnicity. Take one or more of these factors and consider how it affects the socialisation process.

Social control as a social process

Informal social control

As you have worked through the section on socialisation, perhaps you have realised that the agencies mentioned – family, school, mass media, peer group and work – also have a controlling influence on our lives. They all exert pressure to make sure you stick to the laws, rules and norms of society and this is referred to as informal social control. If you stick to the rules you are rewarded through positive **sanctions** such as praise, presents or just general approval. If you break the rules, negative sanctions are applied in the form of disapproval or punishment.

Formal social control

The main agency of formal social control is the criminal justice system. This involves:

- the police who make sure we conform to the laws created by the **legislature** and investigate cases of law breaking
- the **judiciary** who deal with those who are accused of breaking the law
- the probation and prison service who look after people who have been found guilty of breaking the law.

The education system could be seen as an agency of formal social control. Schools, colleges and universities all have formal rules and impose negative sanctions on anyone who breaks them.

Key terms

Sanction: agreed reward for positive actions or penalty for negative actions.

Legislature: the section of the government that is responsible for making laws.

Judiciary: the section of the government that has the power to apply the law, that is, the court system including judges.

Activity

4 Draw out the table below and give three examples of both positive and negative sanctions that could be given from the family, school, peer group and workplace.

	Positive sanctions	Negative sanctions
Family		
School		
Peer group		
Work		

AQA *Examiner's tip*

Remember the links between socialisation and social control.

Check your understanding

1 How can the school exert both informal and formal social control?

2 What is the difference between primary and secondary socialisation?

3 Why might sociologists suggest that socialisation is a lifelong process?

We are all concerned about something

Few people would agree that we live in a perfect society and not everyone can agree on what a perfect society should be like. In a perfect world we wouldn't have concerns about such things as: inequality, discrimination, poverty, pollution and crime. In your perfect society, for example, you might think it is vital to develop embryonic stem cell research but your neighbour or friend might see this as immoral and unacceptable. As individuals and groups look for solutions and become involved in discussion and debate, these concerns become social issues.

Poverty as a social issue

As you have seen earlier, there are noticeable differences between the life experiences of different social groups in modern Britain. It is unrealistic to try to compare the poorest in our society with those who lack the basic essentials of food, clothing and shelter in developing countries. Nevertheless, **poverty** remains an important social issue in contemporary Britain. If you and your family struggle to make ends meet you are already aware of the issue. Others, who enjoy a comfortable lifestyle, perhaps need to be made aware of the inequalities of income and the barriers that deny access to a decent standard of living.

Who is concerned about making poverty a social issue?

- The poor themselves. Those who do not have access to an acceptable standard of living also lack the power to make their situation noticed. They are clearly concerned but do not have a strong enough voice to raise poverty as a social issue.

- The government. There is clearly a need for the state to provide a 'safety net' to prevent those who are financially disadvantaged from hitting rock bottom. All governments since 1945 have pledged to do this through the **Welfare State**. Politicians with a particular interest in social issues have made sure that the concerns about **relative poverty** remain in the spotlight. There has been a determined attempt to reduce the amount of income tax paid by low income families through the introduction of the tax credit system.

- **Pressure groups** and charities. There are a number of organisations that put pressure on governments and businesses to try to bring about change.

    The **Child Poverty Action Group** (CPAG) is the leading charity campaigning for the abolition of child poverty in the UK and for a better deal for low-income families and children.

    The **End Child Poverty Coalition** shows that 3.8 million children – one in three – are currently living in poverty in the UK. The action they are demanding is summed up as follows:

Key terms

Poverty: means being poor (but this can be defined in many different ways).

Welfare State: the government taking responsibility for the health and financial wellbeing of the population.

Relative poverty: a situation in which someone cannot afford to possess the kind of things and participate in the kind of activities considered by members of their society to be a normal part of life.

Pressure group: a group, usually concerned with a single issue, that applies pressure to try to bring about change.

⚭ links

Also see Topic 7.5 to find out more about what it means to be poor in Britain today.

Did you know ??????

The government regards you as being in poverty if your household has 'below 60% of median income'. If all incomes were ranked from highest to lowest you would be in the bottom 40%.

> 66 *Together with all our supporters, we are demanding the Government invests the necessary resources and policy changes to deliver on its promise to all children to eradicate child poverty in the UK by 2020.* 99
>
> End Child Poverty, 2008
> www.endchildpoverty.org.uk

Oxfam has stated that they are:

> 66 *very uncomfortable that in a rich country (UK), 1 in 5 people don't have enough to live on. Many people can't afford essential clothing – or to heat their homes. Children go to school hungry, or to bed without enough food. It's no coincidence that poor communities are in poorer health – and have shorter life expectancy. It's not just outrageous – it's unnecessary. With enough public pressure for change – and enough political will – our politicians can put this right.* 99
>
> Oxfam, 2008
> www.oxfam.org.uk

A *Poor housing*

On an international level such groups as **Christian Aid, Action on Aid, Live Aid**, and the **Catholic Agency for Overseas Development (CAFOD)** all keep the issue in the spotlight.

- Sociologists. Social research by such people as Peter Townsend and Mack and Lansley continues the debate about poverty and, in particular, where we draw the poverty line in the UK today.

Activity

1   Advertise your issue

Let other people who are not studying sociology have a chance to think about social issues. In pairs, design an A3 poster to let others know of the social issue you are investigating. You should make the poster both visually appealing and informative. Then display it where passers-by can see it.

Going further

The Child Poverty Action Group (CPAG) website at www.cpag.org.uk/ not only gives information about the activities of CPAG but from the 'Information & Resources' tab has a Useful Links option to well over 100 websites that you might find of interest.

Fear of crime

There is a great deal of public concern about levels of criminal and anti-social behaviour in Britain today. Certain groups in society see this as a real threat to their own security and feel the need to change and restrict their lifestyle to ensure their own safety.

The social issue that will concern you as a sociologist is that people's fear of crime is often much greater than the actual levels of crime suggest. People are frightened about things that will never happen to them. This is especially so in the case of older, more vulnerable people, as they are the group who are actually the least likely to become a victim of crime.

Asking people about their fear of crime in a questionnaire has the unfortunate consequence of making them frightened. Questions therefore tend to ask about 'concern' rather than 'fear'. How do these concerns become social issues when there is little hard evidence to show that people should be more frightened now than in the past?

Case study

Help the aged

Crime and fear of crime are significant concerns for older people. Older women in particular, report extremely high levels of fear of crime, and many older people cite fear of crime as a significant factor in limiting their ability to get out and about.

Older people are less likely than younger groups to suffer serious personal crime, mainly as a result of their 'restricted lifestyle'. They are rarely to be found in the city centre on a Friday night. It is also true that the rates for most crime categories have been falling in recent years. Nonetheless, many thousands of older people are victims every year and millions are anxious about crime and disorder. They suffer intensively from the emotional, economic, psychological and physical effects of victimisation, and have their lives blighted by worry about being a victim.

B *Staying indoors*

Activities

2 What kind of crimes are older people likely to feel more concerned about in their local community?

3 What do you think can be done to make older people feel more secure in their communities?

Where do we hear the messages and how accurate are they?

We only have personal knowledge of what is going on in our own local community and even then, we rely upon local newspapers and local news programmes to inform us.

Who is it that tells us that paedophiles pose an imminent threat to our children, that Anti-Social Behaviour Orders (ASBOs) are not working or that drug taking is rife in the children's play park?

On both a local and national level it could be argued that the media:

- feed us with information about what is going on in our society and by doing so they highlight particular social issues
- create social issues by exaggerating a set of events and creating a **moral panic** surrounding them
- are selective in the information they present and therefore only highlight social issues that are going to help boost their viewer or reader numbers
- actually increase the level of anti-social and criminal behaviour by publicising it through the process known as **media amplification**.

Key terms

Moral panic: when media coverage of an issue leads to exaggerated public concern.

Media amplification: blowing things out of proportion by over-reporting in the media.

links

Also see Topic 5.4 for more information on media amplification.

Activity

4   Working in groups of three or four, use copies of your local daily or weekly newspaper to examine the following:

a   How many times is there a headline referring to crime or anti-social behaviour?

b   How many times is there a positive headline referring to male youths?

c   How many times is there a story that is likely to make readers feel anxious?

d   To what extent do you think the headlines accurately reflect what is going on in your local community?

'You pick up your knife like you pick up your keys'

Knifeman faces jail

Anti-stab vests given to key staff

Man wanted over two sex attacks held in Cornwall

Police think French pair tortured for pin details

Fatal stabbing near minister's former home

Skinhead gang accused of killing 20

Three charged

Warning to public in hunt for man wanted over two rapes

- Victim's last words after he is chased, cornered and attacked
- Met sets up taskforce to target capital's troubled boroughs

C *Newspaper headlines*

AQA *Examiner's tip*

Remember that some social issues are heavily supported and championed by pressure groups and others are generated through exaggerated media coverage.

Check your understanding

1   Describe why poverty is such an important social issue in Britain.

2   How do pressure groups try to make the public aware of social issues?

3   How do you think the media influence the public in deciding what are important social issues?

Quantitative data is usually gathered from a social survey. A specific group of people (your sample) are asked a set of questions and you base your judgements and conclusions on the information they give you. When the answers to the questions are analysed, they are often turned into numbers, statistics, percentages, tables and graphs. This quantitative data tells you *how many* people gave particular answers to each question and you, as a researcher, look for trends and patterns in the data to help you arrive at a conclusion.

Gathering quantitative primary data

Primary data is data that has been collected, first-hand, by you for the particular purpose of your investigation.

A number of methods are available and you may, of course, use more than one method.

1 Perhaps the most efficient way of collecting quantitative data is through closed or graded response questions in a questionnaire.

2 Structured interviews use a set of pre-prepared questions that are read out either face to face or over the telephone. Comparing responses can generate quantitative data.

3 An observation might involve you counting the number of times a child misbehaves or comparing the amount of time that boys and girls spend on a particular activity in a primary school maths lesson.

4 Content analysis might help you to see how many times individuals from minority ethnic backgrounds are presented in positive and negative ways in newspaper articles, magazines or in 'soaps' on television.

Objectives

You will be able to:

- recognise the features of a quantitative approach to social research

- describe the different types of quantitative methods used by sociologists

- explain why you need to think carefully about who will provide your primary data

- describe the different sampling techniques you can use

- argue for the use of a particular type of sample for a specific piece of research

- create a questionnaire

- assess the strengths and weaknesses of different types of quantitative methods.

Did you know ??????

The main provider of statistics for the government, and a valuable source of quantitative secondary data for the sociologist, is the Office for National Statistics (ONS) (www.ons.gov.uk).

Activity

1 Sometimes the subject being studied determines the best method to be used and the type of data to be collected. Suppose that you were studying the effect that social class has on the achievement of boys and girls at GCSE level.

a What method would you choose to collect your data?

b What kind of data would you most likely collect?

A *...I've torn up the questionnaire but am using the lovely pen you sent me...*

Sources of quantitative secondary data

If you were doing a piece of social research you would be able to look at a lot of statistical information that had already been collected by other researchers and official organisations. You can compare the findings from your primary data with this **secondary data**. The government generates lots of **official statistics** from large-scale surveys. The best known of these is the Census, which takes place every 10 years and asks lots of questions about families, households and work.

The British Crime Survey

The British Crime Survey (BCS) is an important source of information about levels of crime and public attitudes to crime. The results play an important role in informing government policy.

The BCS measures the amount of crime in England and Wales by asking people about crimes they have experienced in the last year. The BCS includes crimes that are not reported to the police, so it is an important alternative to police records. The survey collects information about:

- the victims of crime
- the circumstances in which incidents occur
- the behaviour of offenders in committing crimes.

The interviews also provide information about other topics, such as people's perceptions of anti-social behaviour and attitudes towards the criminal justice system, including the police and the courts. The survey also looks at people's attitudes to crime, such as how much they fear crime and what measures they take to avoid it.

www.homeoffice.gov.uk/rds/

Key terms

Quantitative data: information that is presented as numbers which can be analysed using statistical methods.

Social survey: a collection of information about members of a population. Can be carried out on the street, at home, in an organisation (school, workplace, etc.), by mail, by telephone, online.

Primary data: data collected for the first time by the researcher for a particular piece of research.

Questionnaire: a set of questions used to gather information.

Secondary data: data that exists prior to and independent from the researcher's own research.

Official statistics: a set of statistics generated from data gathered by the government or other official organisations. Often used as secondary data in social research.

Activities

2 After reading the case study above, answer these questions:

a What method of data collection is used in the BCS?

b Who uses this as primary quantitative data?

c Who might use this as secondary quantitative data?

3 Imagine that you have a 4-year-old child who will be starting primary school in September. Find what statistical information there is on the Internet about your local primary schools that will help you choose the right school.

Going further

You might be interested in the findings of some of the other surveys undertaken by different government departments. Most of these are available online. Take a look at the findings of the most recent British Crime Survey at http://rds.homeoffice.gov.uk/rds and have a look at how your local police force are dealing with offences in your area. Look at the statistics published in the latest version of Social Trends at www.statistics.gov.uk/socialtrends to give you up-to-date information on education, health, the environment and much more.

AQA Examiner's tip

Remember that you should always be able to show *why* you have chosen to use a particular method to gather your data when carrying out a piece of social research.

Sampling

As well as deciding on ways of collecting primary data, a researcher conducting a social survey must also think carefully about *who* is going to provide the information that is required.

These **respondents** in the **sample** will be selected from a much larger group of people. In some cases it is possible to choose respondents from a full list of names – a **sampling frame**. An electoral register or a set of class registers are examples of sampling frames that might be used.

All sampling methods rely on the idea that the views of a small group of people will be **representative** of the views of everyone else.

We come across the need for samples in our everyday life. Your doctor would not drain all the blood from your body to test it and a wine taster would be in a sorry state if he/she had to drink the whole barrel to test the quality. They both take small samples and base their judgements on those.

Sampling techniques

Most samples consist of people who have been chosen using a particular technique. We all have inbuilt preferences and biases that could make our choice unrepresentative. So it is important to be careful that you do not avoid asking certain types of people in preference to others.

- **Random sample** – A small group selected from a sampling frame where everyone has an equal chance of being chosen. You give a number to each person in your sampling frame and allow a computer to choose the numbers at random. National Lottery machines draw the winning numbers at random.
- **Stratified sample** – You might want to mirror the distribution of particular groups in your larger population. So, for example, if you want a representative sample from your year group and it is made up of 60 per cent girls and 40 per cent boys you might choose two random samples of different sizes to reflect this.
- **Systematic sample** – You will still use a sampling frame but you choose, say, every 10th or 15th person on the list.
- **Quota sample** – You set your quota controls such as age, gender, ethnicity, social class and then you set about finding people to fit into these slots. Market researchers might stop you on the street because you are a female aged about 16 who is listening to an expensive iPod.

- **Snowball sample** – You choose a small group of people that are probably not contained within a sampling frame, for example, single moms, and then ask them to pass your questions to other single moms they know. The snowball gets bigger as it rolls from one person to another.
- **Opportunistic sample** – This is not a particularly representative type of sampling but a technique that involves just giving your questions to anyone who happens to be available.

Activity

5 Imagine you were carrying out a piece of research into: fan behaviour at a football match, attitudes towards single mothers, and subject choices of boys and girls.

Draw a table as illustrated below and think carefully about the most appropriate responses, giving reasons for your choices. Compare your ideas with those of another student.

B *Carrying out research*

	Fan behaviour at a football match	Attitudes towards single mothers	Subject choices of boys and girls
Which sample type is the most appropriate?			
How would you select your respondents?			
What sample size would you decide on?			
Where would you access your sample?			
When would you gather your data?			
Problems you might encounter			

Designing a questionnaire

A questionnaire is the most commonly used method for collecting quantitative data.

It will probably start by asking some general questions such as: gender, age, ethnic origin, marital status and occupation, as you might think there will be different responses from different groups in your sample.

Different types of questions can be asked in a single questionnaire and these will generate different types of data.

Closed questions

A limited number of possible answers are given and respondents have to choose from the options given to them. These are often presented as Yes/No or Agree/Disagree answers or can be a set of multiple-choice options.

Open questions

Respondents can answer however they like. This often results in lengthy written answers to questions.

Graded response questions

Respondents are asked how much they agree with questions and can record their responses on a scale of say 1 to 6, with 1 meaning strongly agree and 6 meaning strongly disagree.

Key terms
Bias: not taking a neutral view but favouring one side of an argument or debate.
Reliability: data is reliable if it can be repeated and consistently comes up with the same results.
Validity: data is valid if it gives a true picture of what is being studied.
Pilot study: a study on a small scale before the main research is done.

Strengths and weaknesses of questionnaires

Strengths	Weaknesses
• They are a quick way to collect a lot of data.	• Response rates vary depending on the way the questionnaire is distributed.
• They are relatively cheap to produce.	• The researcher has decided what to ask and may choose a **biased** set of questions.
• They can reach a large sample.	
• They produce quantitative data that can be easily converted into statistics.	• If closed questions are asked, the researcher has decided on the range of possible answers.
• They can be designed on a computer, are read by a computer, and computer packages can help to organise the data.	• Questions may be misunderstood and the respondent cannot ask for an explanation.
• People can take their time to think of appropriate answers.	• Open questions take a long time to analyse.
• They produce **reliable** data.	• Respondents might rush through the questions especially if it is a long questionnaire.
• It is possible to cross-reference data from different questions, for example, you can do an analysis by gender and age if you asked those questions.	• If you ask a question you are supposed to analyse the data. You can collect too much data.
	• Responses may lack **validity**.

Testing it out – the pilot study

Having decided on your sample size but before you run off all the copies you need, you should try out your questionnaire on a small group of people. This **pilot study** will let you see if the questions are clear, mean the same to everyone and give you the kind of responses you were expecting.

Ethical considerations

It is important that you understand the **ethical considerations** in your research. You should always remember that it is a privilege for you to be able to ask people about their opinions and experiences, not a privilege for your respondents to be involved in your research.

You must make sure that you do not:

a   put yourself in danger

b   upset anyone by asking questions that are too personal.

You would usually promise **anonymity** and **confidentiality** by not publishing names and not discussing individual responses with anyone. You would be concerned about gaining **informed consent** especially for groups who are more vulnerable than others. In some cases, for example, young children in a primary school classroom, the teacher might act as a **gatekeeper**, giving you permission to question the children after she/he has agreed on the suitability of your research.

Key terms

Ethical considerations: making sure that your research is not offending or harming anyone – that you are doing the right thing.

Anonymity: making sure that no names are mentioned in your finished report or in the data collection process.

Confidentiality: keeping personal details between you and the respondent.

Informed consent: making sure that your respondents know what you are doing and agree to participate.

Gatekeeper: someone who gives permission for others to be involved in your research.

Triangulation: checking the accuracy of data collected through one method (for example, a questionnaire) by comparing it with data collected by using another method (for example, observation).

Activity

6   Working in groups of two or three, design a short questionnaire to explore the television viewing habits of 10 of your friends.

■   Decide how you are going to choose your sample.

■   Use closed or graded response questions and make sure you take ethical considerations into account.

■   Pilot the questionnaire within your design group and make sure the questions are unambiguous and understood by all.

AQA Examiner's tip

Many pieces of social research use evidence that is gathered by using more than one method of data collection. By doing this:

a   they can gain a far more rounded picture of the issue they are investigating

b   the data collected from one method can be used to check the accuracy of data gained through another method.

This process is known as **triangulation**.

You might like to think of the possible advantages of using, for example, an interview and a questionnaire with the same respondents.

Check your understanding

1   What ethical concerns should sociologists consider when collecting data and publishing their findings?

2   What is the difference between primary and secondary data?

3   Why might large samples be more representative than small ones?

4   What methods do sociologists use to collect quantitative data?

5   Why is it important to carry out a pilot study?

Qualitative data

The key idea behind **qualitative data** is that it gives the sociologist a real picture of what is happening. The researcher describes and explains what has been seen, heard or written. Data is not converted into statistics but is usually written up as passages of text or quotations.

Gathering qualitative primary data

Qualitative data can be gathered using a number of methods:

a **Observation** of a group of people. This can be as a participant or non-participant and either overt or covert.

b Conducting an **unstructured interview**. This seems like a relatively informal conversation where the respondent talks freely but the researcher keeps the conversation heading in the right direction. Allowing the interview to wander a little sometimes results in new ideas being developed.

c Including **open questions** in a questionnaire. These ask respondents to write their answer to a particular question or to explain their reasons for giving a previous answer. The detailed written responses often help to make sense of some of the statistics.

d **Focus group**. You may well have been a part of a focus group discussion in your school/college. The opinions of a small group are recorded and taken into account when decisions are made. The comments you make are fed into the analysis of data collected through other (usually quantitative) methods.

You can find all these terms defined in the glossary at the end of this book.

Conducting your own research

These are some questions you need to ask yourself.

What exactly will I study?

Be very clear about what you intend to do and set yourself some clear aims.

Make sure that the questions you ask and the other work you use to support your findings are directly related to the aims you set yourself.

Try to think of some of the key ideas or concepts that are important in your research.

Look at other pieces of social research (secondary data) that might give you useful background information.

How do I collect my data?

Decide on the best method or combination of methods you will use to collect your primary data.

Decide on the size and type of sample you are going to use.

Decide where you are going to find your sample.

Ask for permission whenever it is needed.

Think carefully about ethical considerations related to your research.

Decide on the kind of questions you are going to ask – open, closed, graded response, combination of different types. (questionnaire/interview)

Decide what you are looking for. (observation/content analysis)

How do I organise my data?

Consider using a spreadsheet or database program or stick to tally charts.

How am I going to present my data?

Use graphs and charts to help the reader understand the meaning of your data.

Don't just present the figures but make sure you explain your data.

Look for patterns in your data.

Compare your findings with the findings of other pieces of sociological research.

Have I found anything useful?
Look back at your aims and see if you have achieved them.

Don't be disappointed if your data doesn't show what you expected to find but try to figure out why this might be so.

Enjoy the process – it can be challenging and should be exciting!

Activity

1 A small group of youths regularly meet close to some sheltered accommodation and seem to be upsetting the elderly residents. You want to investigate the problem and make some recommendations to the groups involved.

■ Choose two methods of data collection that seem the most appropriate and explain why you have chosen them.

■ How would you present your findings and what kind of data would it most likely contain?

Sources of qualitative secondary data

A variety of sources exist including:

a Historical documents: particularly useful when you are trying to make comparisons between up-to-date primary data and the past. They allow you to see whether or not things have changed.

b Personal documents: including letters, diaries, reference books, novels, life histories and oral histories.

c Mass media: documentaries on TV, blogs, personal websites, material on the Internet, radio programmes, and films all provide valuable contemporary material that can give essential background information in social research.

Observation

Perhaps the most authentic way of finding out what is happening is to be there and watch it as it happens. This is the real strength of observation. It can lead to the collection of quantitative data by recording the number of times you observe something happening but it also generates valuable qualitative data by watching and listening to the interaction that is taking place in front of you. Observations can be participant or non-participant and can be overt or covert.

Participant observation – As the researcher, you are actively involved in the group's activities as well as making a record of what you see. A study of student behaviour in the classroom could be carried out in the lessons you attend; you would be participating as well as recording events.

Non-participant observation – You watch and record what is happening but are not involved in the group's activities. If you were looking at the way teachers distribute their time between boys and girls in a primary school classroom, you might sit in a corner to observe and record from there.

Overt observation – The group you are observing know why you are there and what you are doing.

Covert observation – You are 'undercover' and the group are not aware of the fact that you are observing them.

Going further

There are some really interesting examples of social research through participant observation. Not only do they uncover events that would remain hidden or private but they also make for good reading.

Ask your librarian to get hold of one of the following and see what you think:

Learning to Labour – How working class kids get working class jobs Paul Willis

Street Corner Society W.F. Whyte

Glasgow Gang Observed James Patrick

Tearoom Trade Laud Humphries

View from the boys Howard Parker

Villains: Crime and Community in the Inner City Janet Foster

Participant observation in action

Undercover

Although all research methods have advantages and disadvantages, participant observation is probably the most controversial.

One of the questions which is always asked of participant observers is how they got in. Like other research of this kind, access for me came about as a result of a chance meeting with Chris. She offered to introduce me to some of her friends who had offended in their youth and socialised in the Grafton Arms, but suggested that the nature of my research should remain covert. I was therefore introduced as Janet, who was a student, and wanted to join the ladies' darts team. Here began the first of many learning experiences (since I had never played darts!) and the first of several ethical dilemmas. I began by visiting the Grafton on ladies' darts night and within a short time was a regular in the pub most evenings of the week. The darts provided me with an excellent opportunity to mix with the men and gave me a 'legitimate' reason for being there. As I was keen to learn they all took a great deal of time and patience (with my appalling subtraction!) helping me.

I never made any attempt to speak or dress differently, and my accent presented few problems. One person described me as 'working class with a nice accent!', while others explained it as a product of my roots. George, for example, defended me when one of her 'mates' commented, 'Your friend's a bit posh, ain't she?' George replied, 'Janet comes from Bournemouth and they all speak like that down there!'

Being small, young, and female was a decided advantage in negotiating most aspects of the field.

Janet Foster, *Villains: Crime and Community in the Inner City*

Strengths and weaknesses of observation

Strengths	Weaknesses
• It produces qualitative data that is a rich source of detailed information about all aspects of a group's activity. It is the method of data collection favoured in **ethnographic** studies.	• It may be difficult to get in, stay in and get out.
• It produces data that can be regarded as highly valid, producing a true picture of behaviour.	• How representative are the findings? Is the data collected from a small group representative of other groups?
• It may be the only practical way of gathering data from some groups.	• How reliable is the data? Would another observer have arrived at the same conclusions?
• Researchers gain an insight which is not gained through surveys, for example,	• The observer effect. Has the presence of the observer changed the behaviour of the group?
As I sat and listened, I learned answers to questions I would not have had the sense to ask. W.F. Whyte	• How objective are the findings? Is the researcher biased or become so close to the group that she/he has 'gone native'?
• It can produce quantitative data.	• In a covert observation, is it right to be secretive and to deceive the group by not telling them that they are being observed?
• It can be used as an additional method to help support or question some of the findings gained from a survey.	• The researcher could be at risk.
• It can be used for the purpose of **triangulation**.	• How do you record what is happening? You might have to rely on your memory and record everything afterwards.

Activities

2 Why do you think the researcher was advised to remain covert?

3 What does she mean by 'ethical dilemmas'?

Key terms

Ethnography: looking at the whole way of life of a group, usually by using a variety of methods of data collection.

Triangulation: checking the accuracy of data collected through one method (e.g. a questionnaire) by comparing it with data collected by using another method (e.g. observation).

B *The observer effect*

Check your understanding

1 If it is so time-consuming and expensive to collect, why do sociologists bother at all with qualitative data?

2 What methods do sociologists use to collect quantitative data?

3 What do you understand by 'the observer effect'?

4 What do we mean when we say that qualitative data is high in validity?

AQA *Examiner's tip*

Look at the topic dealing with quantitative data. Some of the best pieces of social research collect both quantitative and qualitative data and get a much more complete picture of what is happening.

Exam question guidance

As a sociologist there are three questions you need to ask about any item of source material:

- **Who** produced this source material? For example, a sociologist, a journalist or a government department.
- **What** is the source about? For example, a case study of a group of students, a set of statistics, a newspaper article.
- **Why** is the source useful or important? For example, what are the key points and important ideas that we can take from it? Does it provide evidence of the success or failure of government policies? This key question also suggests that you need to think about the intended *audience*: the general public (particularly those who are parents), professional researchers or students.

Example of a source-based question

Item A

Learning to Labour

In a study entitled 'Learning to Labour: How Working Class Kids Get Working Class Jobs', Paul Willis studied a group of 12 working-class boys during their last year and a half at a Midlands' school. He observed 'the lads' in classes, around the school and during their leisure activities and interviewed several of them together. In these group interviews, he was also able to observe the social interaction between these working-class boys.

Adapted from Haralambos and Holborn, *Sociology Themes and Perspectives* 6th edition, Collins, 2004

- **Who?** This source is a description of the work of the sociologist Paul Willis. He has a critical view of the relationship between the education system and the economy.
- **What?** Willis published his book *Learning to Labour* in 1977. He studied a group of students in a comprehensive school serving a working-class community.
- **Why?** Willis argues that education can have unintended consequences and in particular that unsuccessful students have no interest in gaining qualifications, becoming members of a 'counter-culture' that places little or no value on work in school.

| b | i | Identify a research method used by Paul Willis. | *(1 mark)* |

This is a simple comprehension question, answer as briefly as possible. Willis used a range of research methods. You could answer either observation or interviews as both are mentioned in the source.

ii   Identify **one** advantage and **one** disadvantage of using the research method
        you have identified.   *(2 marks)*

The examiners want you to think about the advantages and
disadvantages of either interviews or observation as a research method.
They expect at least two sentences explaining, for example, that
interviews:

- have the **advantage** of allowing the researcher to explore the
  attitudes and beliefs of the interviewee in some depth (*quality* data)
- have the **disadvantage** that the interviewee may change responses
  to give the answers that they think the interviewer wants to hear
  (the interviewer can *bias* the response by appearing to respond
  positively or negatively to certain statements).

Example of an investigation question

You have been asked as a sociologist to investigate the attitudes
towards schooling amongst different ethnic groups.

i   Identify and explain **one** ethical issue which may arise in the course of doing your
        research.   *(4 marks)*
ii   Identify **one** secondary source you might use and explain why it would help.   *(4 marks)*
iii   Explain why the primary research method you would use is better than another
        possible primary method for obtaining the information you need.   *(6 marks)*

These questions are designed to test your knowledge and
understanding of the research methods available to the sociologist
working in the field. The source material (that is, the three items that
are provided in the question), like the example about the work of Paul
Willis, will have been designed to help you with these questions, to
remind you of some of the key ideas and the issues that sociologists
have to deal with when they are completing their research. You should
write in paragraphs. Remember that the final part of the question
carries more marks. This tells you that the examiner wants you to write
more.

Ethical issues are all about the rights and wrongs of research. For
example:

- Do people know why they are being interviewed and do they
  understand that their views might be published (informed
  consent)?
- Has the researcher respected the right to privacy or is it possible to
  identify the individuals concerned?

We would expect Paul Willis not to have identified any of his
informants by name and to have been careful to explain his role as a
researcher.

Secondary sources are sources of information that you have *not* gathered at first hand. They are the work of others, for example, the work of other sociologists or journalists. You need to think about relevant **types** of source for this particular enquiry, for example, published research on ethnicity and schooling that can be used to compare with your own research findings. You do not need to quote particular research studies.

Primary research methods are the techniques and ideas that you might use to gather original data (primary source material), for example, questionnaires, interviews, observations. Why might one method have advantages or disadvantages over another? Interviews enable the researcher to pursue a point of interest; they are flexible and generate **qualitative** data. You might argue that this is important if you are really going to understand the issue of ethnicity and education. Questionnaires enable the researcher to gather more information but are inflexible. They generate **quantitative** data (findings that can easily be compared and are expressed in numbers). You might argue that large-scale research is necessary to provide convincing evidence (numbers) in an area of research that is controversial, for example, ethnicity and education.

■ Questions to try

What follows are examples of the types of questions you will meet in your exam. The letter in each question matches the letter that will be used for that type of question on your exam paper. The number in brackets is only there to help you and your teacher refer to that particular question in this book.

Item B

Researchers from the University of London followed the progress of nearly 3,000 children at more than 800 primary schools from the age of three onwards. Professor Edward Melhuish, who led the research, said that the findings showed that a combination of a good home learning environment, good preschool education and a good primary school were all important. He said that an average child from a poor background who did not have these benefits would be in the bottom 20% at school. This longitudinal study used a variety of research methods including classroom observations, interviews and an analysis of pupils' academic achievements.

Adapted from a report by James Randerson in *The Guardian*, August 2008

a i From Item B, identify **one** of the research methods used. *(1 mark)*

ii Identify **one** advantage and **one** disadvantage of the research method you have identified in (a) (i) above. *(2 marks)*

d(1) Explain **one** way in which a sociological research project investigating divorce might help the government to design policies to reduce family breakdown in Britain. *(4 marks)*

d(2) Explain **one** way in which a sociological research project investigating school absence might help the government to design policies to reduce levels of truancy. *(4 marks)*

e(1) You have been asked as a sociologist to investigate levels of binge drinking amongst 18–24-year-old males and females.

i Identify and explain one **ethical issue** that may arise in the course of doing your research. *(4 marks)*

ii Identify **one** useful secondary source **and** explain why it would help. *(4 marks)*

iii Identify **one** primary research method you would use and discuss why it is better than another possible primary method for obtaining the information you need. *(6 marks)*

e(2) You have been asked as a sociologist to find out how much time women and men spend on childcare.

i Identify and explain one **ethical issue** that may arise in the course of doing your research. *(4 marks)*

ii Identify **one** useful secondary source **and** explain why it would help. *(4 marks)*

iii Identify **one** primary research method you would use and discuss why it is better than another possible primary method for obtaining the information you need. *(6 marks)*

e(3) You have been asked as a sociologist to find out the opinions on masculinity (male identity) of boys aged 15 to 18 at a local school or college.

i Identify and explain **one ethical issue** that may arise in the course of doing your research. *(4 marks)*

ii Identify **one** useful secondary source **and** explain why it would help. *(4 marks)*

iii Identify **one** primary research method you would use and discuss why it is better than another possible primary method for obtaining the information you need. *(6 marks)*

2.1 Why do we have schools?

The education system is a key institution in society. We spend a large part of our lives in education and it has an important influence on us as individuals and on our future lives.

Education means the process of acquiring knowledge and understanding. This process occurs throughout our lives through **formal education** or **informal education**.

What is education for?

The education system serves a very important role in British society. Education provides a function for society (the **functionalist** perspective) and these functions include the following:

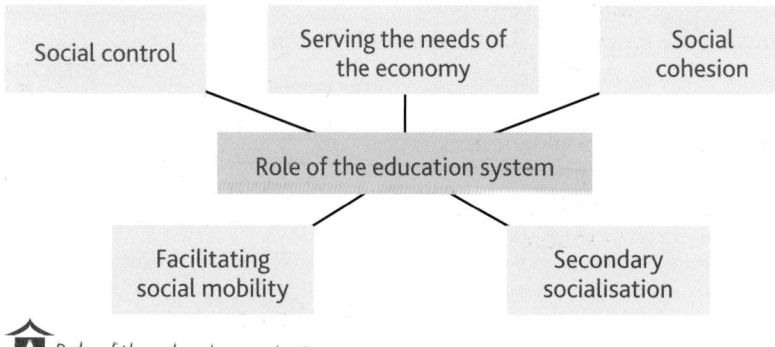

Social control	Serving the needs of the economy	Social cohesion
	Role of the education system	
Facilitating social mobility		Secondary socialisation

A *Role of the education system*

1 Social control

Schools act as an **agent of social control** by teaching acceptance of rules and authority, for example, obeying the teacher.

2 Secondary socialisation

Schools play a role in teaching the values and norms of society to each new generation. It is a continuation of primary socialisation that starts in the family. The norms and values taught in school are reflected in all subsequent organisations people join.

Objectives

You will be able to:

- describe the functions that schools perform in society

- explain the functions of schools from your own experiences

- discuss whether schools have been successful in performing these functions.

Key terms

Formal education: learning particular subjects, for example, maths, English, in organised institutions (schools).

Informal education: occurs through observing what goes on around us, through experiences of life.

Functionalists: argue that the function of institutions such as education is to reproduce culture by socialising individuals into the key values and roles required for social stability.

Agent of social control: individual or group that is responsible for ensuring members of society conform to socially acceptable behaviour.

Social mobility: movement of individuals up or down a social scale.

Social cohesion: 'sticking together'. It describes the integration of a society into a unified whole.

Meritocracy: a social system in which rewards are allocated justly on the basis of merit rather than factors such as class, gender, ethnicity.

3 Serving the needs of the economy

Schools teach the skills and knowledge necessary for work in a modern, technical, industrial society, for example, literacy, numeracy and ICT. Schools need to transmit the skills and knowledge that are required by the economy. There is a close connection between the structure and success of the economy and the skills and knowledge that people acquire in the education system.

4 Social mobility

Schools provide the opportunity to achieve recognised qualifications, enabling students to achieve higher positions in society. The kind of work people do (and their place in society generally) is influenced by what education and qualifications they get.

5 Social cohesion

The norms and values taught in school reflect the norms and values of the culture and give people an identity, for example, 'Britishness'. Shared norms and values bring people together as one society.

Is education always beneficial?

The functionalist approach emphasises the importance of education as a means of transmitting society's values. However, this approach raises various questions:

- There may not be a single set of values to transmit. Society may consist of various groups with different or conflicting interests, each group having its own set of values. Which set of values does the education system transmit?

- This also assumes that the education system gives pupils an equal chance, that they achieve on the basis of merit within a system that is basically fair (**meritocracy**). However, do working-class children have as much opportunity to succeed in education as middle-class children?

- It has also been suggested that schools should be abolished because the compulsory nature of schooling hinders the learning process. Illich (1973) argues that schools stifle creativity and train children to become mindless consumers. This is known as **de-schooling**.

Activity

2 Do schools prepare pupils for the world of work by transmitting norms and values or do schools indoctrinate pupils? What are your views?

Check your understanding

1 What is meant by formal and informal education?

2 Identify and explain three functions of the British education system.

3 Explain whether your own education has been successful in fulfilling the functions you identified above.

4 Explain why education is not always beneficial.

Group activities

1 In small groups, make a list of the norms and values that are taught by parents during primary socialisation and the norms and values that are taught in school during secondary socialisation.

2 In small groups, list any skills you have gained at school that you are likely to use in the workplace.

3 Ask each member of your group whether they think the education system has been successful in performing the following functions: **social control, secondary socialisation, serving the needs of the economy, facilitating social mobility**, and **social cohesion**? For each function answer yes, no or partly.

What do these answers say about the functions of the education system?

Key terms

De-schooling: the idea that schools should be abolished because the compulsory nature of schools hinders the learning process.

∞ links

Also see Topic 2.4 to see the differences in educational achievement between different groups in society.

AQA Examiner's tip

Use sociological explanations for the functions of schools; don't just use your own experiences to answer questions.

How do we measure educational success and failure?

Educational success and failure in contemporary society is measured in many different ways.

The Education Reform Act 1988 introduced the **National Curriculum**. This is a prescribed set of subjects and content that must be studied by all children in state schools. Following this Act, **Ofsted** began to inspect schools and produce publicly available reports on each school.

How do we assess children in schools?

Alongside the introduction of the National Curriculum, various testing and assessment methods were also introduced. Until 2008, all children in the UK were tested at the ages of 7, 11 and 14 with **SATs** and at 16 with **GCSEs**. However, government guidelines in 2008 removed testing at the age of 14. New **diplomas** for 14–19 year olds were introduced in the same year.

Activity

1. In small groups make a list of the National Tests that you have taken since you began school.

   Add the details to a table such as the one below.

Test	Subject	Age

   Discuss these different assessment methods with other students. How successful do you think they were in assessing educational success and failure?

Why do we assess children in schools?

National testing provides teachers with information on pupils' progress, brings public accountability for teachers and schools, and offers government essential data on national standards, providing data for league tables. **League tables** give schools, parents and the students an indication of the success of each school.

Top 100 schools for pupils reaching level 5	
School name	No of pupils
North Cheshire Jewish, Cheadle	36
Hall Meadow, Kettering	11
Whickham Parochial CofE, Newcastle-upon-Tyne	30
Our Lady of Victories Catholic, London	23
Manor Junior and Infant, Bilston	44
Harewood CofE, leeds	14
Ramsbottom Stubbins, Bury	32
Lowercroft, Bury	35
King David Junior, Manchester	90

A League table

Not many years ago, there was a widely held view that children in England were under-tested; now that seems to have swung right round to a belief that they are over-tested. The first National Tests, Standard Assessment Tests (SATs) were introduced at age 7 in 1991 and at age 11 in 1994. The argument for the introduction of national testing was that it would drive up standards.

Case study

SATs scores 'too generous for 1 in 3 pupils'

A third of 11-year-olds in England are getting higher scores in English, mathematics and science national curriculum tests than teachers believe they deserve.

National Key Stage 2 results have already been hit by administrative errors in the marking and provision of results and last night 17,400 Key Stage 2 test results were still missing.

Today's results – the first national test results for children born in the academic year that Labour came to power in 1997 – are expected to show an increase in the proportion of children achieving Level 4, the standard expected of their age, but a drop in the number achieving the above-average Level 5 grades.

From *The Times*, 5 August 2008

Did you know ???????

In 2006, there were almost six million entries at GCSE level.

Activities

2   Using the above case study and other information in this chapter, draw up a table summarising the advantages and disadvantages of the current national assessment tests in schools. Also think about the benefits/drawbacks of publicising these results in leagues tables.

Advantages of national assessment	Disadvantages of national assessment
Advantages of league tables	Disadvantages of league tables

3   From what you have researched, draw some conclusions about the effectiveness of national testing and league tables. Why do you think league tables have been abandoned in Scotland and Wales?

AQA **Examiner's tip**

Make sure you know about the different forms of assessment at different ages. These details will allow you to show a good understanding in the exam.

Going further

1   Access the following website to find out more about the work of Ofsted at **www.ofsted.gov.uk**

School diversity

All children in England between the ages of 5 and 16 are entitled to a free place at a state school. Children normally start **primary school** at the age of 4 or 5 and move to **secondary school** at the age of 11.

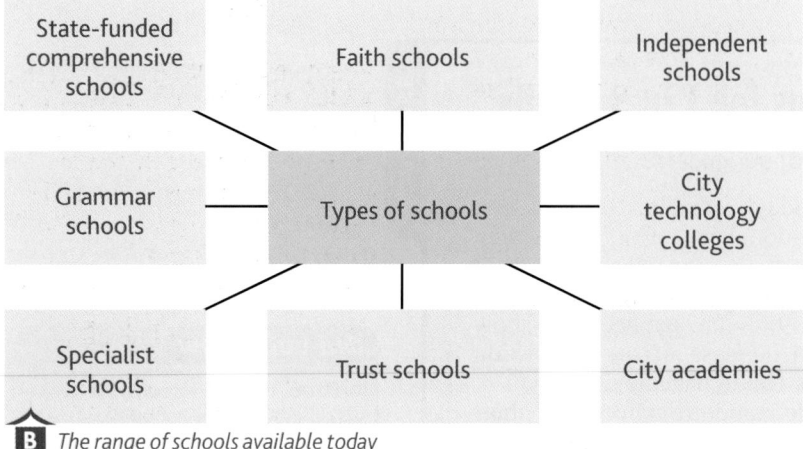

B *The range of schools available today*

State-funded comprehensive schools

Comprehensive schools aim to educate all students, regardless of background or ability, under one roof. The aim is to ensure that all children have access to the same level and quality of education.

Specialist schools

These receive additional funding to support a subject of expertise, and are able to select up to 10 per cent of their students on the basis of ability in this subject. They are an important part of the government's plans to raise standards in secondary education. Specialist status can be in one of eleven specialisms. Special schools can also apply for an SEN (Special Educational Needs) specialism.

Trust schools

These are schools supported by a charitable trust where the school and partners work together for the benefit of the school.

City academies

Ofsted have been given the power by the government to place failing schools under special measures whereby they are re-inspected more regularly. In extreme cases, the government can close down a failing school and reopen it as a city academy with funding from private businesses.

City technology colleges

These are independently managed, non-fee-paying schools in urban areas for pupils of all abilities aged 11 to 18. They are geared towards science, technology and the world of work, offering a range of **vocational** qualifications as well as traditional GCSEs and A-levels.

Key terms

Primary schools (5–11 years): this is the first level of education in the UK. They are generally mixed sex, and usually located close to the child's home. Children tend to be with the same group throughout the day, and one teacher has responsibility for most of their work.

Secondary schools (11–16 years): most children transfer at the age of 11 to secondary school. Most cater for both sexes. Pupils are taught the National Curriculum subjects, normally by specialist teachers.

Vocational: describes a course or qualification designed to provide more of a 'hands-on' approach to learning. This encourages the application of knowledge and understanding of a subject in a practical way.

Did you know ??????

In 2007, nearly 88% of secondary pupils in England and Wales went to comprehensive schools.

Activity

4 Make a list of schools in your local area. Research which of these schools are specialist schools and find out their speciality.

What other schools are there in your local area (for example, trust schools, grammar schools, independent schools)?

Faith schools

Faith schools are mostly run in the same way as other state schools. Their faith status may be reflected in their religious education curriculum, admissions criteria and staffing policies.

- **Advantages**: Faith primary schools offer an advantage over other primary schools in terms of age 11 test scores in maths and English. Children who attend faith schools generally achieve one per cent higher on tests in English and maths. They also receive a religious education supporting their own belief.
- **Disadvantages**: Admission policies may exclude certain groups of children.

Grammar schools

Grammar schools select all or most of their pupils based on academic ability.

Independent schools

Independent schools set their own curriculum and admissions policies. They are funded by fees paid by parents and guardians and income from investments. Independent schools do not have to follow the National Curriculum but most students will take national exams, ensuring that qualifications are consistent and recognised.

Special schools

Special schools for children with Special Educational Needs (SEN) offer a choice to parents who have children that require special education.

Advantages of special school education

- Children can learn appropriate skills to help them with their disability.
- They are taught by teachers who know the techniques to use to help the children.
- Special schools have the most appropriate equipment to help the children develop and learn.

Disadvantages of special school education

- Children are often excluded from other children who do not have their disability.
- They may not have access to the range of the curriculum that may be available in mainstream schools.

Check your understanding

1 Identify and explain three different assessment methods used in schools today.

2 Identify three different types of schools and briefly describe each type of school.

3 Identify one type of school and identify the advantages and disadvantages of attending this type of school.

Going further

2 Research more about city academies. Is there any evidence that they have been successful in raising standards?

Did you know ??????

In 2006, there were more than 2,500 independent schools in the UK educating approximately 615,000 children (roughly 6–7 % of children in the UK).

Group activity

In a small group, discuss the advantages and disadvantages of faith schools. Can you add to the ones listed above?

AQA Examiner's tip

Make sure you know what types of schools there are in the UK today. Be aware of the different types of schools in your area because you could use these as examples in the exam.

Activity

5 Look at the following website which is for a special school for children who are blind or visually impaired: www.newcollegeworcester.co.uk

a Identify some key facts about the school, for example, age range, location.

b Identify the range of subjects the children are offered at the school.

c Identify the range of activities beyond the curriculum that the children are offered.

d List the advantages and disadvantages these children have for being educated in this school compared to a mainstream school.

2.3 What is the hidden curriculum?

The education system provides students with learning through the **formal curriculum**, which is the school's planned programme of learning aims, content, experiences, resources and assessment. However, students also learn through the **hidden curriculum**, which refers to what pupils learn indirectly from the manner in which the school is organised and from teachers' expectations of pupils.

Formal Curriculum	Hidden curriculum
National Curriculum including: • maths • English • science • ICT	• Rules • Obedience • Routine • Dress code • Gender role • Achievement and competition

A Formal curiculum and hidden curriculum

The hidden curriculum reflects society's values and prepares students for their place in society and their future work roles. The hidden curriculum sends messages to the pupils in the school. These messages are coded in many different ways, for example, the structure of the school and the structured timetable.

The school

Structure of schools

Schools are hierarchical institutions. Any hierarchy can be illustrated by using a pyramid. Each layer of the pyramid has more power than the one below it, with the layer at the top having most power. In schools, the headteacher is at the top of the pyramid and holds most power, and the students are at the bottom of the pyramid and have least power.

This structure in schools reflects the hierarchical structure of society in general. In any workplace, there will be a manager at the top of the hierarchy with the most power and workers at the bottom with least power.

Therefore schools guide students to accept this structure, preparing them for work.

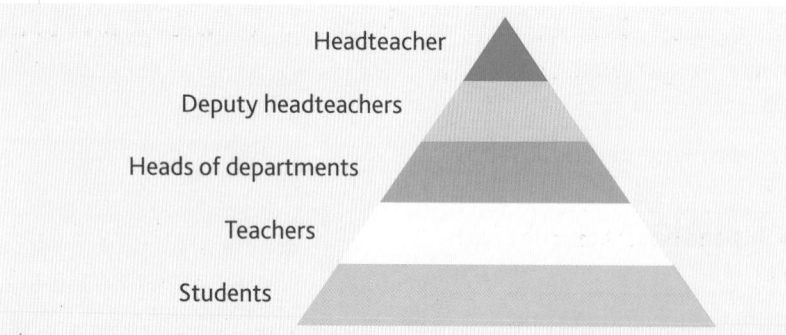

B Structure of schools

Objectives

You will be able to:

- describe the characteristics of the hidden curriculum

- explain the impact of the hidden curriculum on pupils' learning

- explain the impact of the hidden curriculum in preparing you for the workplace.

Key terms

Formal curriculum: what students learn in their timetabled lessons, for example, maths and English.

Hidden curriculum: the ways in which the organisation of teaching, school regulations and routines shape pupil attitude and behaviour, that is, what students learn at school that is not taught in lessons.

Did you know ??????

The term 'hidden curriculum' was first used by sociologist Philip Jackson in 1968, although the concept has been around for longer.

links

Also see Topic 1.1 and Topic 1.4 for definitions of norms, values and socialisation.

AQA Examiner's tip

Clearly show that you understand the differences between the formal curriculum and the hidden curriculum, using examples of what is learnt from each.

Social control

The hidden curriculum consists of rules, regulations and respect for authority. This reflects the social control that operates in society. Students learn to accept society's social controls while they are in the education system. Students need permission to do any activity that is not an assigned task.

Achievement and competition

Schools value and reward individual achievement and hard work, developing the work ethic of society. Pupils learn that differential rewards are earned for different levels of achievement and this encourages competition, for example, in sport. There is also competition between schools, reflected in exam achievements and league tables.

Society is also based on competition, for jobs, material possessions or status. Schools therefore reflect the value that society places on competition and prepares students for their place in a competitive society.

Routine

Schools have a very structured routine. Pupils need to be at school by a particular time and need to register when they arrive. End of lessons are normally indicated by bells and pupils are expected to move from one lesson to another when the bell rings. Lunch times and break times are also at specified times. Good timekeeping and diligence are taught through the discipline of the school routines and are necessary skills for work.

Dress code

Pupils are expected to dress suitably and 'respectably', especially when there is a school uniform. This reflects expectation in the workplace.

Gender role allocation

The way teachers act towards girls, sometimes expecting different behaviour and academic standards from them, means that girls and boys often learn different things at school. Girls are often encouraged to study subjects which are deemed more appropriate for them, for example, biology and English literature, while boys are encouraged into the sciences and technical subjects.

Teachers often have different expectations concerning typical patterns of behaviour for girls and boys. Girls are often expected to be neater, quieter and more studious than boys, who are expected to be lively and more disruptive.

Group activity

In small groups, copy the pyramid from page 48 and add some names to each layer for your school/college. Discuss the role that each person has. Talk to the appropriate staff if necessary.

C *Dress code*

Gender gap still exists

An investigation by the Equal Opportunities Commission into gender segregation in work and training reveals that women are under-represented in key areas including construction, where they make up just 1 per cent of the workforce. While the gender gap has closed in high-status professional sectors such as law, accountancy and medicine, the numbers of women going into building, plumbing, engineering and information technology has barely altered in the last 10 years. Meanwhile, men are barely represented in childcare, another fast expanding sector with a shortage of recruits.

Adapted from Lucy Ward, *The Guardian*, 6 May 2004

Case study

Activity

1   Ask each member of your class what GCSE subjects they are studying. Is there a gender difference?

The classroom

Teaching

Teaching of some subjects, for example, history, gives a student a national identity and a sense that society is something bigger than themselves, for example, 'Britishness'. Subjects are taught separately so that knowledge is fragmented into small segments. This prepares students for the fragmentation of employment, where jobs are broken into component elements.

Labelling

D *Labelling theory*

Students are constantly being assessed and classified. As a result of this testing, they are defined as able or less able and placed in particular classes, entered for particular examinations and given or denied access to certain parts of the school curriculum. Once a student has been given a label (via **labelling**), for example, 'bright', others will respond to them and interpret their actions in terms of this label. The student will often act according to the label, so a **self-fulfilling prophecy** may result.

Setting and streaming

Most secondary schools have a **setting** system for placing students in teaching groups in terms of their perceived ability. These groups include sets in which pupils are placed in subject groups (for example, set 1 for maths) or streams in which they are placed into class groups (class 1, 2, 3) and taught at that level for all subjects.

Streaming has a powerful influence on the formation of pupil sub-cultures, sometimes with negative consequences for the pupils and the school. Most teachers prefer to teach higher ability groups because those in the lower groups tend to develop an **anti-school sub-culture** in which breaking school rules is highly regarded by some students. Teachers spend more time controlling behaviour in these groups at the expense of teaching. They may expect less from these students and these students are often entered for lower level examinations.

This often reflects a social class divide with middle-class students being in the higher sets and working-class students being in the lower sets.

> ### Key terms
>
> **Labelling:** names/labels given to individuals by teachers (and by others, for example, police) which then influence the behaviour of those individuals and also influence the way others respond to those individuals.
>
> **Self-fulfilling prophecy:** people hear labels about themselves from people who are more powerful than they are. They come to believe that the labels are true and then act as if they are true. Therefore, the labels become true.
>
> **Setting:** a way of dividing pupils into groups for particular subjects based on their ability in those subjects.
>
> **Streaming:** a way of dividing pupils according to their supposed ability. A pupil will normally remain in the same stream across all areas of the curriculum.
>
> **Anti-school sub-culture:** these are formed because pupils feel that they are not valued by the school or because they do not identify with the value system and the goals of the school.
>
> **Mixed ability:** pupils of all ability levels are taught as one group.

Arguments for setting and streaming

- Children are judged by their performance as they will be in a hierarchical society.
- Creates a competitive atmosphere that encourages hard work.
- Stretches the brightest pupils whilst allowing the less able to work at their own pace.
- Easier to teach pupils of one ability rather than teaching **mixed ability** classes.

Arguments against setting and streaming

- Labels pupils, which can produce a self-fulfilling prophecy and an anti-academic sub-culture can develop.
- Allocations to groups can result in indirect discrimination, for example, Asian pupils may be put in lower streams than their ability indicates.
- The system is inflexible because transfer up the streams is difficult if the speed and content of the work is different.
- Lower groups are disadvantaged because teachers deny them access to certain aspects of the curriculum and the emphasis is on controlling behaviour rather than teaching.

Activity

2 Using the information in this topic, design a spider diagram to summarise the key aspects of the hidden curriculum.

This would be useful when you come to revise this topic.

Going further

As a class, conduct a survey within your school to identify how successful the school has been in preparing pupils for the world of work through the hidden curriculum.

You may like to design a table as illustrated below to collate your findings.

	Successful	Not successful
Hierarchy (obedience)		
Social control (rules)		
Competition		
Routines		
Dress code		
Gender role allocation		

What do these answers say about the importance of the hidden curriculum?

Check your understanding

1 How does the hidden curriculum differ from the formal curriculum?

2 Identify and explain three ways in which the hidden curriculum shapes pupil attitude and behaviour.

3 Identify and explain how the hidden curriculum has prepared you for the world of work.

What influences educational success beyond school?

When sociologists look at educational achievement they find that there are distinct patterns. Educational success and failure seem to be closely linked to membership of certain social groups.

Social class

Despite all the different government policies since the 1944 Education Act, students from working-class backgrounds, on average, achieve less within formal education than their middle-class peers.

What are the differences in educational success?

The link between achievement and social class is well established.

> A study in 2006 by University College London and Kings College London showed that the overwhelming factor in how well children do is not what type of school they attend, but social class. It reported that in affluent areas, 67 per cent of 11-year-olds were expected to achieve level 5 in the national English tests and 94 per cent of 15-year-olds were expected to get five or more passes at GCSE at grade C and above.
>
> Meanwhile, of the children growing up in more deprived areas, just 13 per cent were likely to get level 5 in the national English tests for 11-year-olds, while only 24 per cent of 15-year-olds were reckoned to achieve the benchmark five-plus GCSEs at grade C and above.
>
> Adapted from Jenni Russell, *The Guardian*, 28 February 2006

In the past, it was generally accepted that there was a relationship between higher qualifications and higher earnings. However, there are more students gaining degrees today and as the number of graduates continues to increase we may well be faced with a situation where jobs that previously required A-levels now require a degree and jobs that required a degree now require a Masters.

Objectives

You will be able to:

- describe different factors that influence success beyond school
- explain how these factors influence success
- discuss the importance of these factors in determining success.

∞ links

Refer to Chapter 1 Studying Society. What did you learn from this chapter on the importance of social class and educational success?

Activities

1 Why do you think these differences in social class and educational success exist?

2 Make a list of possible explanations for these different levels of educational achievement.

Compare your list with others.

A *Higher education and hard times*

Factors affecting these differences in educational success

Home background

- **Material deprivation** – Lack of money can mean a cold and overcrowded house, inadequate levels of nutrition as well as lack of books, computers, etc. This can make it difficult to study at home and may lead to poor school attendance through ill health.
- **Parents' attitude** – The degree of interest and encouragement parents show in their children's education can be a significant element in educational success.
- **Speech patterns** – Middle-class children are more likely to have their writing and speaking skills developed to a higher standard at an earlier age than working-class children.
- **Cultural deprivation** – The norms and values of the working-class child differ from the norms and values of the middle-class institution of schools.

Bourdieu (1977) suggested that middle-class **cultural capital** is as valuable in educational terms as material wealth. The knowledge, values, ways of interacting and communicating ideas that middle-class children possess are developed further and rewarded by the education system. Working-class children may lack these qualities and so do not have the same chances to succeed.

School

- **Teacher/pupil interactions** – Teachers are inevitably involved in making judgements and classifying pupils.

If teachers have low expectations of working-class children, this can affect their progress in school. Equally, if the teacher sees the student as only being capable of reaching a certain level of academic achievement, they may see no point in trying to develop the student's performance any further. This is known as a 'self-fulfilling prophecy'.

Key terms

Cultural capital: the desired skills, for example, language which middle classes pass on to their children.

Did you know ??????

Children from working-class backgrounds are:

- less likely to be found in nursery schools or preschool play groups
- more likely to start school unable to read
- more likely to be placed in lower sets or streams
- more likely to get few GCSEs or low grades
- more likely to leave school at the age of 16.

links

Refer to Topic 2.3 for a definition of 'self-fulfilling prophecy'.

Case study

Equal opportunities?

Despite equal opportunities in the education system it is always going to be hard to change the lives of the most disadvantaged. Teachers preoccupied with delivering the national curriculum had no time for the problems of Kylie, a foul-mouthed four-year-old whose mother smacked her and called her a stupid little bitch on the day school began. Nor did they want to know much about Leroy – the last child of an absentee single parent – who at seven was always hanging around the playground at hometime asking wistfully if he could come back to someone else's house. Leroy and Kylie were still stumbling over simple words at nine because the school relied on parents to do the bulk of the teaching of reading, and neither had a mother who cared. At 16, Kylie's been truanting for much of the past two years, and Leroy has at last found a family of sorts in the gang on his estate. After a dozen years and thousands of hours in education, they'll be lucky to pass any GCSEs. They'll be emerging from the system much as they went in – undersocialised, unwanted, and underskilled.

Adapted from J Judd, *The Guardian*, 5 June 2008

Gender

What are the differences in educational success?

Historically boys outperformed girls, but this situation has changed in recent years. Within three generations, girls have overtaken boys at all levels, and males are now up to seven years behind females in attainment by the end of secondary school.

Girls do better than boys at every stage of the National Curriculum, including SAT results in English, maths and science and in all subjects at GCSE and A-level, except physics.

Figures from the Universities and Colleges Admissions Service (UCAS) show that there are more women than men entering full-time undergraduate courses (in autumn 2006, a total of 390,000 gained a place, of whom 210,000 (54 per cent) were women) and 58 per cent of all degrees were awarded to women.

Key terms

UCAS: University and Colleges Admissions Service. The organisation responsible for the allocation and administration of university and college places.

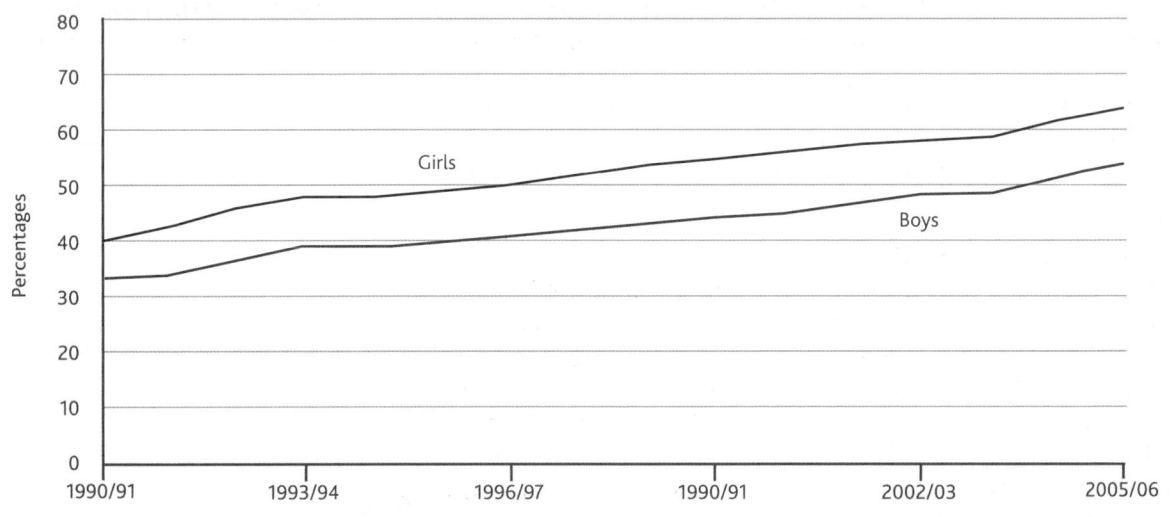

www.statistics.gov.uk

B *Pupils achieving five or more GCSE grades A*–C or equivalent: by sex*

Activity

3 From Graph B:

a Summarise the key differences in educational success between males and females. Why do you think these differences exist?

b Make a list of possible explanations for these different levels of educational achievement.

Compare your list with others.

c Rank the explanations you have identified in order, with the most important first.

Why have you ranked some explanations higher than others?

AQA Examiner's tip

Boys' achievement has not declined; instead girls have improved much more rapidly than boys. When answering exam questions you must be clear that now the focus is on male underachievement and not female underachievement. You need to be clear about why things have changed.

Factors affecting these differences in educational success

Home background

Socialisation

Parents tend to buy girls different toys, which encourage their language skills. Research shows that girls spend their leisure time differently from boys. Boys relate to their peers by doing (that is, being active); girls relate to one another by talking. This puts girls at an advantage because school is essentially a language experience, and most subjects require good levels of comprehension and writing skills. Some boys see schoolwork as 'uncool' and 'unmasculine' and may gain peer group status from not working.

Job market

There are increasing job opportunities for women. Many girls have mothers in paid work who provide positive role models. As a result, girls recognise that the future offers them more choices; economic independence and careers are now available to them. Boys, however, are experiencing a **crisis of masculinity** (Mac and Ghaill, 1994). They are socialised into seeing their future male identity and role in terms of having a job and being a **breadwinner**. However, the decline of manufacturing industries and the increase in service sector jobs, which are often part-time and desk-based, are more suited to the skills and lifestyles of women. Working-class boys' perception of this may influence their motivation and ambition.

School

Teacher/pupil interactions

There are now more career opportunities for women and this has filtered through the education system. With broadening opportunities for girls, more is expected of girls today. Teachers also have different expectations concerning typical behaviour for girls and boys. Boys are expected to be livelier than girls and girls are expected to be more studious than boys. Teachers often respond to these stereotypes.

Curriculum

Since the introduction of the National Curriculum, all girls and boys are required to study English, maths and science up to GCSE level. Girls are therefore studying the same core subjects as boys. Girls tend to spend more time on homework, are more organised and put more effort into their work.

Hidden curriculum

The attitudes created by the wider society about the correct behaviour for females, plus their home socialisation, are strengthened at school through the hidden curriculum. Use of gendered regimes, for example, girls playing netball, boys playing rugby, order of names in the register, uniforms, lining up or seating plans may also reinforce gender roles.

Did you know ???????

In 2005/6, 64% of girls achieved five or more GCSEs at grade A* to C compared with 54% of boys.

Key terms

Crisis of masculinity: the idea that men's perception of what a man is and how he ought to behave has been undermined by social and economic changes.

Breadwinner: the person in the household who is the main income earner.

⌾links

Also see Topic 2.3 for the effect of the hidden curriculum.

Ethnicity

It is easy to assume that because Britain is a multicultural society there are equal chances for all ethnic groups. However, when we look at the performance of Britain's ethnic minorities, a different picture emerges in which huge differences exist between the educational performances of one ethnic minority compared to another.

What are the differences in educational success?

Indian children and Chinese children do extremely well and achieve more than white children. Some ethnicities do, however, tend to underachieve. Pakistani, Bangladeshi and black Caribbean ethnicities often achieve less than white children and each of these groups is under-represented at university.

Key terms

Ethnocentric curriculum: schools are structured in a particular way including such aspects as school assemblies, history and language which reflect the culture of the majority.

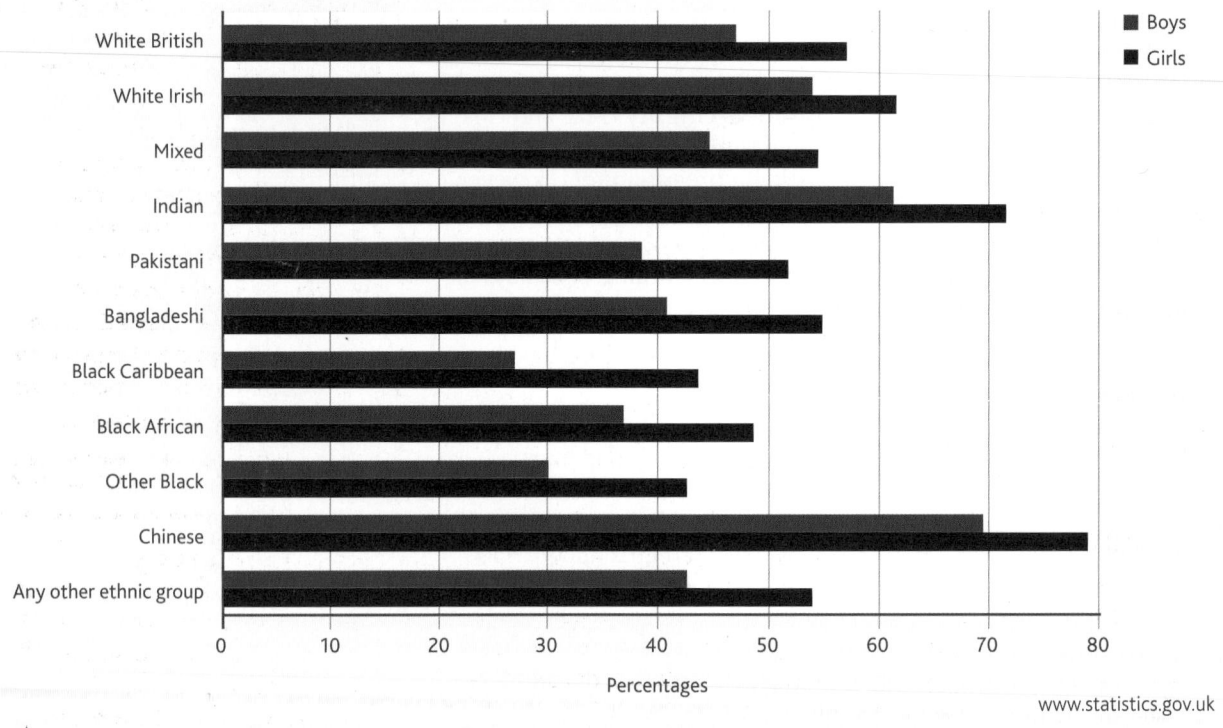

www.statistics.gov.uk

C *Pupils achieving five or more A*–C at GCSE/GNVQ: by sex and ethnic group, 2004, England*

Activity

4   From Chart **C**:

a   Summarise the differences in educational achievement. Why do you think these differences exist?

b   Make a list of possible explanations for these different levels of educational achievement.

    Compare your list with others.

c   Rank the explanations you have identified in order, with the most important first.

    Why have you ranked some explanations higher than others?

AQA Examiner's tip

Remember when considering the differences in educational achievement between different ethnic groups you may also need to consider differences in class and gender, for example, the experience of a white, working-class female in the classroom may be very different from that of an Asian, middle-class boy.

Factors affecting these differences in educational success

Home background

- **Material deprivation**
  The difference in educational achievement between ethnic groups can be partially explained by social class. Many ethnic groups are in lower social classes so suffer material deprivation associated with the lower classes, such as poor housing and lack of resources.

- **Language**
  For many children from immigrant homes, the main language of the home is generally the country of origin. Therefore, their studies are carried out in a 'foreign' language. Afro-Caribbean children may speak English at home but it is sometimes in a dialect that differs from standard English and this can cause confusion in school.

- **Cultural deprivation**
  Working-class and some ethnic minority cultures find it difficult to motivate their children in the education system. As a result they fail to receive the skills and values required to succeed.

School

- **Teacher/pupil interactions**
  Despite the existence of equal opportunities policies in schools, sufficient evidence exists to show that children from ethnic minorities often experience racism within school. This can come from teachers as well as other students.

  Some teachers have stereotyped views and expectations of students, which may be influenced by the child's ethnic origin, for example, some teachers may have higher expectations of Asian pupils as they are considered to be capable and hard working.

  Research has also shown that teachers believe that children from an Afro-Caribbean background are less academic than those from other ethnic backgrounds. Teachers expect less so black pupils are not as encouraged as other students. In this way teachers' labels may lead to a self-fulfilling prophecy through which the students' educational achievement is affected. Teachers inevitably make judgements about and classify pupils. These judgements often affect a child's chances of educational achievement.

- **Curriculum**
  The school curriculum is seen as being **ethnocentric**. Schools are structured in a particular way which tends to reflect British culture, for example, school assemblies, history and language.

Check your understanding

1 Choose social class, gender or ethnicity. What is the difference in educational achievement within this group?

2 Identify two reasons why there is a difference in the educational achievement between the rich and the poor.

3 Identify two ethnicities that achieve well in school and two ethnicities that underachieve. Give reasons for these differences.

4 Describe how patterns in gender and achievement have changed.

Racism in schools?

Very many black Caribbean children in British schools underachieve. Just 29 per cent achieve five good grades at GCSE, although girls do better than boys. A report by school inspectors suggests that racial stereotyping and low expectations amongst teachers are to blame for the poor exam performance of black Caribbean, Pakistani, Bangladeshi and gypsy travelling children. They suggested that there can be a breakdown in communication between the white teachers and black pupils. In some schools, teachers' assessment of black and Asian pupils is considerably lower than their test results, the report said. One student was angry that teachers would not let him take the higher tier GCSE exam for IT and instead made him take the lower tier, which meant he could not achieve higher than Grade C. 'There were white students and Asians who were put in for the higher paper who were not as good as me' he said.

Adapted from Judith Judd, *The Independent*, 11 March 1999

Going further

Choose social class, gender or ethnicity. Carry out your own piece of research to identify whether there is a difference in the educational qualifications achieved within your school.

Design your research, for example, questionnaire, collect your data and analyse your findings. What does your research show about the differences in the educational success of different social groups?

Why is education a political issue?

Education is a political issue because the government is responsible for changes in the law that affect the education system. Local education authorities (LEAs) and places of education, for example, nurseries, schools and colleges, must follow changes in the law.

Social policy timeline

There are continual changes in the education system. However, although each government makes changes and introduces new policies they inherit the policies of the previous government and build on what is currently in place. The information in this topic outlines key educational policies that have been implemented since 1944.

1944 Education Act (Butler Act)

The Butler Act restructured education radically, creating a formal, state-funded secondary sector. The overall aim of this Act was to improve society and the economy through provision of a better education system. It did this by introducing:

- **Tripartite system** with three types of school
  - secondary technical schools for those with a talent in mechanical, engineering or scientific areas
  - grammar schools for more 'academic' students
  - secondary modern schools for those not suited to the other two schools
- Free compulsory state education to the age of 15
- **Eleven plus** exam, which was given to all pupils at the end of primary school.

A *Modern parenting*

Objectives

You will be able to:

- describe how the education system has changed and developed
- explain the current political issues in education
- discuss the impact of politics on education.

Key terms

Tripartite system: three types of secondary school for different types of pupil based on an IQ (Intelligence Quotient) test at the age of 11.

Eleven plus: a type of intelligence test taken at age 11 to determine whether a child should attend a grammar school, a technical school or a secondary modern.

Setting: a way of dividing pupils into groups for particular subjects based on their ability in those subjects.

Streaming: a way of dividing pupils according to their supposed ability. A pupil will normally remain in the same stream across all areas of the curriculum.

New vocationalism: training aimed to equip the young with the skills and education required by a rapidly changing economy.

Marketisation of education: changes to the education system in the late 1980s, so that it became more business-like.

Going further

1 Design a brief questionnaire including questions on the type of education that people experienced, for example, did you take the eleven plus? Ask your parents and grandparents to complete the questionnaire and summarise the findings.

The Eleven Plus

For the vast majority of children in the 1950s and 1960s the eleven plus was the first public examination they took. 'One day in January of our last year in primary school we were marshalled into the gymnasium to take three papers, in mathematics, English language and General Intelligence. The mathematics paper involved simple subtraction, addition, etc. My recollection of this paper was simply dull. The English language paper was more creative: we were invited to write about a recent outing (bad luck if you had the misfortune not to go on them!). General Intelligence was about the recognition of order: numbers and patterns in sequence. All these papers lasted half an hour and so after one and a half hours our educational fate was sealed. Passing or failing these tests was announced three months later.'

'I remember arriving at grammar school on my first day. The most striking characteristic of the pupils was that they arrived in cars, from detached houses and with standard English voices, everyone with the expensive uniform. We needed an entire new wardrobe: from socks to vests to knickers to skirts and hats (one for the summer and one for the winter), three pairs of shoes (one for summer, one for winter, one for indoors), coat, scarf and gloves, all which had to be bought from a specialist school shop.'

Identity and Diversity, Gender and the experience of Education edited by Maud Blair and Janet Holland with Sue Sheldon

Did you know ? ? ? ? ? ?

Gaining a place at a grammar school after taking the eleven plus was influenced by location and gender. For example, due to single-sex schooling, there were fewer places for girls than boys.

Activity

1   Read the case study. What does this extract say about equality of opportunity within the tripartite system?

1965 Comprehensive education

During the 1950s, discontent grew with the way in which the tripartite system limited the opportunities available to many students. The overall aim of comprehensive education was to introduce an inclusive approach where all pupils in a local education authority would attend the same school. It did this by abolishing the tripartite system and putting students into **sets/streams** according to ability when they reached their comprehensive school.

1979 New vocationalism

The issue of whether education was providing the right types of skills for the economy was being questioned. Conservative politicians felt that education had emphasised academic achievement and this was damaging the economy because there was a shortage of skilled individuals. **New vocationalism** was introduced in schools/colleges.

1988 Education Reform Act

The key aim of this act was to introduce competition between schools (**marketisation of education**). Parents were given choice over where to send their children, and schools were encouraged to 'compete' for their children. It was hoped that this would raise the standard of education in the UK. This Act also introduced: the National Curriculum, SATs, league tables and Ofsted.

Going further

2   Some parts of the UK still use the eleven plus as a selection test. Use the Internet to find out where these areas are.

Most recent changes in education

All political parties in power have made changes to the education system but the changes below outline the most recent changes made by the Labour government. Following their election in 1997, New Labour's education reforms built upon the 1988 Act.

1997 New Labour introduced various education policies

1 They retained commitment to parental choice and expanded diversity of available schools. This included specialist schools, faith schools and trust schools.

2 **Excellence in Cities** (EiC) and **Education Action Zones** (EAZs) were created to improve achievement in the most disadvantaged areas. By doing this they tried to address systematic underachievement in some schools, particularly in the inner cities.

Case study

Education Action Zones

ATHENA EiC Action Zone in Birmingham has developed an intervention programme which provides targeted support in numeracy and literacy for pupils who are a borderline Level 4 when they enter Year 6. They use innovative ICT (Information and Communication Technology) programmes as well as an interactive whiteboard to support the programme of study.

In this programme targeted children attend literacy and numeracy sessions at the ATHENA Learning Resource Centre based in Harborne Hill School up until their SATs in the summer term.

3 Curriculum 2000. Changes were made to the structure of A-levels by splitting A-levels into AS and A2. Also, as part of Curriculum 2000 the teaching and testing of key skills were introduced in numeracy, communication and ICT. To encourage students to continue in education after the age of 16, a payment is given to students who are from less wealthy backgrounds. This is known as the **Educational Maintenance Allowance (EMA)** and can be worth up to £30 a week.

4 Ofsted were given the power to place failing schools under special measures where they were re-inspected more regularly and given additional freedoms. In certain cases, the schools would be closed and reopened as an academy. The aim of academies was to raise standards of education.

5 Changes were made to the post-compulsory sector with the pledge that 50 per cent of young people will be in some form of higher education by 2010.

6 They abolished grants for attending university and introduced student loans.

Going further

3 Research other EiC Action Zones and Education Action Zones and summarise the key points. Share this information with others in your class.

Key terms

Excellence in Cities (EiC): the Excellence in Cities programme, launched in March 1999, made a unique contribution to the raising of attainment of disadvantaged pupils in our most deprived cities, towns, and rural areas.

Education Action Zones (EAZs): are built around groups of schools that are determined to raise educational standards in the most challenging areas in the UK.

Educational Maintenance Allowance (EMA): money paid directly to students who stay on in education after the age of 16. The amount received depends on parents' income.

links

Also see Topic 2.2 for more information on the different types of schools.

2006 – Raising Skills, Improving Life Chances

To encourage young people to stay on in education after the age of 16 this policy was introduced to improve skills for industry, employment and the economy, including skills for enterprise and self-employment. Every further education institution was instructed to develop at least one specialism. The sixth form sector was promoted to encourage young people to continue their education.

2007 Children's Plan

The Children's Plan aims to ensure that every child gets a 'world class education' and to encourage parents to become more involved in their children's education. The links between family life and the education of children have been identified as paramount and this is evident in the creation of a new government department in 2007: The Department of Families, Schools and Young People.

"My dog ate my homework, so I couldn't study for the test. So, as his punishment, he'll be taking the test for me."

B

C   *Education is essential*

Activity

2   Draw a timeline that includes all the key dates of the education policies. Add the key points relating to each policy. Complete this in groups and display it on the wall or do this as a revision exercise.

1944_____   1965_____

Tripartite system   Comprehensive education

(Eleven plus)

> **AQA** *Examiner's tip*
>
> There are continuing changes in the education system. Examiners will expect to see up-to-date information in your answers.

Going further

4   Keep up to date with changes in education. Read newspapers, listen to the news or check websites.

Check your understanding

1   Identify and explain the key aspects of two different education policies prior to 2000.

2   What impact have these policies had on the education of young people?

3   Identify and explain the key aspects of two different education policies since 2000.

4   What impact have these policies had on the education of young people?

What does social research tell us about education in contemporary Britain?

There are various research methods available when studying education and the method used depends on what the sociologist is trying to find out.

As you saw in Chapter 1, in order to build or test theories, sociologists need to collect data. They can do this in two ways: collecting and analysing data that already exists – **secondary data** or by collecting data themselves – **primary data**.

Sources of secondary data on education

Source	Examples
Official statistics These are statistics produced by government bodies, for example, league tables.	www.statistics.gov.uk
Unofficial statistics These are statistics produced by charities etc.	Joseph Rowntree Foundation (www.jrf.org.uk)
Mass media News stories can be used as a source of information.	www.bbc.co.uk
Life documents Personal records of thoughts and feelings such as diaries, letters, etc. Life documents tend to be qualitative documents as they tend to be about what people think and often how they feel.	Hey (1997) examined girls' personal diaries to explore girls' friendships in two London schools. She also used participant observation (primary data).

The education and employment of disabled young people

Disabled young people have not always been encouraged to see themselves as having a valuable role in adult society. Previous research on a sample of young people born in 1958 reported that the proportion of disabled youngsters aspiring to semi-skilled and unskilled jobs was six times that of non-disabled youngsters with those aspirations (A Walker, *Unqualified and underemployed: handicapped young people and the labour market*, Macmillan, 1982).

A study by the Joseph Rowntree Foundation (2005) asked whether the gap between disabled and non-disabled young people's aspirations, and the even larger gap in their subsequent attainment, has persisted for those born more recently. The research analysed data from cohort studies of children born in 1970 and in the early 1980s.

Key terms

Secondary data: data that has been produced by other researchers.

Primary data: data collected for the first time by the researcher for a particular piece of research.

Did you know

In 2006/7, there were nearly 33,900 schools in the UK, attended by 9.8 million pupils.

The research was based primarily on analysis of data from two sources. The 1970 British Cohort Study (BCS70), a nationally representative study of all children born in one week in 1970; and cohorts 9 and 10 of the Youth Cohort Study (YCS), a nationally representative study of people of school-leaving age, who were born in 1982/3 and 1984/5. BCS70 was selected because it is a very rich dataset and follows young people through to their mid-twenties. The YCS was selected because it is more recent (age 16/17 surveys in 1998/2000). The study found that in general:

- three in five young people wanted to stay on after 16, whether or not they were disabled
- one in three disabled young people aspired to a professional occupation, compared with one in four non-disabled
- the average weekly pay that disabled and non-disabled 16/17-year-olds expected from a full-time job was similar.

Adapted from T Hope, *Building Success in Post-Compulsory Education: The Effectiveness of the Education Maintenance Allowance (EMA)*

Activity

1. List the research methods you have used during this chapter on education.

B   *Higher education can lead to better employment*

Going further

1. Design a questionnaire to discover what aspirations fellow students have. Include questions on further/higher education, type of job, salary, etc. Also include questions about ethnicity, gender and social class and disability. Do any of these factors make a difference?

Check your understanding

1   What was the aim of this research?

2   What secondary sources were used in this research?

3   What is meant by a 'cohort'?

4   Why were these two sources used in this research?

5   What were the key findings of this study?

∞ links

Refer to the Studying Society chapter for more information on research methods and to the Mass media chapter to read more about the mass media as a source of secondary data.

AQA *Examiner's tip*

An understanding of different research methods is important because whatever topic you are studying in sociology you will be conducting research. You will therefore face the same challenges whatever the topic area. This means that the act of research raises common issues that can be used as a way to think about studies.

AQA *Examiner's tip*

It is necessary to show a clear understanding of the differences between primary and secondary sources. It is also a good idea to use examples to clarify the differences.

Sources of primary data on education

Source	Examples
Laboratory experiment A highly controlled situation where the researchers try to isolate the influence of each variable.	Davis (1989) explored gender roles within literature and the perceptions of these stories from young children. Stories were read to children over two years to assess the children's response to the stories.
Field experiment An experiment conducted in the participant's natural environment, for example, school.	Rosenthal and Jacobson (1967) gave students intelligence tests. Teachers were told that the test was a predictor for very sudden increases in ability. Names were given at random to teachers, who were told these particular children would show significant improvement in ability over a six-month period. The children were then retested and it was claimed that the children whose names were given to the teachers as 'bloomers' or improvers showed improvement. This shows how the attitude of teachers to children could affect their success.
Interview There are two types of interviews: structured/formal and unstructured/informal. **Structured/formal interviews** are similar to a questionnaire where the questions are asked by the interviewer. **Unstructured/informal interviews** are where the interviewer has a topic and an outline of questions to be asked but may ask other questions depending on the answers given by the respondent.	Hope (2000) conducted interviews with students who were receiving an **Educational Maintenance Allowance (EMA)** at a college in Truro to explore whether the receipt of an EMA affected participation in further education. It was found that 62 per cent of EMA students did not believe that the EMA affected their participation in further education.
Questionnaire/survey A way of obtaining information in a standardised manner from a large group of people.	Lees (1986) conducted a survey and found that girls are more career oriented but still wanted to become wives and mothers.
Participant observation The observer becomes part of the group they are observing.	Hey (1997) used participant observation to explore girls' friendships in two London schools. She also examined the girls' personal diaries (secondary data).
Non-participant observation The observer observes the individual or group from a distance without interfering with the participant's behaviour.	Paul Willis (1977) carried out observations of 12 'lads' from a Midlands school over a period from their last year in school to their first months of paid employment. He found that the 'lads' adopted a 'preparation for future work culture'. The 'lads' rejected school and the rules that went with it which was in a way preparing them for their lives in the workplace.

links

Also see Topics 1.6 and 1.7 for definitions of the different research methods.

Remuneration, Recruitment, Retention: The Educational Maintenance Allowance as an incentive to learn

At Truro College in 1999/2000 research was conducted to identify the extent to which a financial incentive (EMA) can improve post-16 recruitment and retention in the College. Truro College, Cornwall is a tertiary Further and Higher Education College with 1,950 full-time students in Years 1 and 2 of Further Education courses.

Quantitative data was collected on the participation and retention rates for the student Advanced Level cohorts 1998–1999 and 1999–2000. The 1998–1999 cohort acted as a base line, or control, for student participation and retention without the discretionary financial award incentive of the EMA. The 1999–2000 cohort was the first year to be given access to the EMA and was therefore used for comparative analysis (against cohort 1998–1999) to examine the effect of the EMA on participation and retention levels.

Qualitative data was collected using semi-structured interviews based on an opportunity sample of 43 EMA recipients in Year 1 (1999–2000) of a two-year full-time Advanced Level FE course. A pilot interview was conducted in order to establish the final interview structure. The researcher had intended to use a randomly stratified sample of Year One Advanced Level EMA recipients, but of the 74 selected for interview, only 10 turned up (despite two weeks notice, a reminder three days before the interview and permission to miss lessons). Consequently the final student interview sampling technique emerged out of necessity.

Adapted from *Remuneration, Recruitment, Retention: The Educational Maintenance Allowance as an incentive to learn* **www.educational-research.co.uk**

Key terms

Educational Maintenance Allowance (EMA): money paid directly to students who stay on in education after the age of 16. The amount received depends on parents' income.

Activity

2   Read the section on the EMA and then answer the following questions.

a   What is the difference between qualitative and quantitative data?

b   What quantitative research method was used in this research?

c   What qualitative research was used in this research?

d   What is a control group and why was it important to use a control group in this research?

e   What is a pilot study and why is it important?

f   What is a randomly stratified sample?

Going further

2   Design a questionnaire to discover how fellow students feel about receiving payment to continue with their education. Include questions about ethnicity, gender and social class. Do any of these factors make a difference?

Check your understanding

1   What is the difference between primary and secondary data?

2   Identify one way education has been studied using a primary source. What are the advantages and disadvantages of this method?

3   Identify one way education has been studied using a secondary source. What are the advantages and disadvantages of this method?

Exam question guidance

Example of a source-based question

∞links

See the Exam question guidance section in Topic 1.8 on page 38 for general advice on answering source-based questions.

Item A

Faith schools

The debate about faith schools and whether they help to create a divided society is not simple. Many people have seen Muslim faith schools as reinforcing the way in which some communities have become isolated. Others believe that parental choice and population changes are more important factors. The government wishes to encourage faith schools within the state sector, seeing them as able to raise educational standards.

Adapted from an article in *The Guardian*, 26 September 2007

- **Who?** This source is from a newspaper article. The paper concerned is *The Guardian*, a liberal 'broadsheet' with a long tradition of championing social reform.

- **What?** The neo-liberal reforms of the Labour government have encouraged a market in education with different types of provision including involvement from the private sector and faith-based groups. The idea appears to be that competition and variety in the educational 'market place' will drive up standards.

- **Why?** Faith-based schools are particularly controversial and are seen by some commentators as allowing extremism to establish a secure state-funded foothold in education. It is not only Muslim schools that are a matter of concern. Extremist Christian groups have also made the headlines as a consequence of their belief that 'creationism' (the literal truth of the Bible) should be given equality of status with evolutionary biology in the **science** classroom.

---

a   Identify one possible disadvantage of faith schools.   *(1 mark)*

Answer as briefly as possible. The article refers to the possibility that faith schools might encourage a **divided society** reinforcing the **isolation** of some communities from the mainstream.

---

c   Identify **two** reasons why parents may wish to send their children to faith schools.   *(2 marks)*

The examiners want you to think about the reasons **why** some parents send their children to such schools. Relevant reasons might include:

- a belief that such schools maintain traditional standards of discipline and/or that they achieve high levels of academic excellence

- the concern that educating children from religious or ethnic minority groups within the mainstream may expose them to cultural values that the parents disapprove of or anti-social behaviour that they wish to avoid. This behaviour could include criminality, different standards of sexual morality and drug or alcohol abuse.

Example of an extended-answer question

These questions are designed to test your knowledge and understanding of the relevant sociology **and** your ability to construct an argument in response to the question. The source material (that is, the three items that are provided in the question) will have been designed to help you think about some of the issues and to remind you about current areas of debate. The best advice anyone can give to a student tackling an extended answer is to stick to a number of basic principles (the rule of three):

1 Say what you are going to do: **introduce** the key ideas and review the focus of the question.

2 Do what you said you would do: make an **argument** based on the evidence you have from your course of study.

3 Say that you have done it: write a **conclusion**, return to the original question and sum up your thoughts.

> g   Discuss how far sociologists would agree that encouraging pupils to adopt British values has become the most important function of the education system in recent years.
>
> *(12 marks)*

- The examiner would expect you to be aware of the importance that the government has placed on citizenship education. You also need to be aware of concerns about the loss of a distinct 'cultural identity' for the British in a society that is generally tolerant of the beliefs of others and allows minority groups to retain their distinctive cultural identity (multiculturalism).

- The question clearly raises the issue of **extent. How far** would sociologists agree? From a sociological point of view there are a number of important issues to be addressed. These include the fact that any national educational system must reflect the *core values of a particular culture at a particular point in time, including an element of social control.* This might bring your argument back to the idea of allowing certain minority groups to 'opt out' of mainstream education and whether there is in fact anything new about this. For example, students from privileged and wealthy backgrounds have long been able to purchase a very different form of education to the vast majority of the population. A Marxist sociologist might even argue that this whole question misses the point: fundamentally state education systems are largely about creating a *compliant* workforce equipped with the basic skills needed by industry. Ultimately these are not British values as such but the values of global capitalism. You might discuss the fact that Muslim schools appear to be particularly worrying to some. This is because they are seen, rightly or wrongly, as potential breeding grounds for extremism. On the other hand, Christian fundamentalism is tolerated because it is not seen as a threat to the security of the state.

▪ Remember to avoid the trap of only referring to the sources in the question. The examiner wants to see evidence that you have studied the sociology of education and thought about the issues.

Questions to try

What follows are examples of the types of questions you will meet in your exam. The letter in each question matches the letter that will be used for that type of question on your exam paper. The number in brackets is only there to help you and your teacher refer to that particular question in this book.

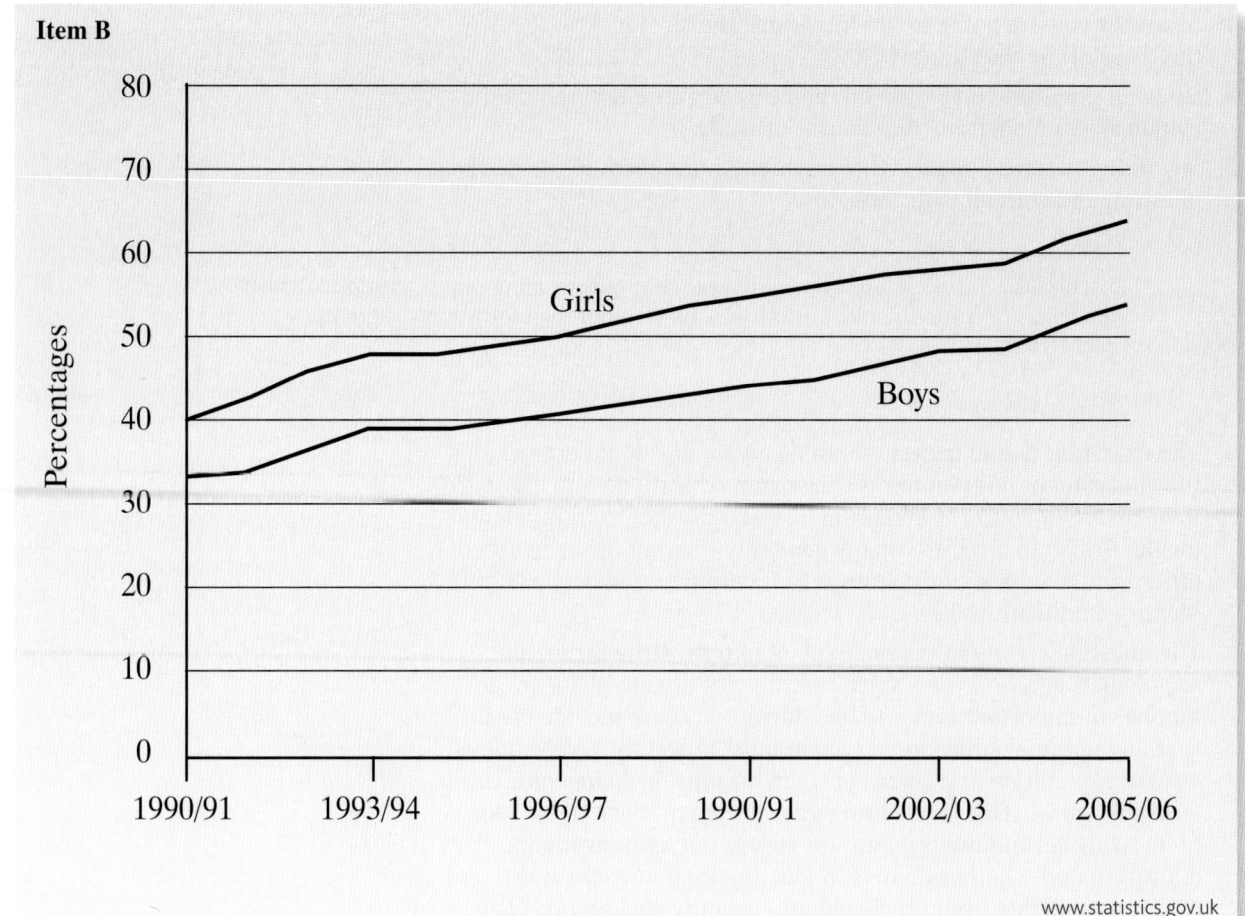

Item B

www.statistics.gov.uk

a From **Item B**, which gender group has consistently achieved the highest proportion of GCSE grades A*–C? *(1 mark)*

d(1) Explain what sociologists mean by the self-fulfilling prophecy in schools. *(4 marks)*

d(2) Explain what sociologists mean by the hidden curriculum. *(4 marks)*

d(3) Explain what sociologists mean by selective education. *(4 marks)*

e Describe one way in which recent governments have attempted to raise standards in schools and explain how successful the policy has been. *(5 marks)*

g(1) Discuss how far sociologists would agree that differences in educational achievement between individuals result from differences in home background. *(12 marks)*

g(2) Discuss how far sociologists would agree that a pupil's social class is the most important influence on his or her educational achievements. *(12 marks)*

g(3) Discuss how far sociologists would agree that the improvement in girls' achievement in examinations has been the result of educational reforms. *(12 marks)*

3 Families

3.1 What is a family?

We all have one. You are likely to have been brought up in one, you are probably living in one now and you will probably form one of your own in the future – but for each of you, your **family** is unique. You can see your family as:

- all the people who are related to you and to each other either through blood (they were born into your family) or through marriage (they married someone who was a blood relative). This collection of related individuals is sometimes called your kinship system.
- the people who are related to you and live with you in your **household**.

Some interesting questions arise when we really try to define the 'family'. Do you include your pet cat, dog or hamster? Do you need adults of the opposite sex in a family? Do you need to have children to be called a family?

What is a household?

This is the term used to describe the group of people living together in the same domestic dwelling. For you, your family and your household may be the same thing but they may be different. A group of students living in the same house, a lodger renting a room in a 'family home', an au pair or a nanny looking after children, a couple providing foster care are all examples of households that contain people who are not necessarily related.

It is also worth considering that, in an increasing number of cases, mothers, fathers and children might not live in the same household.

Different family structures

If we look at the variety of families that exist in Britain today we could say we are looking at **family diversity**. The two types of family we hear most about are extended and nuclear families.

A **nuclear family** is traditionally seen as made up of mother, father and young or **dependent children**. It also assumes that husband and wife will act out traditional roles with the male being the **breadwinner** and the mother staying at home to look after the home and the children.

An **extended family** is a family consisting of parents and children, along with either:

- grandparents – three **generations** make it vertically extended or
- aunts and uncles – a horizontally extended family.

Objectives

You will be able to:

- recognise the difference between a family and a household
- explain the essential features of different types of family structures
- recognise that a variety of family forms exist in Britain today
- assess your own journey through the family life cycle.

Key terms

Family: a group of two or more persons associated by birth, cohabitation, marriage, or adoption.

Household: all the people living together in a domestic dwelling.

Family diversity: the idea that there are many different types of family structure.

Nuclear family: a family group consisting of the father, mother, and their dependent children.

Dependent child: a person living in the household who is under 16 years of age or aged between 16 and 18 but in full-time education.

Breadwinner: the person in the household who is the main income earner.

Extended family: a family composed of the nuclear family and other relatives.

Generation: a group of people who live during the same time period.

A *Nuclear family*

B *Extended family*

In its pure form, these family members live under the same roof, in the same household. However, even if we don't live with our relatives we can still feel as though we are part of an extended family as we can constantly keep in touch through:

- modern communication technology, for example, mobile phone, text, e-mail, video link
- transport by private car and regular short or long-distance rail and air links.

There are differences in family structures between different cultural and ethnic groups in modern Britain. Although most families of Asian origin tend to be nuclear families, they do maintain very close links with their extended family network. Families with Bangladeshi and Pakistani origins tend to be larger than those from other ethnic groups. A high percentage of families with an Afro-Caribbean background are headed by a lone parent. These **matrifocal** households are organised and run largely by women and men are not involved.

∞ links

Also see Topic 3.2 for a fuller discussion of the nuclear family.

Key terms

Matrifocal: a family organised by and focused on the mother.

Census: a survey of all people and households in the country, held every 10 years (UK).

Activity

1 Researching your family history is called genealogy and the best way of recording what you find is in the form of a family tree. Draw out a family tree to include all the relatives you know in your own, your parents' and your grandparents' generations.

Going further

1 Find out where your ancestors were living between 1841 and 1901. **Census** records for 1841, 1851, 1861, 1871, 1881, 1891 and 1901 are available online through **www.ancestry.co.uk** and free access to the actual census pages is available from the computers in most libraries in the UK. The information here gives you some idea of where your ancestors lived and their ages and occupations. You might like to invite another member of your family to view the information with you.

AQA Examiner's tip

Make sure you are able to identify the similarities and possible differences between a family and a household.

Family and household structures in modern Britain

There are many different types of family structures in modern Britain. These family structures are not settled; they change over time. If you ask people to describe their family, it will give you a snapshot of that family at a particular time and any statistics on family structures do the same.

The modern nuclear family

Married couples or **cohabiting** couples with or without children, about 70 per cent of the UK population, currently live in these types of family.

The reconstituted family

With the rise in the divorce rate over the last 50 years, many of the couples in these families have remarried and have formed what is referred to as **reconstituted families** with step-parents and stepchildren.

The lone parent family

This is the fastest growing family structure in modern Britain. Lone parent families can be the result of:

- the divorce of a couple who have children. Recent figures show that two in five marriages will ultimately end in divorce – a considerable rise over the last 50 years.
- a mother choosing not to marry the father of the child. The fastest growing group of lone parents is single or never-married lone mothers. However, only 15 per cent (or one in seven) lone mothers have never married or lived with their child's father.
- a father not wanting to be involved in the welfare of the child.

Statistics only give a snapshot in time. For many adults and children, lone parenthood will only be a temporary phase in their lives. Figures show that this 'stage' in family life lasts on average about five and a half years.

Same sex families

Although they account for a very small proportion of all families, those headed by two people of the same sex have increased in number recently. The Civil Partnership Act came into force in 2005 and granted legal recognition to same-sex relationships. Adoption, surrogacy and in-vitro fertilisation (IVF) technology have given these families the opportunity to include children.

links

Also see Topic 3.2 for more detail on the development and characteristics of the nuclear family.

Did you know

The General Household Survey 2007 showed that 39% of single individuals aged 25 to 34 were cohabiting.

Activity

2 Lone parent families are often presented in the media in a negative light. They are portrayed as presenting a problem both for society and for the individuals involved. Having read the facts and figures below, to what extent do you agree with this?

Data for 2006/7 showed that:

- About 10 per cent of families in Britain are headed by one parent.
- 24 per cent of all dependent children live with one parent (22 per cent with their mother and 2 per cent with their father).
- A third to a half of all dependent children will spend some time in a one-parent family.
- Nine out of ten lone parents are women.
- Never-married lone parents tend to be younger than other lone parents and are more likely to be on benefit. However, this group does tend to have smaller families and they take paid work and re-partner sooner.
- 50 per cent of lone mothers are in paid work and nearly half of these work more than 30 hours a week.
- The average age for a lone parent is 35.
- 35 per cent of lone parents have experienced violence in their last relationship with three-quarters of them sustaining physical injuries.
- At any one time, less than 3 per cent of all lone parents are teenagers.

Focus on Families, 2007, ONS
National Council for One Parent Families (NCOPF)

Empty nest families

When children have grown up and left home, the parents continue to live together in the family home. This type of family structure is on the increase as a result of longer life expectancy, with parents now likely to live into their 80s and beyond.

Beanpole families

Rather than having a wide, bushy family tree, many modern family trees will be tall and thin – something like a 'beanpole'. The tree is made thinner because families are having fewer children than in the past and longer because older relatives are living longer.

Activity

3 In groups of three, design an A3 display to show the structure of your three families. Make joint decisions on what you mean by 'family' and who or what is to be included.

Going further

2 The General Household Survey (GHS) is a continuous national survey of people living in private households, conducted on an annual basis by the Office for National Statistics (ONS). The main aim of the survey is to collect data on a range of core topics, covering households and families. This information is used by government departments and other organisations and presents a picture of households, families and people in Great Britain. The GHS Reports for each year can be viewed and downloaded from *Results from the General Household Survey (GHS)*:
www.statistics.gov.uk/StatBase/Product.asp?vlnk=5756

AQA Examiner's tip

We all have relationships with important individuals throughout our lives. This means that we belong to different family structures at different points in our lifetime. You should be able to identify the stages you are likely to pass through during the course of your lifetime.

Check your understanding

1 What are the similarities and possible differences between a household and a family?

2 What are the basic differences between nuclear and extended families?

3 List the ways in which someone can be closely attached to their extended family.

4 Explain why mothers may choose to belong to a lone parent family.

What is the conventional nuclear family?

The stereotypical image of the nuclear family

When you look at the variety of family structures that can be found in modern Britain, the nuclear family stands out as being a popular choice. In its conventional or traditional form it consists of a mother and father in their first (or primary) marriage together with their dependent children. The image that we traditionally see also involves some agreement about the roles that mothers and fathers should play in the family.

- The father takes on the role of provider (the instrumental role) by being the chief wage earner or breadwinner.
- The mother is less likely to work and takes on the dominant role of carer and homekeeper (the expressive role), staying at home to look after the home and the children.

When many people think of a family, this image of the nuclear family is the one that usually comes to mind. It is often seen as the ideal, typical or normal family type in a society such as ours. It has also been referred to as the **cereal packet** image of the family with mum giving her smiling children their breakfast bowl of cornflakes and with dad waving goodbye as he goes out to work.

The perfect fit?

Some sociologists, especially functionalist sociologists, see the nuclear family as being a perfect fit in a modern industrial society for the following reasons:

- Our working world is based on the idea that we will all be trained to do particular jobs. We can't be expected to be specialists in everything, so we choose the education and training we need for a particular profession or occupation. We must be willing to move around the country if the skills we have are needed in areas other than the one in which we live. Living in a small nuclear family allows us to uproot and settle somewhere else, to be geographically mobile.
- Some jobs carry more **status** than others. In a large extended family, fathers and grown-up sons, mothers and grown-up daughters may have jobs that are seen as more or less important and this could cause conflict. The role and status of the father, for example, could be threatened if the son's job carried much more status than the father's job. Living in a small nuclear family means that this conflict doesn't arise because, by the time the son has achieved a status, he has left the family and probably started a nuclear family of his own.
- Living in the warm, cosy nest of a nuclear family strengthens the **conjugal bond** between husband and wife and provides a secure base for the children. Children receive a warm and affectionate upbringing and gain their primary socialisation in the supportive atmosphere of the nuclear family.

Objectives

You will be able to:

- recognise the key features of a conventional nuclear family
- explain how this image of the family is used in the world of media and advertising
- assess the reasons for this family structure being a political favourite
- explain some of the features of the nuclear family in modern Britain.

∞ links

See Topic 1.2 for more about functionalist sociologists.

Key terms

Cereal packet family: the traditional image of the nuclear family presented through the media involving clearly defined male and female roles.

Status: the honour or prestige attached to a person's position in society.

Conjugal bond: the attachment that exists between marriage partners.

∞ links

See also Topic 7.1 for information on achieved status and ascribed status.

Did you know ??????

In 2006, 65% of all dependent children were living in a family headed by a married couple with an average of 1.8 children per family.

Case study

Dean and Jayne are moving

Dean and Jayne are married, have children aged 6 and 3 and live in a house they are buying in the north-east of England. Dean is a welder by trade and Jayne has a part-time job as a nursery assistant. Dean has just been made redundant and there are few job prospects for him where they live but there are well-paid jobs in south-east England.

Activities

1 How easy will it be for Dean and Jayne to move? What complications might they face if they were to consider moving from one part of the country to another?

2 What other issues related to status conflict and relationships within the family might arise?

Key terms

Stereotypical: oversimplified and sometimes exaggerated view.

AQA Examiner's tip

Although there are lots of family structures in modern Britain, don't lose sight of the fact that most people live in some form of nuclear family.

■ Family houses, family cars and family-sized packets of cornflakes

Some argue that the family presented by advertisers, politicians and the media is almost always the cereal packet image of the nuclear family.

The family in advertising and the media

When you see a 'family house' advertised it usually has three bedrooms with planned space for two parents and two children. A 'family car' will comfortably take two people in the front with child seat points for two in the rear. Although some changes are being made, a 'family ticket' to many visitor attractions in the UK allows entry for two adults and two children.

The media in general, and television in particular, has been accused of presenting a **stereotypical** image of the family that is based around the roles of mother, father and children in the traditional nuclear family.

Activity

3 All the images in Figure A use the family as their focus.

a Look in magazines, newspapers and on the shelves of your local supermarket.

b Make a record of the products that use an image of the family in their promotional material.

c What type of family structures can you identify and which are used the most often?

d Compare your list with other members of your group.

A Stereotypical images of the family

The family and politics

All political parties promote the benefits to individuals and to society of living in a family. They all have tax, health and welfare schemes that are aimed directly at the family. Although they accept that other family structures exist, they sing the praises of marriage and the conventional nuclear family.

Political speeches

66 *We will uphold family life as the most secure means of bringing up our children. Families are the core of our society. They should teach right from wrong. They should be the first defence against anti-social behaviour. The breakdown of family life damages the fabric of our society.* 99

1997 *Labour Party Manifesto*

The Conservative Party in the 1980s and 90s stressed the importance of traditional values and more recently they have made the importance of marriage and stable family life a central theme in their policies:

66 *And what is the institution that, in so many cases, holds families together? Most of all, it is marriage. After a child is born, half of all unmarried parents split up within five years. For married parents, it's just one in 12… Most people want to get married and stay married. Married families are most likely to survive the birth and upbringing of a child.* 99

David Cameron MP, Leader of the Conservative Party, 11 July 2007

Key terms

Neo-conventional families: the new nuclear family headed by a married or cohabiting couple who are both working.

Reconstituted family: a new family formed when two adults remarry or cohabit and live together with children from a previous relationship.

▨ How is the nuclear family changing?

Seven out of ten of the UK population currently live in a household headed by a married or cohabiting couple. Those that contain children are sometimes referred to as **neo-conventional families**. They don't exactly fit the old definition of the nuclear family for these reasons:

- More families now than in the past rely on two wages coming into the family and could be called dual-breadwinner families. The male sole breadwinner and female homekeeper roles of the traditional nuclear family are disappearing.

- More couples decide not to marry but just to live together.

- With the rise in the divorce rate over the last 50 years, many of the couples in these families have remarried and have formed what is referred to as **reconstituted families** with step-parents and stepchildren.

Going further

Look at the websites of the main UK political parties and find out what they are currently saying about marriage and the family: www.labour.org.uk, www.conservatives.com and www.libdems.org.uk

Are nuclear families still important?

The proportion of children in Great Britain living in a two-parent family unit has remained steady since the late 1990s and was 76 per cent in 2007. If you remember that statistics just give you a snapshot of where you are in the family cycle at any one time, then you will come to the conclusion that most people will belong to a nuclear family at some time during their life. You may not be living in one now but you may have lived in one in the past and may well form one of your own in the future.

B *A nuclear family*

Activity

4   Working in pairs:

a   Choose a popular soap opera and a family-based sitcom.

b   Discuss the structure of the families in each of them and the roles played by males and females.

c   To what extent do these match what you would expect to find in the following family types?

■   The conventional family

■   The neo-conventional nuclear family

AQA Examiner's tip

Make sure that you can both support and question the importance of the nuclear family and don't forget the other family structures you already know about.

Check your understanding

1   Is there really such a thing as an ideal or typical family? Give reasons for your answer.

2   What are the differences between the conventional and neo-conventional nuclear families?

3   Explain how, according to some sociologists, nuclear families prevent status conflict.

4   Why are politicians in favour of marriage and stable, two-parent families?

3.3 Is marriage in decline?

Different types of marriage

In our society, the accepted form of **marriage** is **monogamy** and involves individuals having only one **spouse**. Having more than one marriage partner at any one time is illegal in our society. Anyone doing so would be committing the criminal offence of **bigamy** with a maximum sentence of seven years' imprisonment. Many people do marry a number of people through their lifetime but their current marriage must be ended through the death of their partner or through **divorce** before they can marry again. This form of marriage is called **serial monogamy**.

Most marriages involve individuals choosing their own partner but **arranged marriages** do take place in some families with an Asian cultural heritage. Many will agree to an arranged marriage but will be able to reach compromises that are suitable for everyone.

Other societies practise some form of **polygamy**, the accepted practice of having more than one spouse. **Polygyny** involves a man having more than one wife. Although polygyny is legally allowed in these societies, most men now choose to marry monogamously.

Polyandry involves a woman having more than one husband. This usually takes place in areas where there are more men than women as a result of **female infanticide** and a wife is often 'shared' by brothers.

What is happening to marriage in Britain today?

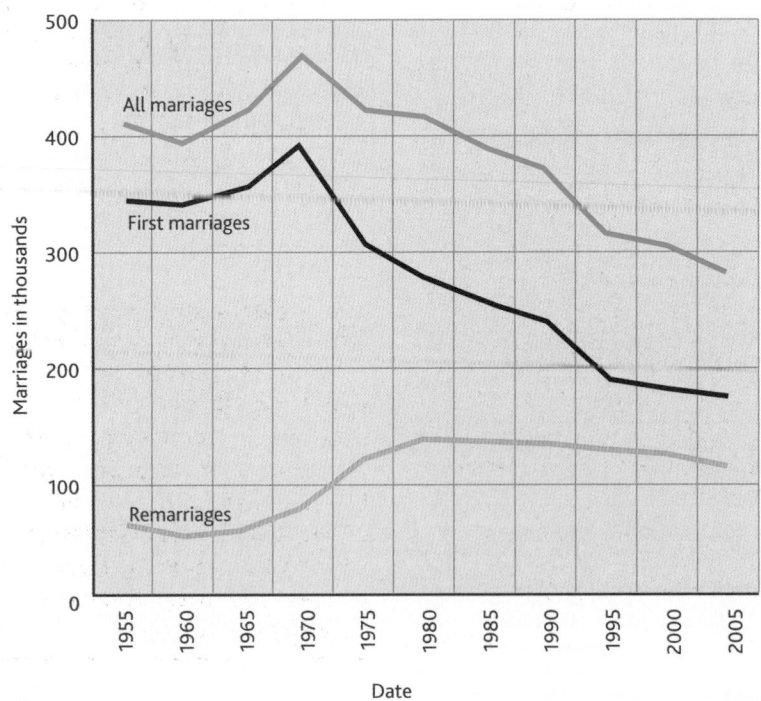

A Marriages in the UK

Objectives

You will be able to:

- recognise different types of marriage seen in different societies

- discuss the recent changes in attitudes to marriage in Britain

- analyse the key reasons for the rise in the divorce rate

- discuss the consequences for family members of an increased divorce rate.

Key terms

Marriage: a legally recognised union of a man and a woman by religious or civil ceremony.

Monogamy: the practice of being married to only one person at a time.

Spouse: a marriage partner, husband or wife.

Bigamy: the illegal practice in a monogamous society of having more than one spouse.

Divorce: the legal ending of a marriage.

Serial monogamy: a pattern of divorce and monogamous remarriage.

Arranged marriage: a marriage in which the parents have a say in the choice of a bride or bridegroom for their son or daughter.

Polygamy: the accepted practice in some societies of having more than one spouse.

Polygyny: the accepted practice in some societies of a man having more than one wife.

1　In pairs, look at Graph **A** and answer the following questions:

a　What has happened to the total number of people marrying between 1970 and 2005?

b　What has happened to the number of people marrying for the first time?

c　What has happened to the number of people remarrying?

Polyandry: the accepted practice in some societies of a woman having more than one husband.

Female infanticide: the intentional killing of baby girls due to the preference for male babies.

The age at which people decide to marry has shown a steady increase as Table **B** shows. Recent figures show that only 25 per cent of women aged 20 to 29 are married compared with 75 per cent 30 years ago.

The rise in cohabitation

Many people are deciding to live together in a cohabiting relationship and this is having an impact on the number of marriages that take place. Recent survey data has shown that 39 per cent of single people aged between 25 and 34 are cohabiting.

Cohabitation can be seen as either:

▣　something that happens before a couple decide to get married. Latest figures show that 21 per cent of women aged between 20 and 29 are cohabiting compared with only 1 per cent 20 years ago.

▣　an alternative to marriage. Of those aged between 35 and 49, 30 per cent of single people and 41 per cent of divorced men and women are cohabiting.

Married in a church?

Only 36 per cent of marriages now take place in a church. More people now marry in a Register Office or, since 1995, in approved premises. This usually means a local hotel but could also involve more unexpected venues. UK citizens do not have to register marriages that take place abroad and there is some evidence that marrying abroad is becoming popular, perhaps accounting for up to 10 per cent of marriages in England and Wales.

B	*Average age at which people married*	
	Male	**Female**
1961	25.6	23.1
2005	31.4	29.1

2　**How much does it cost to get married?**

In groups of three, do some research and plan out the cost of a 'conventional' wedding with a guest list of 40 people. Add up the cost of all the items you think you would need and display the list and costs on an A3 sheet of paper. When all groups have finished, compare your final costs. Who do you think should pay for it all?

C *Nearing the end of an exciting and expensive day*

1　Use the Internet to find areas of the world where polygyny and polyandry are practised.

These are all approved premises in which you can get married:

The London Eye, Blackpool Tower, Chester Zoo, Manchester United FC, Chelsea FC, Wookey Hole Caves, Concorde at Manchester Airport, the National Railway Museum, the Science Museum and Madame Tussauds.

Divorce and family breakdown

What do the statistics show?

- The number of divorces has risen over the last 50 years.
- A dramatic rise in the early 1970s with figures reaching their highest in the 1980s and 1990s.
- A recent reduction in the number of divorces. 2006 figures were the lowest on record since 1977.
- Since the mid-1970s, over twice as many divorces granted to women than men.

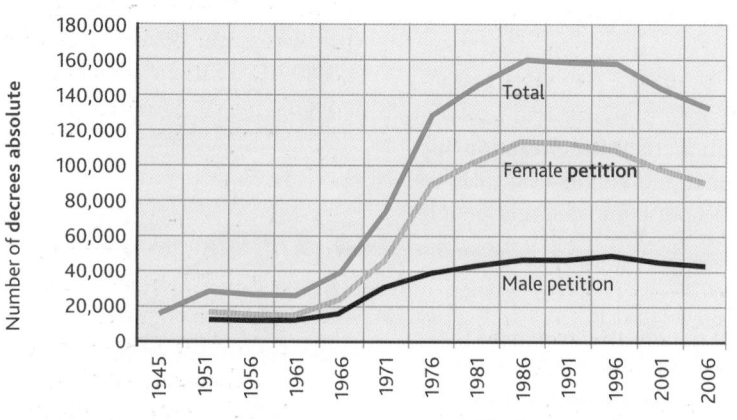

Office for National Statistics, 2006

D *Divorces and who asked for them*

Why are there more divorces now than 50 years ago?

- Changing social attitudes mean that the **social stigma** attached to divorce has declined.
- New laws changed the **grounds for divorce** making divorce easier to obtain. The rapid rise in the early 1970s was largely a result of the 1969 Divorce Reform Act. It introduced 'irretrievable breakdown' as the grounds for divorce, to be proved through adultery, desertion or unreasonable behaviour. New grounds allowed 'no-fault' divorces if partners had been living apart for two years (five years if only one agreed). In 1984, divorce was allowed after one rather than three years of marriage.
- Do people expect too much from marriage and, when it disappoints, resort straight to divorce? Can marriages constantly deliver the romance and happiness stressed in the media, through films and magazines?
- Fewer couples marry in church and fewer have religious objections to divorce.
- The role of women in society has changed. Equal educational opportunities and the ability to control family size means they can move into occupations giving them financial independence. Feminist sociologists see them challenging **patriarchal** relationships and show that women no longer need to feel trapped within an **empty shell marriage**.

Key terms

Decree absolute: this is the legal ending of the marriage. Once this has been granted, your marriage has been dissolved and you are legally single.

Divorce petition: the formal request to start divorce proceedings.

Social stigma: branding something with negative feelings of shame and disgrace.

Grounds for divorce: the legal reasons given for wanting a divorce.

Patriarchal: a situation where men dominate society and its institutions.

Empty shell marriage: when a couple are still married and live in the same house but lead separate lives.

Activity

3 In pairs, discuss and record how the role and status of women has changed over three generations: your grandmothers', your mother's and your own.

E *Children can be pulled in two directions by divorce*

What are the consequences of an increased number of divorces?

For husbands and wives

- More remarriages: divorced men are more likely to remarry than divorced women – perhaps they have more to gain from being married.
- More cohabiting relationships: 34 per cent of divorced men and 24 per cent of divorced women are cohabiting.
- More decisions about how to divide property and possessions.
- Having to agree on who will care for children and where they will live.
- Financially: usually having to manage with less money coming into the home.
- Emotionally: either a change for the better or a stressful change of circumstances.

For the family

- An increase in lone parent families or shared parent families.
- Children living with one parent but keeping in regular contact with the other.
- An increase in the number of reconstituted families. Most children stay with their mother if she remarries. 84 per cent of stepfamilies in Britain have a stepfather and a natural mother.

For children

- Adjusting to a new set of relationships especially in a reconstituted family.
- Keeping in contact with the parent they are not living with.
- They may have the best of both worlds as they are now attached to two families (and two sets of birthday presents?).

Did you know ??????

Two out of five marriages are likely to end in divorce. The other three will continue throughout the lifetime of the couple.

Activity

4   Many of the stories you hear about divorce concentrate on the difficulties people face in arriving at a settlement over property and children. Assume that the divorcing couple have dependent children then list as many positive consequences of divorce for both the parents and the children involved.

Saw-in-two cabinet to aid divorce

Case study

A student from Northumbria University has designed a piece of furniture that comes with a saw, which divorcing couples can cut in half.

The 1950s-style cabinet can be cut in two with the help of pre-drilled cut lines across the top. There are pull-down legs, ensuring that each half of the cabinet can still be used.

F *The saw-in-two cabinet*

Check your understanding

1 Why do you think there are fewer church weddings now than in the past?

2 What do the cohabitation patterns of different age groups tell you about the way those groups view marriage?

3 What were the grounds for divorce introduced in the 1969 Divorce Reform Act?

4 Which partner is the one who usually petitions for divorce?

5 Which partner usually gains custody of the children after a divorce settlement?

Going further

2   How do levels of divorce in the UK compare with those for other countries in Europe and beyond?

Use the Internet to look for statistics that allow you to make some comparisons.

What are role relationships in the family and how have they changed over time?

Traditional roles and power relationships in the family

Men have traditionally taken the role of main breadwinner in families whereas women have taken the main responsibility for the home and children. When partners do not share housework, childcare, decisions and leisure time, they have **segregated conjugal roles**. Families based on roles such as these are often seen as having unequal power relationships between the partners because the male has control of money coming into the household. Feminist sociologists in particular suggest that these relationships are patriarchal and that women, and perhaps children, suffer as a result.

What about relationships in the family today?

Sociological research in the 1970s suggested that role relationships within the family were changing and that families were developing joint or **integrated conjugal roles**. These involved couples sharing childcare and housework and both were involved in paid employment. Power relationships between partners were becoming more equal or **egalitarian**. Some research saw the roles and relationships as so similar that they referred to the families as **symmetrical families**. These changes were happening because:

- Women were having fewer children, having them earlier in their lives and, as a result, had the time and desire to go out to work.
- Men were spending more time in the home because they were working shorter hours and were in jobs that were less physically demanding.
- The home and their children were becoming their central focus. Families were becoming child centred. Homes were comfortable and had entertaining spaces in which to relax after work.

What evidence is there to support the view that families have continued to move towards symmetry?

Activity 2 will allow you to:

- assess the contribution of members of your household to the **domestic division of labour**
- make a decision about the gendered nature of roles in your own household and your generation
- consider the debate about the move towards integrated conjugal roles and symmetrical families in relation to your household.

Key terms

Segregated conjugal roles: husband and wife perform different tasks and have a number of separate interests and activities.

Integrated conjugal roles: husband and wife perform similar tasks and have a number of common interests and activities.

Egalitarian: the idea that all are equal.

Symmetrical family: family where responsibilities and tasks are equally shared between husband and wife.

Domestic division of labour: how household tasks are divided between family members.

Dads 'cling to traditional role'

Case study

Most fathers still think of themselves as the breadwinner rather than being equally involved with running a home and family.

The Equal Opportunities Commission (EOC) has identified four types of father.

A *Enforcer dad*

- **Enforcer dad**. Not involved with the day-to-day care of children. He provides a role model and clear rules for his children.
- **Entertainer dad**. Often entertains the children while mother does things like cooking and cleaning.
- **Useful dad**. Helps with day-to-day childcare and household tasks, but still takes lead from mother about what needs doing.
- **Fully involved dad**. Equally involved with running the home and family, at least some of the time. Mother and father roles are virtually interchangeable.

Fully involved dads were more likely to enjoy flexible working arrangements and were more likely to leave work on time, the research suggested.

The EOC said most fathers fell into the middle two categories.

Norwich Union, 2002

Activity

1 In small groups, discuss the four types of father described in the case study and consider the following:

a Is the age of the father likely to affect his attitudes to his role in the family?

b Are there likely to be any differences between fathers from different ethnic backgrounds?

c Are there likely to be differences in levels of participation between social classes?

d Are there other social factors that will affect the way a father sees his role in the family?

Activity

2 Copy out the table then put ticks in the appropriate columns to show who usually does or last did the following tasks in your household. Leave blank any columns that are not relevant to your household.

Task	Female adult	Male adult	Female child(ren)	Male child(ren)
1. Cleaning the bathroom				
2. Vacuuming				
3. Taking the bins out				
4. Washing up				
5. Cleaning the windows				
6. Washing the car				
7. Changing the bed linen				
8. Doing the ironing				
9. Cooking the evening meal				
10. Shopping for food				
11. Buying birthday cards				
12. Managing the money				
13. Listening to your problems				
14. Helping with homework				
15. Mowing the lawn				
16. Looking after family pets				
TOTALS				

a When you have allocated all the tasks, add up the totals for your household and for the whole group.

b What conclusions can you draw from your results?

c Would you have included tasks other than those listed?

d Lone parent households will only have ticks in one of the adult columns. Do children in these households do more to help out?

e What about the frequency of tasks and the gender allocations? Some tasks are done every day whereas others are done infrequently.

f Can you do a rough estimation of the time spent on tasks per week by the males and females in your household?

■ The debate continues

Has there been any noticeable change in what is expected of women by the members of their families?

The dual burden

Most research shows that women are increasingly involved in full-time paid work and are also expected to be responsible for the bulk of the housework. Women still do the boring, dirty, repetitive tasks around the home. Men do not take an equal share of the burden of running the home but 'help' when it is convenient to do so. It is debatable whether there is any change on the horizon as it looks as though this gender division is continuing in the current younger generation. Girls and young women do much more around the house than their brothers do.

The triple shift

As well as working full-time and doing the bulk of the housework, it has been suggested that mothers are also largely responsible for what has been called 'emotion work' in the household – making sure everyone is happy, resolving arguments and holding relationships together.

Invisible work

To add to all of this, women are shown as thinking about family issues much more than men. Deciding what to make for dinner and what to include on the shopping list or remembering birthdays and what to buy as birthday presents all take up time and energy.

Decision making

Women make most of the day-to-day family decisions but the big decisions are often made by the person who earns the most money. In many families the man's wage is still the one used to pay the bills and buy the essentials, whereas the woman's wage is used for holidays and extras.

Money management

Rather than one partner having control of family finances there is much more evidence now of money being 'pooled' from the earnings of both partners and going into a joint account.

Parenting and childcare

In recent years, we have seen the development of 'work rich/time poor' households. With both parents working, families are finding it difficult to spend time together. Recent **longitudinal studies** don't support the notion of a 'new dad' who spends more time with his children. In fact, they seem to suggest that fathers today are actually taking a smaller role in childcare. Although fathers are spending less time with their children than mothers, they say that they want to be more involved in their child's upbringing. However, due to other pressures, they find this is not possible.

Activity

3 Consider all the members of your family and then decide:

■ Who makes the big decisions in your family?

■ Who holds the power in your family?

Compare your responses with other students in your group.

B *Who really controls the household finance?*

Key terms

Longitudinal studies: studies that follow the same people over a long period of time.

Life expectancy: the age to which a person can be expected to live. Current UK figures are: male: 76.6; female: 81.

Children in families

Children are at the very core of most families and family life has become very child-centred. Children are increasingly experiencing different types of family structures and different kinds of family relationships as they grow up. The experiences that children have are affected by factors such as social class, ethnicity and gender. A lot of children live very happy family lives but a significant number live in poor conditions and are not well cared for. Limitations are placed upon what young people are allowed to do. However, they also have far more rights now than in the past and their opinions are taken very seriously.

The third age

The rise in **life expectancy** has resulted in an increasing number of families having older members who are no longer in paid employment. Around 20 per cent of the UK population are aged 65 and over. As their children are likely to have married and had children later in life, this often results in an older generation being grandparents of young children. As well as enjoying their own retirement, they regularly provide unpaid childcare and support for single and two-parent families.

C *Grandparents provide family support*

Going further

Find out more about the feminist approach to housework.

An Internet search for feminist+housework will identify a number of interesting articles that should be fairly critical of this taken-for-granted element in the lives of many women.

Check your understanding

1 State the difference between integrated and segregated conjugal roles.

2 What evidence is there for the widespread existence of symmetrical families?

3 What do you understand by the expression 'work rich/time poor' in relation to family life?

AQA Examiner's tip

Most of us belong to a family of some kind and experience role and power relationships in our families every day. Use this experience to bring some of the ideas in this topic to life.

Did you know ??????

Some sociologists have suggested that women don't want to relinquish the power they have around the home and with their children. They say that women have a maternal instinct that makes them closer to their children and that in most homes it really is the woman who is in charge.

Did you know ??????

Men say they do more than they really do!
52% of fathers say that cooking the evening meal is either done by them, or is shared broadly equally with mum.
'Not true' say the mothers!
70% of mothers say that they cook the evening meal.

Did you know ??????

Of working parents, mothers are far more likely to be the ones who take time off work to look after children if they are ill and cannot attend school/nursery. 47 per cent of mothers say that if their children were ill they would take time off to look after them. Only 17 per cent of fathers say that they would.

Not living in a family

We have relations and are attached to families but whether we decide to form one of our own is a personal decision.

- We may decide to live on our own as a single person and may continue to do so throughout our lifetime.

- More young people are staying in their family home for longer but, when they do move out, an increasing number are living on their own.

- Many young people move away from their family when they move into higher education and may decide to live in that location when they finish their studies.

- Older people may be living on their own or with other single people in sheltered or residential accommodation.

Do young people increasingly want to maintain their individual, single lifestyle? Some debate currently exists as to the existence of the 'lad culture'. This is the idea that many males don't want to settle down but prefer to follow masculine pursuits in 'perpetual adolescence'.

Chart **A** shows the percentage in each age group who live alone. Remember that, for most people, this is a temporary stage in their lives. Many older people will have been part of a family in the past and many of those in younger age groups will be part of one in the future.

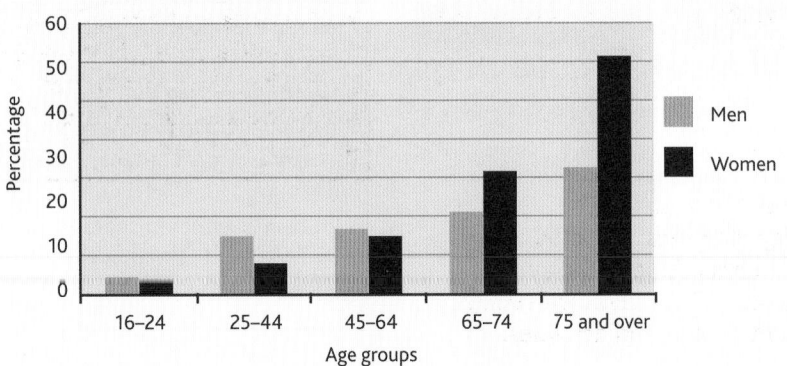

General Household Survey 2007 (Longitudinal), Office for National Statistics

A *People living alone*

Forms of communal living

Communes

A very small proportion of the UK population decide not to live in families but in some form of **commune**. These involve shared ownership of property, shared skills with other members and shared responsibility for people living in the community.

In some communities, children attend local schools whereas in others they are educated 'at home'. Some take shared responsibility for childcare, looking after children while parents get on with other tasks.

Kibbutz life

Most **kibbutzim** were established in the 1940s in what became the newly created state of Israel in 1948. They aimed to provide communal living for those who wanted it.

Today there are some 270 kibbutzim in Israel. Most have a population of around 500. About 2.5 per cent of the population (130,000 people) live in a kibbutz.

There have been changes in kibbutz life that have seen a move away from some of the basic principles that led to their formation.

B *Childcare on an Israeli kibbutz*

Jewish Virtual Library, 2006

Then	Now
People living in these communities were monogamously married.	They also contain young volunteers who live in the kibbutz in exchange for work.
Children were brought up in children's houses with sleeping quarters, play and study rooms. Parents spent time with their children only after work.	Since the 1970s, kibbutz life has become 'family-centred' with all children being raised by their parents and living at home.
When kibbutzim were smaller, social and cultural life was characterised by togetherness and being 'one big family'.	With the advent of cable and satellite television, videos and personal computers, entertainment has become more home-based and family-centred.

Activities

2 Make a list of the advantages and the disadvantages of living in a community like a kibbutz.

3 How might you be involved in community living at some time during your life?

AQA *Examiner's tip*

You need to decide if it is the family that is under threat or just one type of family structure that is being challenged. Although there are alternatives, these would seem to be either short-lived or still involve some kind of family structure.

Co-housing

If someone has the money to buy a house but wants to live communally with other households, they may consider co-housing. People have their own self-contained accommodation in a large converted mansion or estate but also involve themselves with other families and individuals who share common aims and activities.

◼ Alternatives?

All of these alternatives appear to lead back to a structure that looks suspiciously like a family!

Check your understanding

1 Why is there such a difference between the numbers of men and women living alone who are aged 75 and over?

2 Explain why living alone is just a temporary phase for many people.

3 Give three differences between family life in a kibbutz now and in the past.

Going further

Where is the nearest commune to you? Where can you find out about co-housing projects in your area?

You might find these two websites useful:
www.cohousing.org.uk and
www.diggersanddreamers.org.uk

What does social research tell us about families in contemporary Britain?

Some sociologists argue that the family is in turmoil and responsible for the problems society currently faces.

The underclass and family breakdown

> " By **underclass**, I do not mean people who are merely poor, but people at the margins of society, unsocialised and often violent. The **chronic** criminal is part of the underclass, especially the violent chronic criminal. But so are parents who mean well but who cannot provide for themselves, who give nothing back to the neighbourhood, and whose children are the despair of the teachers who have to deal with them.
>
> One of the leading reasons that children have not been socialised is that larger numbers of British children are not being raised by two mature, married adults, which brings us to the most important of the indicators of an underclass, births to unmarried women.
>
> Does it make any difference? Jack Straw assured us that: 'We shouldn't get in a paddy about the decline of formal marriage.' Other kinds of families, he said, 'can do just as well for their children'. Many would understand him to mean that on average the children of these non-traditional families do just as well as the children of two formally married biological parents. That would be factually wrong – no alternative family structure comes close to the merits of two parents, formally married.
>
> The debate in the US has turned to 'how much' rather than 'whether' the two-parent family is better for children. It makes no difference whether we are trying to predict a child's criminality, school grades, income as an adult, or psychological well-being; it makes no difference how carefully the analysis controlled for the family's socioeconomic status.
>
> Taken as groups, the children of two married biological parents are found to do much better than the children of single parents, and the children of divorced mothers are found to do much better than the children of never-married mothers.
>
> In Britain, nearly 40 per cent of births are out of wedlock and illegitimacy is overwhelmingly a lower-class phenomenon. Fifteen per cent of births among the professional classes are out of wedlock, while that figure is likely to be well over 50 per cent among the unskilled and unemployed. Similar comments can be made about the effects of divorce – in affluent neighbourhoods, divorces are not only fewer than in low-income neighbourhoods, but many of them occur after the children are grown. "

Adapted from Charles Murray, *Underclass + 10, Charles Murray and the British Underclass 1990–2000*

Objectives

You will be able to:

- explore the relationship between research and matters of controversy and debate

- argue that the family is constantly adapting to keep pace with changes in society.

Key terms

Underclass: the group of people at the very bottom of the social structure who, either by their economic situation or culture, are cut off from the rest of society.

Chronic: a continuous problem that extends over a period of time.

A *Criminal behavior*

A separate underclass or just disadvantaged families?

> *Smaller scale qualitative studies of poor families living on benefit have questioned the existence of an 'underclass' in the sense of a group with a distinct sub-culture. Bradshaw and Holmes, for instance, dispute the notion of an 'underclass', arguing that the families they studied 'are just the same people as the rest of our population, with the same culture and aspirations, but with simply too little money to be able to share in the activities and possessions of everyday life with the rest of the population'.*
>
> *Kempson concludes from her review of 31 research studies supported by the Joseph Rowntree Foundation that 'people who live on low incomes are not an underclass. They have aspirations just like others in society: they want a job; a decent home; and an income that is enough to pay the bills with a little to spare. But social and economic changes that have benefited the majority of the population, increasing their incomes and their standard of living, have made life more difficult for a growing minority, whose fairly modest aspirations are often beyond their reach.'*

Adapted from Ruth Lister, *Charles Murray and the Underclass: The Developing Debate*

Going further

1. The concept of the 'underclass', presented by Charles Murray, has promoted a great deal of discussion and debate. Many sociologists, politicians and journalists have seriously questioned the legitimacy and the value of the ideas that Murray has presented.

- What have you already learned about cohabitation, marriage and divorce that prepares you to question some of the suggestions made about the development of an underclass?

B *A young person with alcohol*

Check your understanding

1. What does Murray mean when he uses the term 'underclass'?

2. What kind of family is Murray suggesting is the best for children?

3. What is illegitimacy?

4. What is socialisation?

5. Why does Murray see family breakdown as a key reason for the development of an underclass?

6. What does Murray suggest are the differences in rates of divorce and illegitimacy between social classes?

7. Why does Lister think that poor families do not form part of an 'underclass'?

The future of the family

Some sociologists argue that the family is constantly adapting to keep pace with changes in society.

> " There is an alternative view to the doom-laden prophecy that families are falling apart. In fact, the future of the family is stronger than ever. All the research shows that families are hugely valued and will continue to be.
>
> Successive British Social Attitude Surveys, show clearly that while family members live further apart, they turn to each other when important life events take place. Hardyment points to the fact that families are still responsible for the bulk of socialising in British life and that family members talking to each other account for a large proportion of telephone usage.
>
> Fiona Williams says 'People will have different experiences over their lifetimes – of marriage, of cohabitation, of single parenthood – but in many of them they are negotiating complex and deeply held commitments. Parents and children have more emotional investment in each other. Children and their parents talk of each other as friends whom they can talk to – now, fathers want as much of that quality of relationship as mothers have. The relationship between parents and children has got stronger.'
>
> What goes along with the greater emotional investment is a longer **financial dependency**. Children used to be off their parents' hands by 18, but the combination of student loans, university fees and rising property prices has already reversed that, and the trend is likely to continue. Parenthood is well on its way to becoming a minimum 25-year deal.
>
> The way generations in the family are connected by vertical links is sometimes characterised as the 'beanpole family' – long and thin. As family sizes shrink, the number of siblings and cousins will dwindle while the **intergenerational** relationships become more intense.
>
> Webcams might by 2020 be playing the role the telephone did in the 20th century, a vital communication link for families who might live hundreds of miles apart. Already some nurseries are linked up to their parents' office by webcam so they can see their children at play. More and more communication within the family is likely to be mediated by technology – the Internet, email or the mobile phone. Already, technology has facilitated the family life of people who have migrated from their home country. For example, a South African nurse working in the UK can now be involved in daily decisions about the upbringing of her children and care of her parents. Involvement in family life no longer requires **geographical proximity**. "

Adapted from Madeline Bunting, *The Guardian*, 25 September 2004

Key terms

Financial dependency: relying upon someone else for money.

Intergenerational: between or across generations.

Geographical proximity: not being far away.

Social research and the family

Much of what you have read throughout this topic has been a collection of ideas, arguments and debates that all have their roots in one piece of social research or another. Some research that is now quite dated is still useful because we can see whether what was suggested has actually happened. Also we can compare what is happening now with how things were in the past. New social research makes us constantly question the things we sometimes take for granted.

CHOCOLATE DESCRIPTIONS

MILK & DARK
Layers of smooth milk chocolate and 70% cocoa dark chocolate. The best of both worlds.

LEMON MOUSSE
Light lemon truffle covered in white chocolate with a dark chocolate drizzle.

ALMOND MARZIPAN
Almond marzipan smothered in intense dark chocolate topped with a whole almond.

ORANGE DUO (GOLD FOIL)
Fruity orange crème with a tangy centre covered in dark chocolate.

SOFT CARAMEL (RED FOIL)
Rich soft caramel covered in milk chocolate. An all time favourite.

CARAMEL FUDGE
Caramel fudge in smooth milk chocolate.

BISCUIT IN CARAMEL
Smooth caramel with crunchy biscuit pieces encased in milk chocolate.

HAZELNUT PRALINE
A nutty praline in a milk chocolate shell.

TURKISH DELIGHT
Turkish delight in milk chocolate with a dark chocolate finish.

COFFEE TRUFFLE
Truffle made with ground coffee, double coated in dark and white chocolate.

CHOCOLATE TRUFFLE
Melt in the mouth truffle in milk chocolate.

CHOCOLATE TOFFEE
A chewy toffee centre smothered in smooth milk chocolate.

P69618

AQA *Examiner's tip*

Try to make your written answers 'evidence based'. In other words, make sure that your ideas are supported by research evidence wherever possible. It isn't necessary to remember a list of sociologists' names but it is important to keep up to date with current trends and ideas.

... technology managed to keep ...

... the relationship between ...

3 In what ways are children financially dependent on their parents?

4 How would you describe the 'beanpole' family?

5 Why do families no longer have to be geographically close to feel involved in each other's lives?

Going further

2 You can download the full version of Charles Murray's article on the underclass in Britain from: **www.civitas. org.uk/pdf/cw33.pdf** It makes for a challenging but interesting read if you can find the time.

Exam question guidance

Example of a source-based question

⚭ **links**

See the Exam question guidance section in Topic 1.8 on page 38 for general advice on answering source-based questions.

Item A

Household Division of Labour Among Married or Cohabiting Couples in Great Britain 1990s

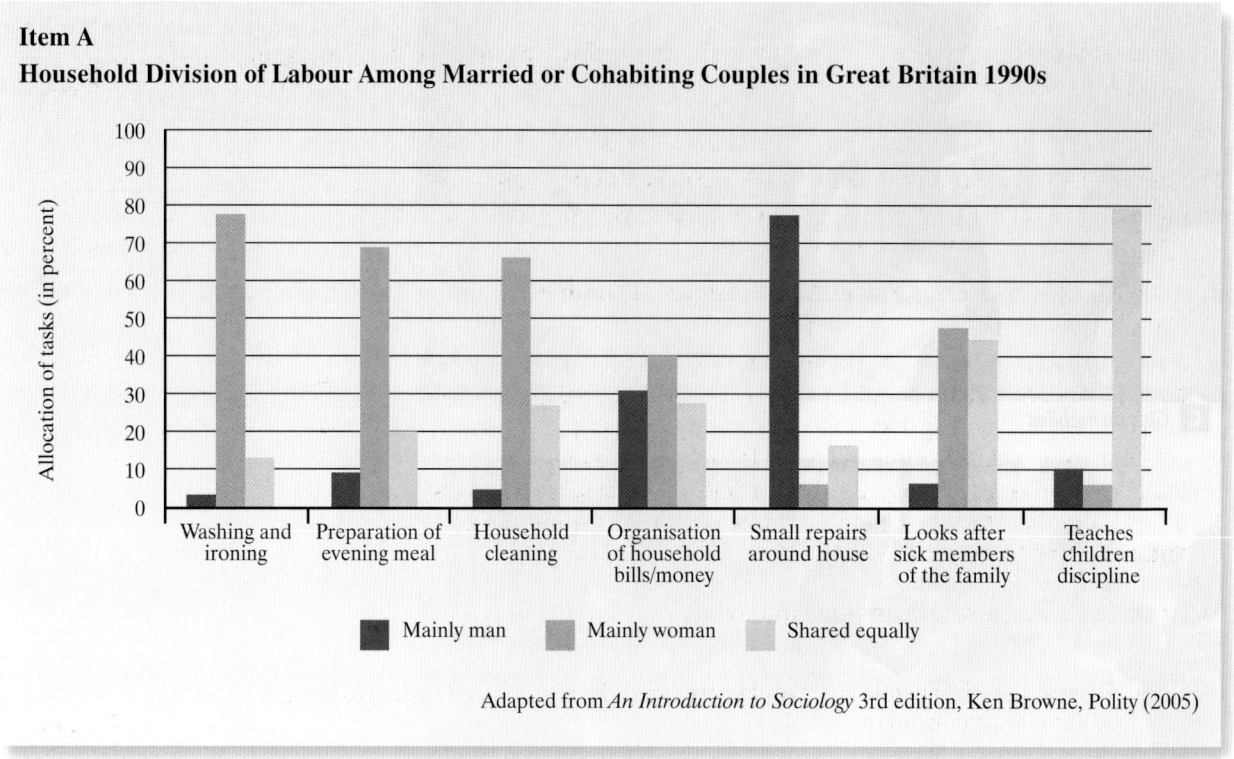

Adapted from *An Introduction to Sociology* 3rd edition, Ken Browne, Polity (2005)

- **Who?** This source is taken from a textbook and is likely to be based on material from the Office for National Statistics (government research data). The material is presented as a bar chart with a key. The vertical scale refers to the percentage of those studied. The horizontal scale refers to the variety of domestic tasks.

- **What?** The source reviews the share of domestic tasks between married and cohabiting couples during the 1990s. It distinguishes between those tasks that are primarily performed by the male or female partner, or equally shared between partners.

- **Why?** Sociologists have long been interested in the division of domestic labour. Concern has been expressed that the equal status of working women in society is undermined by a **double shift**. They complete a full day's work and then return home to shoulder the main burden of domestic tasks, for example, childcare, cooking and cleaning. The argument that the '**new man**' is more prepared to share such tasks equally has been undermined by research that shows men overestimating their contribution to domestic life.

a   From **Item A**, which household task is most shared?   *(1 mark)*

Answer as briefly as possible. Remember to bring a ruler or straight edge into the exam room. This can be placed on the chart or table to help avoid the simple error of reading the wrong column on the chart or selecting the wrong number from a table. In this case the answer is 'teaches children discipline'.

Example of a 2-mark question

c   Identify **two** reasons for the general rise in the divorce rate in Britain during the last 40 years.   *(2 marks)*

The examiners want you to think about the reasons **why** the number of divorces has risen over a specified time period (this will take you back to the 1960s). Relevant reasons might include:

- changes in the law. Prior to the 1960s, divorce was both expensive and difficult to obtain.
- changing social attitudes. As divorce reform made the legal process easier, this both reflected and encouraged changing social attitudes. Divorce became socially acceptable both because it was far more common and because people were no longer prepared to tolerate unhappy marriages (**empty shell marriages**). These social changes particularly reflected the changing status of women (**equal rights and women's liberation**).

Example of an extended-answer question

g   Discuss how far sociologists would agree that living in a family tends to benefit men more than women.   *(12 marks)*

- The examiner would expect you to be aware of the general increase in levels of divorce and continuing changes in the status of women in society. Women are liberated from men economically and socially, yet they often retain primary responsibility for the emotional and physical wellbeing of family members.

- The question clearly raises the issue of **extent. How far** would sociologists agree? From a sociological point of view there are a number of important issues to be addressed. These include the fact that family life in the 21st century is fundamentally different from the idealised '**cereal packet norm**' of the 1960s. Men undoubtedly benefit from family life and many can expect to live longer and healthier lives when they are partnered in a stable, domestic relationship. However, for women the benefits are less certain: while many women continue to seek an idealised relationship, the reality is often far less satisfying. Women who work frequently return home to shoulder a greater share of the domestic burden than their male partner. However, research shows that men overestimate the part they play in cooking, cleaning and childcare.

⊂⊃ **links**

See the Exam question guidance section in Topic 2.7 on page 67 for general advice on answering extended-answer questions.

The very high levels of divorce and single parent families in our society would seem to reflect, at least in part, unwillingness by women to tolerate relationships that are unsatisfactory let alone those that are abusive.

▪ Remember to avoid the trap of only referring to the sources in the question. The examiner wants to see evidence that you have studied the sociology of families *and* thought about the issues.

◼ Questions to try

What follows are examples of the types of questions you will meet in your exam. The letter in each question matches the letter that will be used for that type of question on your exam paper. The number in brackets is only there to help you and your teacher refer to that particular question in this book.

Item B

Divorce rates in England and Wales are at their lowest for 26 years according to official statistics. Research by the Office for National Statistics found that the number of people getting divorced had fallen for the third year running, down from 12.2 divorces per 1,000 married men and women in 2006 to 11.9 in 2007. However, the research also showed that more people aged 60 and over, and couples in their mid to late 40s, split up. Marilyn Stowe, of Stowe Family Law, said that the rise in 'silver haired divorce' may be linked to longer and healthier life. 'People now have more energy in their later years and realise there is nothing left in their marriage once they have had their career and the children have left home.'

Adapted from *The Guardian*, August 2008

---

a	From **Item B**, what was the total number of divorces per 1,000 married men and women in 2007?	*(1 mark)*
d(1)	Explain what sociologists mean by primary socialisation.	*(4 marks)*
d(2)	Explain what sociologists mean by a reconstituted or blended family.	*(4 marks)*
d(3)	Explain what sociologists mean by the term segregated conjugal roles.	*(4 marks)*
e	Describe one way in which recent governments have attempted to support low income families and explain how successful this policy has been.	*(5 marks)*
g(1)	Discuss how far sociologists would agree that the roles of men and women in the family have changed in the last 40 years.	*(12 marks)*
g(2)	Discuss how far sociologists would agree that changes in social attitudes have been responsible for the increase in the divorce rate since the 1960s.	*(12 marks)*
g(3)	Discuss how far sociologists would agree that the married couple family is no longer the typical family.	*(12 marks)*

◼ Revision Advice – Short Course

AQA GCSE Sociology is divided into two elements: the first is the **Short Course** (Paper 1) as detailed below:

Written paper – 1 hour 30 minutes

Covers 100% of Short Course or 50% of Full Course

90 marks available in total

∞links

Also see Revision Advice – Full Course for information on Paper 2 on page 198.

You must answer all questions in **all three** compulsory sections:

- Studying Society (social research and the basic ideas of sociology)
- Education
- Families

Each section consists of one question, sub-divided into part-questions.

The Education and Families sections offer two options for the final part-question, where extended writing (an essay style answer) is required.

The basic rule you must follow is that the more marks a question carries the **more you should try to write** in the time available. If a question is worth one mark, answer as briefly as possible as the examiner does not want to read a long answer (you are wasting time). If a question is worth two marks, you will probably need to write one or two sentences. If it is worth four marks, a paragraph (a useful guide is five to ten lines, but this is only a guide). If a question is worth twelve marks, try to write at least three paragraphs. Some students will be able to write more than others in the time available. You must try to **finish** the exam paper – anything you leave out because you run out of time will be marks you throw away.

In order to be successful in the exam in terms of the **Studying Society** section, you must be able to answer 'yes' to the following:

- Can you describe how to design a basic research project?
- Are you familiar with the basic research tools available to the sociologist? Do you know how to use them and the problems you might encounter?
- Have you attempted an observation (as a participant in the group you observed or as an outsider)? What problems did you encounter? Have you read about sociologists who have tried this approach?
- Have you read about the work of other sociologists? Do you know what official statistics and opinion polls are and have you made use of them in your studies?
- Can you read and make sense of the way in which sociological data is presented? Have you attempted a small-scale research project of your own and attempted to analyse and present the data?
- Do you understand that sociology is about more than just common sense? A good sociologist looks for evidence to test their understanding of the social world; they aim (as far as possible) to achieve an objective scientific approach.
- Have you designed and carried out simple research projects as part of your programme of study? If so, all the ideas above will come alive and begin to make sense to you. You do not need to worry about submitting this work.

Obtain a copy of the specification – you can find a copy on the AQA website. Go through the remaining Short Course content: Education and Families. Use **three highlighting pens**. Colour code a topic **red** if you do not know very much about it, **orange** if you need to know more about it and **green** if you are confident about it. Plan your revision timetable around this.

4 Crime and deviance

What is crime and deviance?

Crime is usually associated with behaviour that breaks the formal, written laws of a given society.

Deviance is behaviour which does not conform to the dominant norms of a specific society.

It is useful to think of deviance as a wide category, of which crime is a smaller part. An act can be criminal and deviant – breaking both social and legal rules. For example, battering an old lady to death is both criminal and deviant and deserves a punishment such as imprisonment.

An act can be deviant but not criminal – breaking social, but not legal rules. For example, a male manager wearing a dress in the office.

Can an act be criminal but not deviant? You may think that all crimes are deviant but is this always the case? What about speeding? Breaking the speed limit is a criminal offence but if someone is found guilty of a minor speeding offence and fined, are they subject to social disapproval?

Objectives

You will be able to:

- describe the difference between crime and deviance

- explain when behaviour is deviant or criminal, using examples

- discuss criminal and deviant behaviour in different contexts.

Key terms

Crime: behaviour that breaks the law.

Deviance: behaviour that does not conform to the dominant norms of a specific society.

Socially defined behaviour: thought of as natural but is actually the product of cultural expectations.

A *Criminal and deviant behaviour*

Social codes Deviance	Criminal and deviant	Criminal codes Crime
These are acts that are not against the law but which are generally considered to break the rules and norms of society.	These are acts that are immoral and illegal such as murder, rape and theft.	These are acts that break the law of a society.

Activity

Discuss these and decide whether you think any of this behaviour is deviant, criminal or both.

Add some more examples of your own.

Behaviour	Criminal or deviant (or both)
Stealing a bottle of milk from a doorstep	
'Burping' after a meal	
Drinking a can of lager on the bus	
Taking paper clips home from work	
Crossing a pedestrian crossing when the 'red man' is displayed	
Keeping money you have been given in error in your change in a supermarket	
Parking on double yellow line	
Not paying for a chocolate bar in a shop	

Crime and deviance are believed to be **socially defined behaviour**. Whether an act is seen as criminal or deviant depends on the particular social setting/culture in which it takes place. Let's take the example of 'nudity'. There is nothing deviant about nudity in itself, in the shower or bath, for example. However, in a supermarket or at a football match, nudity would be seen as deviant. In certain situations and contexts, nudity is seen as appropriate whereas in other situations it would be seen as deviant and might also be illegal.

Criminal activities are defined by the laws of a particular society. Therefore, whether an action is seen to be criminal or deviant can depend on the time, place, social situation and culture in which it occurs:

B *Criminal or deviant?*

- **Time**. When the act takes place, for example, drinking alcohol in the morning compared with nine o'clock in the evening. What is considered deviant or illegal also changes over time, for example, in July 2007 the UK government introduced a smoking ban in all public places in the UK. Prior to this, smoking in a restaurant whilst others were eating could be classified as deviant. Now it would be illegal.
- **Place**. Where the act takes place, for example, an adult running naked across a nudist beach as compared with at a cricket match.
- **Social situation**. The context in which the act takes place, for example, chanting and flag-waving at a funeral as compared with the same behaviour on a football terrace.
- **Culture**. Different cultures have different expectations of appropriate behaviour, for example, the use of cannabis in many Arab states is perfectly legal while alcohol use is a serious crime. The opposite laws apply in Britain.

It is vitally important to recognise that crime and deviance is relative. The context in which behaviour occurs is crucial to how it will be identified. This means that there is not a universal way of defining a criminal or deviant act. Crime and deviance can only be defined in relation to a particular standard of behaviour in a particular culture at a particular moment in time. No standards are fixed forever.

⬭**links**

Refer to the Studying Society chapter for more information on norms and values.

Did you know ??????

The Law Commission was set up in 1965. It is responsible for sifting through the old and irrelevant laws of England to bring them up to date. For example, it is still illegal for cab drivers to carry rabid dogs or corpses.

Going further

Different cultures have different laws and classify different acts as illegal. For example, the following cultures have the following laws:

- In Texas, it is illegal to have a pair of pliers in your possession.
- In France, it is illegal to call a pig Napoleon.
- In San Salvador, drunk drivers can be put to death by a firing squad.

Search the Internet for some 'strange' laws and list them. What do these laws say about the 'social construction' of crime and deviance?

AQA *Examiner's tip*

The examiner will expect you to explain the difference between crime and deviance with the use of appropriate examples.

Check your understanding

1 Explain the difference between crime and deviance.

2 Give one example of a criminal act and one example of a deviant act.

3 Explain what factors may influence whether an act is seen as deviant or not.

4.2 How do we measure the amount of criminal behaviour in society?

There are three different ways to build up a picture of crime: **official crime statistics, victim surveys** and **self-report surveys.**

▉ Official statistics

Official statistics are drawn from records kept by the police and other official agencies. They are published by the Home Office annually. Sociologists use these statistics as a secondary source of data to obtain information on a range of crime-related issues, for example, the number of offences recorded.

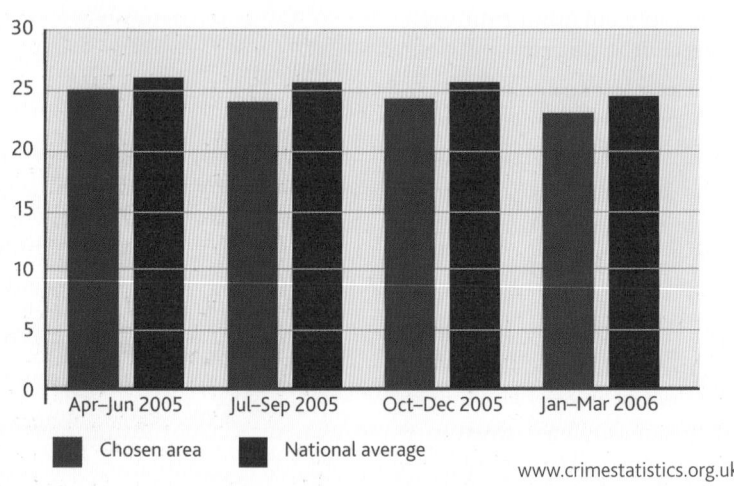

A *All crime for West Midlands Region, Apr 2005–Mar 2006*

Chosen area   National average

www.crimestatistics.org.uk

Why do sociologists use official statistics?

Official statistics on crime are a useful resource as long as they are used critically.

▪ Official statistics provide a cheap and easily available resource.
▪ They can show change over time.
▪ They contain a large amount of information.
▪ The data can be combined with the results of victim surveys and self-report studies to estimate the 'real' rate of crime.

Problems with official crime statistics – do they tell the whole story?

Although statistics appear to be a straightforward measure of the real level of crime, they need to be treated with caution. Crime recorded by the police represents only a partial picture of the total amount of crime committed.

Objectives

You will be able to:

▪ describe the different ways of measuring crime

▪ explain some of the difficulties in accurately measuring crime

▪ discuss the advantages and disadvantages of different methods for measuring crime.

Activity

1 Look at Chart **A**. What does it say about crime rates in the West Midlands compared to the national average?

Research some crime statistics for your area of the country. How do they compare to the national average?

Key terms

Official crime statistics: the way crime is officially measured, based on statistics collected by the Home Office.

Victim surveys: surveys of the public which ask them to report any crimes they have experienced, whether or not they have reported them.

Self-report surveys: surveys of the population which ask them to confess to crime they have committed but for which they have not been caught.

Reported crime: crime that is reported to the police. Not all crime is reported.

Reasons why not all crimes are included in the official crime statistics

Detection

Is a crime detected? If a crime is observed and identified as a crime, the police may be informed. However, if crime has not been detected, it cannot be reported to the police and cannot be counted in official statistics. Many crimes therefore go undetected and are not included in official crime statistics, for example, a thief taking £5 from a wallet containing £85 may go undetected by the owner and would not be detected as a crime.

Reporting

Someone reports to the police that a crime has been committed or the police observe or discover a crime. However, many crimes are not **reported** to the police and so they cannot record them. Reasons for not reporting a crime include the following:

- The victims may fear the consequences from the criminals if they report the crime.
- The victims may fear the police.
- The crime is considered too private, for example, domestic violence.
- The victim suffered no loss.
- The crime is considered too petty, for example, theft of £5.
- It is thought that the police will not be interested and will do nothing.
- It may be too sensitive or embarrassing, for example, rape.
- Crime in the workplace may not be reported because the company may prefer to dismiss the person rather than involve the police.

However, one of the reasons for the apparent increase in certain crimes is that people are now more willing to report them to the police. The number of rape cases reported to the police rose from 1,200 in 1980 to 5,039 in 1994. Increased police sensitivity, specially trained police officers and change in attitudes have all led to an increase in the reporting of such cases.

Recording

The police decide to **record** the report of a crime. However, only about 40 per cent of the offences reported to the police are actually recorded by them.

The police may not necessarily record an act as a crime for several reasons:

- The reported crime is seen as too trivial.
- The reported crime was not actually a crime.
- The complainant may decide not to proceed with a complaint.
- The police may decide there is not enough evidence of an offence having been committed to justify a criminal investigation.

Official crime statistics therefore lack **validity**. They do not measure all crime that occurs and therefore they obscure the true extent of crime. Sociologists argue that official statistics ignore the **dark** (or hidden) **figure of crime**. A very small proportion of actual crime is ever reported and recorded in official statistics.

Key terms

Recorded crime: crime that is recorded by the police. Not all reported crime is recorded.

Validity: data is valid if it gives a true picture of what is being studied.

Dark figure of crime: a large amount of criminal activity never appears in the crime statistics.

Activity

2 What sort of crimes are people most likely to report to the police? Explain why.

Did you know ??????

Recorded crime: the tip of the iceberg. In 2006, about 30% of all crime was recorded.

Unrecorded crime: the hidden figure of crime. In 2006, about 70% of crime was 'hidden'.

AQA Examiner's tip

It is important that you know the different ways that crime is measured. You should also know the advantages and disadvantages of each of these methods of measurement.

Going further

1 Access the following document from the Home Office website and compare the latest crime figures from the British Crime Survey and police recorded crime.

Crime in England and Wales 2006/07 – A summary of the Main Figures

www.homeoffice.
gov.uk/rds/pdfs07/
crime0607summ.pdf

Alternative ways to measure crime

Victim surveys

These are generally large scale surveys of the population in which people are interviewed and asked what crimes have been committed against them in a given time period. **The British Crime Survey (BCS)** is a large scale victim survey. It measures the amount of crime in England and Wales by asking people about crimes they have experienced in the last year. The BCS includes crimes that are not reported to the police, so it is an important alternative to police records. The survey collects information about:

- the victims of crime
- the circumstances in which incidents occur
- the behaviour of offenders in committing crimes.

The first BCS that was conducted in 1981 estimated that there were 11 million crimes in England and Wales. However, there were less than three million crimes recorded by the police in 1982. This gap is the 'dark figure' of crime.

Case study

Northern Ireland Crime Survey

The Statistics and Research Branch of the Northern Ireland Office commissions a survey of approximately 3,000 individuals aged sixteen and over living in private households. It was first carried out as a one-off survey in 1994/5 and was repeated in 1998, 2001 and 2003/4 and has been running as a continuous survey since January 2005. The structure of the survey is very similar to the British Crime Survey (BCS).

The main purpose of the survey is to collect information about levels of crime and public attitudes to crime. The information is collected by interviewing people to find out about crimes they may have experienced, including those that were not reported to the police. Respondents are also asked their views about the level of crime and how much they worry about crime.

The results play an important role in developing and monitoring government policies and targets

The findings of the 2003/04 survey showed:

- Over a fifth of respondents and their households were victims of at least one crime during the 12 months prior to interview,
- Increases occurred between this survey in 2001 and 2003/04 in the proportions of households victimised by vandalism (from 6.4% to 7.1%), vehicle vandalism (from 3.4% to 3.6%), and domestic burglary (from 2.0% to 2.4%). Decreases occurred in the victimisation rates for theft of a vehicle (from 1.4% to 1.2%), attempted theft of or from a vehicle (from 1.7% to 1.5%) and other household theft (from 3.9% to 3.4%).
- Among crimes against the person, there were increases between the 2001 survey and 2003/04 in the proportions of adults falling victim to common assault (from 2.1% to 2.6%), and mugging (from 0.4% to 0.6%). A decrease occurred in the victimisation rate for wounding (from 1.1% to 0.5%).

Key terms

British Crime Survey (BCS): a victim survey conducted annually by a team of researchers at the Home Office. The BCS measures the amount of crime in England and Wales by asking people about crimes they have experienced in the last year.

Did you know ??????

According to official statistics, the typical criminal is young, male, working class, black, poorly educated, and likely to have had a disturbed childhood. However, is this really the case or can it be argued that the official statistics do not provide a valid picture of crime and criminals?

B *A criminal is arrested*

Activity

3 Divide into groups. Discuss the key findings of the 2003/04 Northern Ireland Crime Survey (NICS).

⚙ **links**

Refer to page 99 for the definition of dark figure of crime.

Going further

2 Look at the Home Office website to find the results of British Crime Surveys: **www. homeoffice.gov.uk**

■ A comparison of the results of NICS 2003/04 and the 2003/04 British Crime Survey (BCS) shows that, while the risk of becoming a victim of crime remains lower in Northern Ireland (21.4%) than in England and Wales (25.7%), the gap has narrowed. Whereas the victimisation rate in Northern Ireland increased between NICS 2001 and 2003/04, from 19.7% to 21.4%, that in England and Wales fell between BCS 2001/02 and 2003/04, from 27.5% to 25.7%.

Activity

4 Using all the information on official crime statistics, victim surveys and self-report surveys, draw up a table to show the advantages and disadvantages of all three methods of collecting crime statistics.

Draw some conclusions about the accuracy of each method.

C *What are the advantages and disadvantages of victim surveys?*

Advantages	Disadvantages
May uncover some of the hidden figure of crime.	Not all crimes will be reported for various reasons, for example, a victim is embarrassed to reveal they have been the victim of certain crimes, such as rape.
Focuses on the problems as people experienced them.	
Identifies local, geographically focused figures.	Participants may lie.
	In some cases, the victim cannot be questioned, as in the case of child abuse.

The BCS does not claim to provide a complete picture of crime. However, it does claim to give a more accurate figure than police statistics and to provide a more accurate indication of trends in crime.

■ Self-report surveys

The basic approach of the self-report method is to ask individuals if they have engaged in delinquent or criminal behaviour, and if so, how often they have done so. They include lists of criminal or deviant acts that are given to people and they are asked to tick off the activities which they have committed within a given time period. It is always given anonymously so that people can feel free to admit to crime. Self-reporting suggests that criminal activity is more common than official statistics indicate.

Check your understanding

1 Identify three reasons why official statistics do not give an accurate picture of crimes.

2 What are the differences between victim surveys and self-report surveys?

3 What are the advantages of conducting victim surveys?

4 What are the advantages of conducting self-report surveys?

Activity

5 The following is an example of a self-report survey.

a Complete this survey. Have you committed any of these acts in the last two years?

■ I have ridden a bicycle without lights after dark.

■ I have, aged under 16, driven a car or motorbike.

■ I have played truant from school.

■ I have, aged under 15, smoked cigarettes.

■ I have dropped litter in the street.

■ I have broken into someone else's property.

■ I have had a fight with someone in a public place.

■ I have carried a weapon.

■ I have, aged under 18, drunk alcohol in a pub.

■ I have stolen something from a shop.

b Now that you have completed this survey, list the advantages and disadvantages you have identified with this type of self-report survey.

For example:

■ Advantage: may uncover some of the hidden figure of crime.

■ Disadvantage: people may lie.

4.3 How do we explain criminal and deviant behaviour?

There are many different explanations for crime including biological, psychological and sociological. Although we are particularly interested in the sociological explanations, it is important to have an understanding of the other explanations for crime.

Are criminals born or made?

Biological explanation

It has been argued that some people are naturally inclined to be criminals. This means that biological factors are responsible for their behaviour. They are born criminals.

A study published in 1876 claimed that criminal behaviour was a result of biological factors. Lombroso studied a large number of prisoners and concluded that a person's character could be assessed from the shape of the skull and other physical characteristics. He believed that criminals were less evolved than normal people. This view, however, is no longer considered as offering a satisfactory explanation of crime.

A geneticist, Steve Jones (1994) believes that our genes are a complex set of chemical instructions that shape our behaviour. They do this in interaction with the environment. Any influences of biology are always developed by society. Therefore, attempts to explain human behaviour only in biological terms will never provide a complete answer.

However, this nature/nurture debate is crucial to understanding a sociological approach to crime. Sociologists are interested in explaining how crime and criminals are **socially constructed**.

Key terms

Socially constructed: views of what is criminal or deviant behaviour are influenced by the values and norms of the society we live in.

Case study

Biological explanation for criminal activity?

Shortly after midnight on 17 February 1991 Mobley robbed Domino's pizza store and shot John C. Collins, the store manager, in the back of the head. Over the next three weeks, Mobley committed six additional armed robberies. Approximately three weeks after the crimes, Mobley used the pistol while robbing a dry cleaning store, and tried to dispose of it by tossing it out his car window onto the side of a road when he realised he was being followed by an unmarked police car. The pistol was later recovered and Mobley arrested. Mobley made statements to the police confessing to the murder of Collins and the robbery of the pizza store. His lawyer claimed that the murders were a tragic consequence of a genetic predisposition. The genes of Tony Mobley, his lawyer argued, meant he was born to kill. Mobley was however, found guilty and executed on 1 March 2005 by lethal injection in the state of Georgia, USA.

http://www.clarkprosecutor.org/html/death/us/mobley950.htm

Activity

1 Read the robbery case study.

a Do you believe that a person could be born a criminal? Explain your view.

b Make a list of other reasons why you think people commit crimes.

c Compare your list with others.

Psychological explanations

Various explanations have been put forward by psychologists to explain crime.

- **Premenstrual tension (PMT)**
  Stress caused by menstruation can make women act irrationally and so they cannot be held responsible for their actions. It is believed that 80 per cent of female crime occurs around the period of menstruation.

Case study

On 9 November 1981 a London barmaid walked out of the Old Bailey a free woman, although she had threatened to kill a policeman when she was already on probation for stabbing another barmaid to death. The reason for her release was that she was stated to have suffered from severe premenstrual tension, which had had a 'Jekyll and Hyde' effect on her life, and that she was now on daily injections of progesterone which would keep her 'safe and benign'. On the next day another English woman, who had killed her lover by running her car into him deliberately after a quarrel, was acquitted of murder, again on a plea of premenstrual tension.

Did you know ???????

Research conducted in Denmark (2000) with adopted children appears to show that criminality can be inherited. Research by Mednick consisted of over 14,000 adoptions and he argued that the adopted children's behaviour showed more similarity to their biological parents than to their adopted parents.

- **Maternal deprivation**
  Research has shown that early childhood deprivation, lack of emotional security and lack of secure attachment in childhood could also lead to a person developing a criminal personality as they seek affection and attention from elsewhere.

A *A criminal in prison*

■ Sociological explanations

There are many different sociological explanations for crime and deviance.

Socialisation

Society has accepted norms and values which most people know and follow. However, some young people may have been inadequately socialised into the norms and values of society or they may have learned criminal norms and values in the family and may have had criminal role models.

Functionalists believe that shared norms and values in society are important for the success of society. Functionalists see crime and deviance as a threat to this success. However, they also see that crime can be functional for society by having clear boundaries of acceptable behaviour which are made known by the arrest of those who do not follow the accepted norms of society. Crime and deviance strengthens bonds between people and reaffirms values when they are drawn together by horrific crime.

Peer groups and sub-cultures

Some sociologists explain deviance and criminal behaviour in terms of the influence of peer groups (**peer group pressure**). Being part of a group gives individuals a sense of belonging. Individuals within the group are likely to follow the norms and values of the majority, particularly if they want to feel accepted by the group.

Many of these groups are likely to develop their own norms and values which may differ from the norms and values of society. These groups then become known as **sub-cultures**.

Relative deprivation

Growing up in a poor environment and lacking certain resources that the majority of others in society have, for example, mobile phone, laptop, could lead to criminal activity.

Marxists explain crime by examining the type of society in which we live. They are critical of our society (**capitalist society**), which is based on values such as materialism (valuing material possessions), consumerism (wanting more and better goods, for example, designer clothes, car) and competition between individuals to achieve these possessions. The media also reinforce these values through advertising. In this sort of society it is likely that some people will attempt to obtain material goods through any means, including illegal means, leading to criminal and deviant behaviour.

Labelling

A label is a tag which is often attached to an individual or group. Labelling a person as a criminal can have serious consequences for a person's identity. If the negative label of criminal is successfully applied, it tends to stick and people see the person as this label. After constant reinforcement, the individual comes to believe the label and takes on this role. The label then becomes a **self-fulfilling prophecy**.

Key terms

Functionalism: an approach in sociology that seeks to explain the existence of social structures by the role they perform for society as a whole.

Peer group pressure: a group of a person's own age who are important to them and often influence them to behave in a particular way.

Sub-culture: a group with a set of values and ways of behaving which are distinctive from the generally accepted cultural values of society.

Marxist: someone who believes in the ideas of Karl Marx and sees the main divisions in society based on social class operating in a capitalist system.

Capitalist society: an economic system where the production of goods is organised for profit and sold to a free market.

Self-fulfilling prophecy: people hear labels about themselves from people who are more powerful than they are. They come to believe the labels are true and then act as if they are true. Therefore, the labels become true.

⊙⊙ links

Refer to Chapter 1 Studying Society for explanations of relative deprivation.

Activity

2 Does the labelling of certain groups in society affect crime statistics? Are individuals targeted because they are involved in higher rates of crime or because of the way people are stereotyped by the police?

Let them wear hoodies

In May 2005, the Bluewater shopping Centre in Kent banned the wearing of hooded tops and baseball caps as part of a crackdown on anti-social behaviour. Managers of the centre have drawn up a code of conduct which bans the wearing of such clothing. People contravening it will be asked to leave the centre.

B *Are 'hoodies' menacing?*

Media

The media reports criminal activities in a highly selective way. Cohen (1973) argued that through several stages, a group is identified and portrayed by the media as being 'troublemakers', for example, which leads to public outcry and the determination by the authorities, for example, police, to tackle this 'problem' group. This is known as amplification of deviance.

> The amplifiaction of deviance process:
> actual event reported by media
>
> ↓
>
> report raises concerns amongst population, who demand something is done about it
>
> ↓
>
> police respond by putting more police in area concerned
>
> ↓
>
> more people caught doing illegal act
>
> ↓
>
> media reports increase

Activity

3 Divide into groups. Discuss what the case study on hoodies has to say about labelling and teenagers.

⃝⃝ links

Also see Topic 5.4 for information on deviancy amplification and the media.

Activity

4 Which of the explanations of crime do you agree with most? Write out a summary of the explanation and why you think this explains criminal behaviour more than the other explanations.

Use this as the basis of a discussion with others in your group.

AQA *Examiner's tip*

Your answers should focus on sociological explanations of crime and deviance. However, it is a good idea to have an understanding of biological and psychological explanations. These can be used as comparisons to sociological explanations.

Check your understanding

1 Identify and explain, using examples, two different sociological explanations of criminal behaviour.

2 Identify one biological and one psychological explanation of criminal behaviour. Explain why these explanations are not sociological.

3 Identify one explanation and explain, using examples, why you think this is the most important explanation for criminal behaviour.

Going further

Read newspapers on a regular basis and identify any issues relating to current crime figures, criminal activity, etc.

4.4 How do we attempt to control anti-social behaviour?

■ Social control

Societies can only exist if there is some order and some predictability otherwise society would be in chaos. Order is applied by the use of rules and laws. Social control refers to the methods that are used to control individual and group behaviour, which leads to conformity to the rules of a particular society.

Informal social control

This form of control is based on the approval or disapproval of those around us, for example, family, friends and peer group. If they disapprove of our behaviour, they will tell us and criticise our behaviour. In extreme cases we may be excluded from the group for our behaviour. For example, swearing amongst a group of people who do not swear.

Formal social control

Formal social control is where behaviour is controlled through organisations that exist to enforce order, for example, the police.

Social control in action

Agents of social control attempt to control anti-social behaviour.

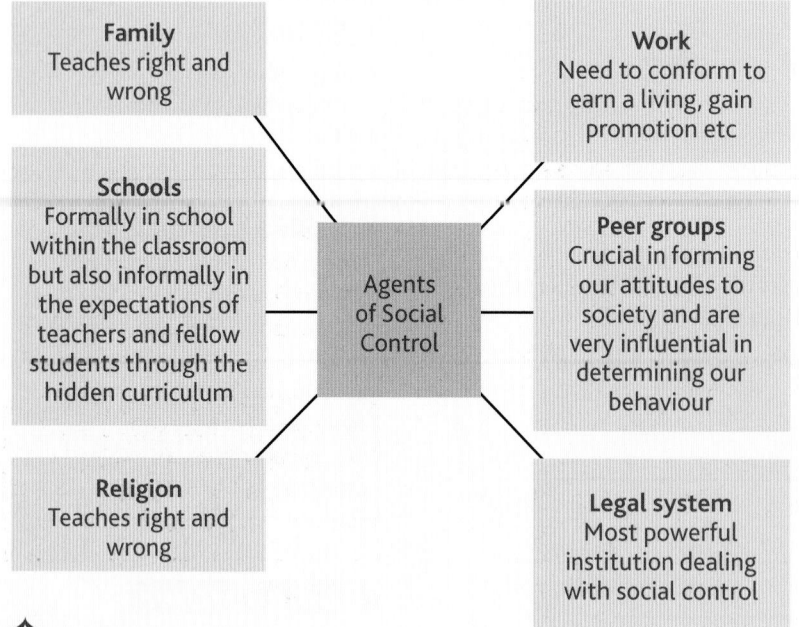

Family
Teaches right and wrong

Schools
Formally in school within the classroom but also informally in the expectations of teachers and fellow students through the hidden curriculum

Religion
Teaches right and wrong

Agents of Social Control

Work
Need to conform to earn a living, gain promotion etc

Peer groups
Crucial in forming our attitudes to society and are very influential in determining our behaviour

Legal system
Most powerful institution dealing with social control

A Agents of social control

Objectives

You will be able to:

- describe the different methods of social control

- explain the differences between formal and informal social control

- discuss the effectiveness of the different methods for criminals, victims, communities and society as a whole.

Key terms

Agent of social control: individual or group that is responsible for ensuring members of society conform to socially acceptable behaviour.

Surveillance: is the monitoring of the behaviour of people and objects within society.

CCTV (Closed-circuit television): a television system often used for surveillance.

∞ links

Also see Chapter 2 Education for information on the hidden curriculum.

links

Also see Chapter 3 Families for information on primary socialisation.

Activity

1 Think of some examples of informal social control and discuss these with other students.

A new agent of social control? Surveillance and CCTV

In an attempt to prevent anti-social behaviour, there is greater **surveillance** of our everyday lives.

CCTV

Case study

The introduction of public Closed Circuit Television (**CCTV**) has been successfully introduced into many towns and cities to fight crime and disorder. It has been proved effective in both cutting and detecting crime and because of this people now feel safer when they are out and about.

However, CCTV is not just used for crime, problems and the 'bad' side of society, it can be used for many 'good' things too such as helping visitors find their cars in car parks, informing the public about traffic flow problems and even reuniting children with their parents.

Going further

1 Research the use of CCTV cameras in your local area. Where are they and what are they used for?

Activities

2 Design a questionnaire to investigate the opinions of students in your group on the influence of family, peer group, school, etc on their behaviour. How influential have these agents of social control been in influencing behaviour? For example, some students may be strongly influenced by religion whereas this may play no part in the social control of others.

3 The UK has more CCTV cameras per person than anywhere else in the world and the use of CCTV raises data protection and wider privacy concerns. It can be used in intrusive ways to put ordinary individuals under surveillance as they go about their everyday lives.

a Do you think CCTV cameras are a good idea or do you think they intrude on our lives?

b Using the CCTV case study, and other information you can find, what are the advantages and disadvantages of CCTV cameras?

AQA **Examiner's tip**

When answering exam questions on crime and deviance don't forget that you could use information from other topic areas, for example, family, education, which are influential in the socialisation and control of children's behaviour.

Did you know

It is thought that the average person is caught about 300 times a day on a CCTV camera.

Ways of dealing with anti-social behaviour

The judiciary

The role of the police is to act as 'gatekeepers', deciding which acts should be classified as crime or not. It is from the police figures that the criminal statistics are derived. The influence of the courts is to decide, not what criminal acts have been committed, but if the persons accused are guilty.

The British judiciary system could not work without a huge number of the accused pleading guilty. Eight out of ten people appearing in court plead guilty, which allows the courts to concentrate on those who plead not guilty. If convicted of a criminal offence, the criminal may be sentenced to a jail term, the length of which will vary depending on the crime committed.

Alternatives to a jail sentence

A **police caution** is an alternative to prosecution (legal proceedings). It is intended to act as an official warning to deter people from getting involved in further crime. There are two forms of caution:

- Formal caution: may be given to adults who admit they are guilty of first-time minor offences, such as vandalism or petty theft, and counts towards a criminal record.
- Informal caution: an oral warning given by a police officer and does not count towards a criminal record.

A **reprimand** is a formal verbal warning given by a police officer to a young person who admits they are guilty of a minor first offence.

Community service is a service that a person performs for the benefit of his or her local community in place of a prison sentence.

Probation is the suspension of a jail sentence. A person may have committed a crime but they are given 'probation' where they can live in the community and follow certain conditions set by the court under the supervision of a probation officer.

The ASBO or 'Anti-Social Behaviour Order' is seen by some as the solution to much of the inappropriate and anti-social behaviour in society today. ASBOs are court orders which are issued to people for anti-social behaviour including rowdy and nuisance behaviour, yobbish behaviour, vandalism, dealing and buying drugs on the street and anti-social drinking. An ASBO can ban a person from continuing the behaviour, spending time with a particular group of friends or visiting certain areas. ASBOs are issued for a minimum of two years.

> **Key terms**
>
> **Police:** agents of social control with the power to enforce the law.
>
> **Prosecution:** conduct of legal proceedings against a defendant for criminal behaviour.
>
> **ASBO (Anti-Social Behaviour Order):** an order made by the courts against a person who has been shown to have engaged in anti-social behaviour, for example, drinking on the streets.

Case study

Do ASBOs work?

A report in November 2006 by the Youth Justice Board (YJB) into ASBOs and under 18s, found that some teenagers view anti-social behaviour orders (ASBOs) as a 'badge of honour'. The report claimed that young people given ASBOs are sometimes seen by peers as glamorous, and that in half of all cases of ASBOs issued to youths the conditions attached to them were violated. Home Office figures show that one ASBO in four is breached.

Activity

4 What do you think about ASBOs? Do you think they work?

   a List the advantages and disadvantages of ASBOs.

   b Discuss your answers with other students and draw some conclusions on the effectiveness of ASBOs.

Did you know ??????

The total number of ASBOs reported to the Home Office between April 1999 and December 2006 stands at 12,675.

But what about the victims and the communities affected by crime?

Social control is important in society not just to control the individuals who take part in deviant or criminal behaviour but also for society as a whole. Some areas are greatly affected by criminal behaviour, for example, inner cities. The crime in the area has a huge effect on the individuals in that area, for example, not feeling safe to go outside or destroying community life.

B *The police enforce the law*

Activity

5 What effect does criminal behaviour have on victims, communities and society in general?

   a Draw a table as illustrated below and complete it showing the effects of crime.

Victims	Communities	Society
For example, loss of self-esteem	For example, closure of play area	

   b Draw some conclusions as to whether methods of social control are working to improve the lives of victims, communities and society as a whole.

Going further

2 Research cases of people who have been given ASBOs. Is it just young people who are issued with ASBOs?

Check your understanding

1 Identify and explain the role of two agents of social control.

2 What is the difference between formal and informal social control?

3 Identify and explain two methods of controlling anti-social behaviour.

When sociologists look at crime statistics, they find that there are distinct patterns. Crimes, and indeed different types of crime, seem to be closely linked to membership of certain social groups.

■ Crime and gender

What are the differences?

Statistics show that men commit more crimes than women. In 2006, male offenders in England and Wales outnumbered female offenders by more than four to one. About 90 per cent of people found guilty of burglary, robbery, drug offences and criminal damage are male.

The Offending, Crime and Justice survey clearly indicates the crime rates of males and females.

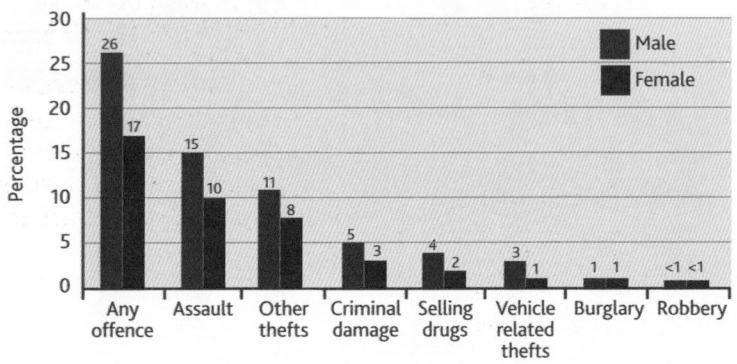

www.homeoffice.gov.uk/rds/offending_survey.html

A *Proportion of 10- to 25-year-olds committing an offence in the last 12 months by sex, 2006, OCJS*

Why do these differences exist?

■ **Different socialisation**
Boys are more likely to be brought up with the values of toughness and aggressiveness whereas girls are generally brought up in such a way that they come to possess qualities and expectations that lead them to behave in a law abiding way.

■ **Opportunity to commit crime**
In adolescence, girls are more likely to be confined to the home and subject to greater parental supervision.

■ **Social control**
Men may constrain women in their lives often enforcing them into family-centred roles.

■ **Chivalry thesis**
There is a common belief that the male-dominated police and courts are easier on women. Males, for example, are more likely to be prosecuted whereas females are cautioned.

■ **Inaccurate statistics**
Statistics that show that males commit more crime than females could be a reflection of the labelling of male youths by the police.

∞links

Also see Topic 4.2 for information on crime statistics.

Is this pattern changing?

Ladette drinking culture condemned

"**Ladette**" culture — young urban women with large disposable incomes, few responsibilities and an ability to drink as much as men has been boosted by awareness among breweries. Since the mid-1990s breweries have increasingly taken women into account when deciding the style and location of bars. Research showed that women wanted an airy interior, polished wood floor, unintimidating glass front, smart bathroom and music that does not get in the way of conversation.

Drinks are also devised for the female market. The UK's ladettes knock back £1.5 billion worth of alcopops and ready-to-drink brands each year — 75% of total sales.

B *Ladettes drinking*

Did you know ??????

'Ladettes' was introduced to the revised version of the Concise Oxford Dictionary in 2001. This reflects the change in the behaviour of women.

AQA Examiner's tip

It is tempting to assume that because women are less likely to be criminal than men, they cannot be criminals. Women have been charged and convicted of all crimes including serious sexual abuse and murder.

Activity

2 What does this case study say about the changing behaviour of women in today's society?

■ Crime and location

Crime rates tend to be higher in inner city areas and some 'problem' housing estates because the people concentrated in these areas are often from working-class backgrounds. Consequently the explanations given later about working-class crime are especially true here.

Inner city areas may have more pubs and clubs which means that the area is likely to be more heavily policed and therefore more crime is detected, reported and recorded for these areas.

Rural surveys suggest that crime does not only occur in urban areas but the nature of crime appears to be different in rural areas to urban areas.

Going further

1 Use the Internet to investigate the nature of urban crime in comparison to rural crime.

Going further

2 Are the figures an accurate reflection of the amount of male and female crime?

Research more about the **chivalry thesis** and discuss it with other students.

■ Crime and age

What are the differences?

Statistics tend to suggest that most people receiving criminal convictions will be between 14 and 24 years of age.

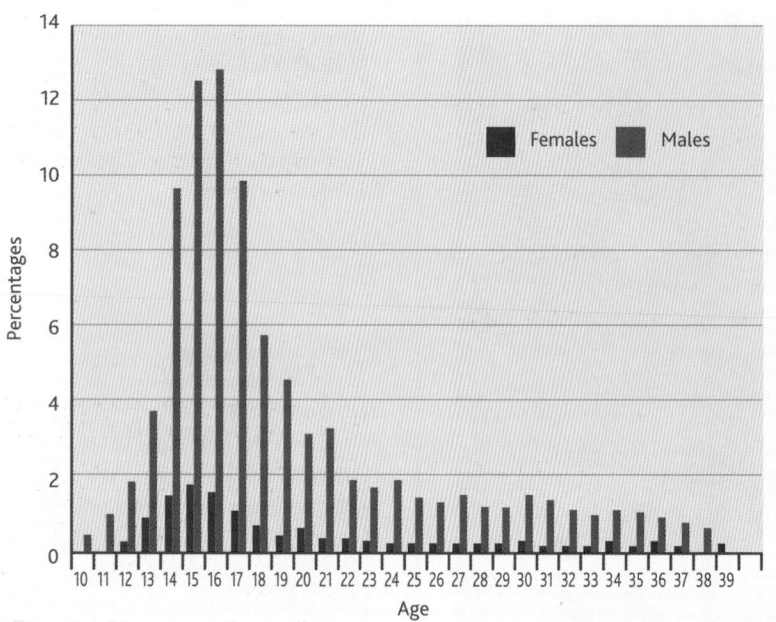

C *Distribution of offenders by age and gender*

Key terms

Injustice: when a person is accused of a crime of which they are not guilty.

Institutional racism: occurs when the everyday practices and procedures of an organisation, for example, the police, lead to discrimination against ethnic groups either intentionally or unintentionally.

Activity

3 Study Chart **C** which shows the distribution of offenders by age and gender.

a What do these figures say about the crime rates of young people?

b Can you suggest sociological reasons for the patterns you have described?

Case study

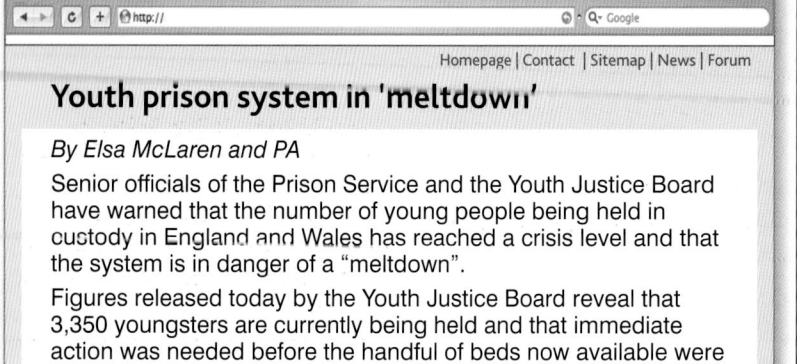

| Homepage | Contact | Sitemap | News | Forum

Youth prison system in 'meltdown'

By Elsa McLaren and PA

Senior officials of the Prison Service and the Youth Justice Board have warned that the number of young people being held in custody in England and Wales has reached a crisis level and that the system is in danger of a "meltdown".

Figures released today by the Youth Justice Board reveal that 3,350 youngsters are currently being held and that immediate action was needed before the handful of beds now available were filled.

Dozens of children and youths from London are being held in South Yorkshire and the Scottish borders because of the shortage of beds, contravening rules that young offenders should not be held more than 50 miles from home.

From *Times Online*, October 24, 2006

Did you know ??????

In 2005, it was reported that:

- Twenty five per cent of all recorded crime was committed by children aged between 10 and 17.
- Forty per cent of all crime was committed by people under the age of 21.
- Forty per cent of male prisoners left school before the age of 16.

Activity

4 Do you think youth crime is a problem in society today?

What suggestions do you have to reduce youth crime? Discuss your suggestions with other students.

D *Young black people are eight times more likely to be stopped and searched than white people*

Crime and ethnicity

What are the differences?

Statistics tend to suggest that Afro-Caribbean males and Asian males are over-represented in the prison population.

In Britain today there are 55 million people. Of these, 5 per cent are Afro-Caribbean and 2 per cent are Asian. This would mean that the prison population should be 5 per cent Afro-Caribbean and 2 per cent Asian, but it is not. The actual figures are 10 per cent Afro-Caribbean and 9 per cent Asian. Of the 2 million people arrested, 16 per cent are Afro-Caribbean and 7 per cent are Asian.

Activity

5 There are various ways to explain these crime statistics among ethnic groups.

- Ethnic groups commit more crime.
- The police are more likely to arrest and charge ethnic groups, who therefore experience **injustice**.

Take these points and discuss them in groups. Some points you might like to consider in your discussion may include:

- Accuracy of figures.
- Police labelling certain groups.
- Institutional racism.
- Police mishandling enquiries because of their own views and beliefs (Stephen Lawrence enquiry).
- Discrimination.
- Afro-Caribbeans are more likely to be working class.
- Many Asians are also likely to be working class and discriminated against.
- Media reinforcing views.

Did you know ??????

At the end of June 2002, ethnic minority groups made up 22% of the male prison population and 29% of the female prison population.

AQA *Examiner's tip*

You don't necessarily need to remember actual figures/ percentages for the exam, but an idea of trends and patterns will be helpful.

It is clear that, although statistics offer a view of the typical criminal as being working class, young and male, this may tell us more about how criminal statistics are gathered than about crime and criminal behaviour.

Crime and social class

There is a clear link between a person's social class and the likelihood that they will be convicted of a crime. In the UK, official crime statistics don't refer to the social class of convicted people.

However, studies do show that more working class than middle and upper class people are convicted. There are various explanations for this:

Socialisation

Children develop the norms and values of their parents. Children of working-class parents will therefore develop different norms and values from middle-class children. Children from working-class families may also suffer from material deprivation which may influence them to turn to crime.

Anomie

If a society fails to provide enough ways for people to be successful, then they will feel frustrated and possibly turn to crime.

Education

Working-class youths are more likely to fail at school and be in the bottom streams. They are therefore more likely to be in lower-paid jobs. Lack of money in some cases could lead to criminal activities.

Although studies show that most crime is committed by working-class young people, there are other types of crime which probably cost society more than the value of the burglaries and bank robberies put together. **White-collar crime** is committed by middle-class people in the course of their work. The term 'white-collar crime' was introduced by Sutherland in the 1940s. This crime takes several forms:

Occupational crime

This is carried out by individuals in work and ranges from minor theft of an organisation's property to large scale fraud.

Professional crime

Carried out as a lifetime career such as drug running.

Corporate crime

Carried out by executives of organisations to increase profit and can include such activities as selling harmful products.

Computer crime

This is increasing as more financial transactions are conducted via computers. In one case, a bank employee transferred £45,000 from dormant accounts in Kuwait, to be placed in accounts of his own once he had left the bank. In order to prevent detection, he programmed his computer to delete all records of these transactions.

White-collar crime is hard to research due to difficulties in identifying it and the unwillingness of individuals and organisations to discuss it. Many crimes are 'without victims'. Organisations such as banks are reluctant to report offences for fear of losing public confidence. If white-collar crimes are detected, offenders may be sacked and given time to pay back the money they may have stolen. They escape prosecution which avoids publicity and maintains public confidence in the company's good name. In many cases, the public never hears about the offence.

White-collar criminals may be brought to court but they tend to be treated rather differently from other criminals. This may be for the following reasons:

- Judges have similar social backgrounds to many white-collar criminals.

Key terms

Anomie: a situation where large numbers of people fail to follow generally accepted values, instead adopting various deviant forms of behaviour, such as theft.

White-collar crime: criminal acts committed by middle-class people in the course of their work.

Identity theft: the misappropriation of the identity (such as the name, date of birth, current address or previous addresses) of another person, without their knowledge or consent. These identity details are then used to obtain goods and services in that person's name.

E *White-collar crime: easy to spot?*

- Compared to the burglar, mugger, etc, white-collar criminals are not considered to be a danger to the public.
- The victims of white-collar crime are not harmed as seriously as the victims of many other crimes.
- The media tends not to portray white-collar crime as serious.

Case study

Identity theft hits 135,000 a year

A survey suggests that every year 16,000 tonnes of documents with potentially valuable personal details are dumped in London dustbins by the public.

David Lennox, of CIFAS, the national fraud-prevention service, said the number of victims had risen from 20,000 in 1999 and most were often unaware that anything was amiss until they received demands for loan repayments or bills for goods that they had never bought.

The cost of identity crime is estimated at £1.3 billion a year but it could be more, and up to 18 million households could be failing to protect themselves.

From *The Times*, 18 October 2005

AQA *Examiner's tip*

White-collar crime raises important questions about the nature of crime and challenges the view that crime is mainly a working-class activity.

Activity

6 **Identity theft** is increasing in the UK. In small groups discuss:
- the reasons why identity theft is increasing
- suggestions for protecting your own identity.

Going further

3 Find out about some famous white-collar crimes, for example, Guinness, Enron.

Check your understanding

1 Choose social class, gender, age or ethnicity. What is the difference in crime statistics within this group?

2 Explain why these differences exist.

3 Explain what is meant by white-collar crime and explain why this crime is treated differently from other crimes.

4.6 What does social research tell us about crime and deviance in contemporary Britain?

There are various research methods available when studying crime and deviance and the method used depends on what the sociologists are trying to find out.

The fear of crime

A 2008 study of the fear of crime funded by the Economic and Social Research Council (ESRC) aimed to build on previous research showing that the fear of crime is not as widespread as previously thought and may even have been misrepresented.

The main objectives of the study were to explore the fear of crime, taking into account gender, age, type of area, ethnicity and social background.

Interviews were conducted about the fear of crime, specifically the fear of burglary, robbery and car crime. Twenty-three interviews were conduced with experts on the fear of crime. Twenty-four interviews were conducted with residents of one West London borough. Sixty-four interviews with residents in an area of Glasgow, carried out as part of an earlier ESRC study, were also used in this study. The data collected was then compared with data from the **British Crime Survey (BCS)**.

This study identified two types of fear about crime:

- The first was a fairly rare, everyday worry about crime. These people experienced intensely frightening episodes where they felt in real danger from crime. They tended to live in high crime areas and they may have experienced crime either directly or indirectly. They were worried about behaviour and social disorder in their own communities.

- The second type of fear was one of general anxiety about crime, a feeling that 'it could happen'. It was more common among people leading protected lives in lower crime areas. These people were concerned about society's problems but were not terrified of crime as an immediate threat.

People tend to associate the issue of crime with concerns about the breakdown of society and the flouting of society's rules. To be afraid of crime is to show disapproval for the way society seems to have loosened its moral standards.

Adapted from www.crimereduction.homeoffice.gov.uk/crimereduction025.htm

Objectives

You will be able to:

- describe different research methods used by sociologists when researching crime and deviance

- discuss the advantages and disadvantages of these research methods when investigating crime and deviance

- describe studies of crime and deviance that have used different research methods.

Key terms

British Crime Survey (BCS): a victim survey conducted annually by a team of researchers at the Home Office. The BCS measures the amount of crime in England and Wales by asking people about crimes they have experienced in the last year.

Indictable offences: serious crimes, generally those for which an accused person may be sent to prison if found guilty.

Non-indictable offences: less serious crimes such as parking offences.

Check your understanding

1 Who was this research conducted by?

2 What were the main objectives of this research?

3 What primary research method was used in this research?

4 Identify advantages and disadvantages of using this primary research method.

5 What secondary source was used in this research?

6 Why was it important to take into account such factors as gender, age, type of area, ethnicity and social background?

7 What conclusions could be drawn from this research?

⦾ links

Also see Topic 4.2 for how we measure the amount of criminal and deviant behaviour in society.

A *Youths hard at work*

Going further

1 Design a questionnaire to explore the fear of crime in your local area. Include questions on gender, age, type of area, ethnicity and social background. Do any of these factors make a difference?

■ Youth crime

The number of young people found guilty by the juvenile courts has fallen in England and Wales during the past 15 years. Between 1983 and 1993 the proportion of 10- to 13-year-old boys who were found guilty or cautioned for serious **indictable offences** dropped by 42 per cent, with a 15 per cent decline among 14- to 17-year-olds.

However this apparent decrease seems to be an illusion. Police-recorded crime statistics and national surveys of the victims of crime both agree that the types of offence most often committed by young people, such as burglary and taking vehicles, have risen dramatically over the same period.

The reasons for the apparent decline is a reluctance to take juveniles to court and an increasing tendency of police to issue unrecorded warnings rather than formal cautions, treating indictable offences as **non-indictable offences**.

Criminal careers

The life-time likelihood of getting a criminal conviction is greater than generally realised. More than 4 out of 10 males and 1 in 10 females are likely to be found guilty or cautioned at some point during their lives.

'Self-report' studies show that individuals more often break the law when they are young. The 'peak' ages at which they are most likely to be found guilty or cautioned are between 15 and 19. Criminal involvement typically starts before the age of 15, but declines once young people reach their 20s. However, young people who become involved in crime at the earliest ages – before they are 14 – tend to become the most persistent offenders, with longer criminal careers.

Interviews with young offenders suggest that their crimes are most commonly committed for material gain. However, a minority of offences, especially vandalism and taking vehicles without the owner's consent, are committed for excitement, enjoyment or to relieve boredom.

Risk factors

Research has identified thousands of factors that point to an increased risk that children and young people will become criminally involved in the future. The major risk factors for juvenile offending are as follows:

- Early child-bearing increases the risk of low school attainment, anti-social behaviour, substance use and early sexual activity.

- Personality including impulsiveness, hyperactivity, restlessness and limited ability to concentrate are associated with low attainment in school and a poor ability to foresee the consequences of offending.

- Harsh or erratic parental discipline and cold or rejecting parental attitudes have been linked to delinquency.

- Living in a home affected by separation or divorce is strongly related to delinquency.

- Social and economic deprivation are important predictors of anti-social behaviour and crime.

- Delinquents tend to have delinquent friends. However, it is not certain whether membership of a delinquent peer group leads to offending or whether delinquents simply gravitate towards each other's company (or both).

- The risks of becoming criminally involved are higher for young people raised in disorganised inner city areas.

Adapted from www.jrf.org.uk/knowledge/findings/socialpolicy/SP93.asp

Check your understanding

1 Why does the number of young people found guilty by the juvenile courts, or formally cautioned by police, differ from police-recorded crime statistics and national surveys of the victims?

2 Identify two different methods that were used in this research.

3 What is a self-report study?

4 What are the advantages and disadvantages of self-report studies?

5 What are risk factors?

6 Identify and explain two different risk factors and explain why they may lead to criminal behaviour.

Going further

2 If risk factors have been identified, it should be possible to develop strategies/prevention techniques to reduce their influence. Divide into groups. Work out some strategies that could be developed to reduce the influence of these risk factors and so reduce youth crime in the UK. Discuss these strategies with the other groups.

4.7   Exam questions for Crime and deviance

■ **Exam question guidance**

∞links

See the Exam question guidance section in Topic 1.8 on page 38 for general advice on answering source-based questions.

Example of a source-based question

Item A
Teen Survey Results

Of the children who have done this	Percentage of their parents who think they haven't
tried drugs	65
smoked	52
drunk alcohol	45
shoplifted	65
played truant	39

Adapted from the article 'You don't know the half of it',
The Guardian Weekend, 24 February 2007

▦ **Who?** This source is based on the results of a survey conducted for *The Guardian* newspaper by the market research organisation ICM in 2007. The source is presented in the form of a table. The column on the left refers to children who have had certain experiences. The column on the right refers to what their parents believe.

▦ **What?** ICM interviewed a sample of over 1,000 people from random geographical locations. Half of these were aged between 11 and 16 and lived in the same household as their parents.

▦ **Why?** The researchers asked young people to fill in confidential questionnaires about issues such as alcohol and drug use, sex and the Internet. Their parents, who gave permission for the research, gave separate answers about what they believed their children had experienced. The research revealed a significant gap between what teenagers said they had done and what their parents believed their children had experienced.

a   From **Item A**, what percentage of parents think their children have not shoplifted?   *(1 mark)*

Answer as briefly as possible. The answer is 65 per cent. Remember to bring a ruler or straight edge into the exam. You can place this on the chart or table to help avoid the simple error of reading the wrong column in a chart or selecting the wrong number from a table.

Example of a 4-mark question

d   Explain what sociologists mean by deviance.   *(4 marks)*

The examiners are expecting you to be able to demonstrate your understanding of a key sociological idea. The best place to start is by stating that while all crime is deviant, not all deviance is criminal. Deviance is a social construct. Some sociologists have argued that there is nothing, no matter how terrible or unusual, that is impossible for human societies to accept. For example, in the past, human societies have tolerated human sacrifice, forced marriage and even cannibalism. You could make the point that **social norms and expectations** vary over time and between one society and another. Forms of behaviour that deviate from these norms and expectations are measured between extremes. Some behaviours are simply disapproved of while others are viewed as serious threats to the social order.

⊂⊃ **links**

See the Exam question guidance section in Topic 2.7 on page 67 for general advice on answering extended-answer questions.

Example of an extended-answer question

g   Discuss how far sociologists would agree that teenage crime and deviant behaviour
result from parents failing to socialise their children correctly.   *(12 marks)*

- The examiner would expect you to show your knowledge of the current debate about levels of criminality and anti-social behaviour among young people in our society. Remember that the question is not just about behaviour that would be considered criminal. It is also about deviant behaviour. Don't fall into the trap of defining 'socialise' in a common-sense way. Here it means the process of socialisation (social learning), not about making friends. You could question why people believe that there is a particular problem with young people in our society. Are people's perceptions based on direct experience or reports in the media? Such reports have created a moral panic linking young people to knife and gun crime and images of hoodie-wearing youths rampaging around inner cities. We live in a remarkably safe society and yet any attempt to provide a balanced view of the problem does not receive much attention in the media.

- The question clearly raises the issue of **extent. How far** would sociologists agree? From a sociological point of view there are other reasons for criminal and deviant behaviour among young people. Rising levels of unemployment and persistent poverty may have considerably more to do with the root causes of the problem. Social commentators frequently look for someone to blame for the ills of society (**scapegoats**). For example, in the recent past, single parents have been held responsible for a range of social problems. Blaming criminal or anti-social behaviour among the young on poor parenting is undoubtedly a further development of this tendency to look for simple solutions to complex problems.

■ Remember to avoid the trap of only referring to the sources in the question. The examiner wants to see evidence that you have studied the sociology of crime and deviance *and* thought about the issues.

■ Questions to try

What follows are examples of the types of questions you will meet in your exam. The letter in each question matches the letter that will be used for that type of question on your exam paper. The number in brackets is only there to help you and your teacher refer to that particular question in this book.

Item B

Beliefs about the change in the national crime rate in England and Wales[1]

	Percentage				
	1996	**1998**	**2000**	**2001**	**2001/02**
Little or lot more	75	58	66	57	64
Same	21	32	28	36	30
Little or lot less	4	10	6	8	6

[1]Respondents were asked how they thought the recorded crime rate for the country as a whole had changed over the two previous years.

Source: British Crime Survey, Home Office
Source: Office for National Statistics

a   From **Item B**, what percentage of respondents in 2000 thought that national crime had increased over the previous two years?   *(1 mark)*

d(1)   Explain what sociologists mean by informal social control.   *(4 marks)*

d(2)   Explain what sociologists mean by norms and expectations.   *(4 marks)*

d(3)   Explain what sociologists mean by a victim survey.   *(4 marks)*

e   Describe **one** way in which recent governments have attempted to reduce the level of crime in society and explain how successful the policy has been.   *(5 marks)*

g(1)   Discuss how far sociologists would agree that an act some people would see as deviant might not be seen as deviant by other people.   *(12 marks)*

g(2)   Discuss how far sociologists would agree that high rates of criminal, anti-social and deviant behaviour can be blamed on features of the modern family.   *(12 marks)*

5.1 What are the mass media?

The mass media and its audience

When you watch a television programme, read a magazine or a newspaper, watch a film or use the Internet, you are experiencing a form of **mass communication**. The information and ideas you meet are specifically designed to reach large numbers of people. Sociologists have long been interested in this area of social life. They are interested in how individuals and groups use the media and respond to its influence. They are also aware that the speed of **technological change** nowadays is transforming the media. The Internet, for example, might make the idea of a 'mass' medium less relevant. This is because people interact with it rather than passively consuming a product designed to appeal to the widest possible audience. Using this new medium, individuals can easily contribute their own content in the form of **blogs** that reflect their own experiences, interests and prejudices.

People who use the Internet want to make contact with and influence the views of others. They are using a relatively cheap and readily available alternative to old technologies. Historically the process of technological development connects the printing press to the Internet, via radio and television. These technologies are different in form but share a common purpose – to provide information and communicate ideas. *All* these technologies have had at least one common effect: each technological innovation has made it easier for people to access ideas and information and to communicate with the widest possible audience.

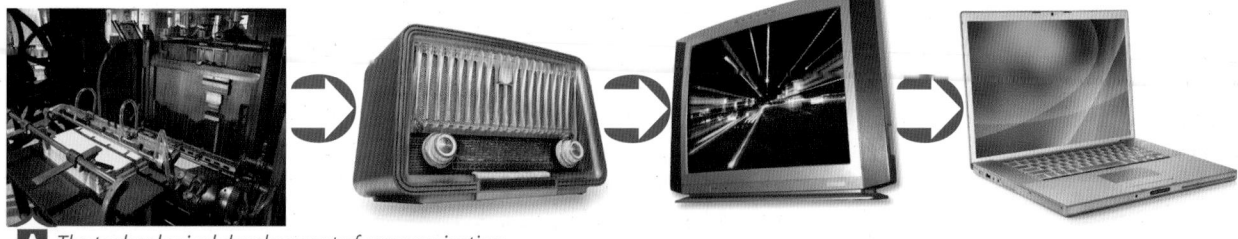

A *The technological development of communication*

Did you know ??????

US border agents can search your laptop, or any other electronic device, when you are entering the country. They can take your computer and download its entire contents, or keep it for several days.

Did you know ??????

Project Gutenberg is the oldest digital library in the world. Started in 1971, it now holds more than 25,000 items all freely available to more than 1 billion people worldwide.

Key terms

Mass communication: reaching an audience of thousands or perhaps millions.

Technological change: the changing technology of communication, for example, the printing press and television.

Activity

1 Divide into groups of about six.

a Write down whether everyone in your group has a computer at home.

b Does everyone have Internet access? If so, which year did they first have it? What made them get it? Was it for work? Was it to communicate with friends? Was it to shop online?

c Collate and discuss your findings with those of other groups. How do your findings compare with the information in Chart **B**?

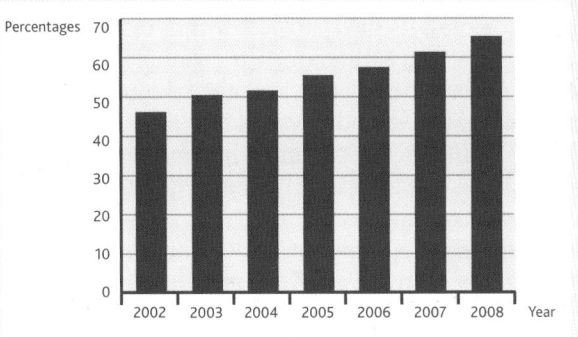

Office for National Statistics

B *Households in Great Britain with access to the Internet*

The mass media as an agency of social change

Some sociologists have argued that the development of communication is the most important **agency of social change**. The publishers of the first books, for example, were often motivated by the idea of religious reform. They wanted to allow people to have an immediate and personal contact with the word of God. In order to achieve that aim, they believed that the Bible should be published in a language that people could easily understand. However, once this technology became available, it produced unexpected outcomes, spreading ideas that challenged the foundations of religion.

This unpredictability lies at the heart of the idea of communicating with a 'mass' of people. Early social scientists believed that individuals in large groups were unthinking and open to manipulation. Sociologists today recognise that individual responses to the media are more complex. For example, the **social class**, gender or **ethnicity** of an individual can have a big effect on how they respond to the media.

Changing technology and the mass media

Case study

Old technology has a noble history of refusing to die. For decades, vinyl has defied the march of the compact disc. Radio was not killed by television. Nearly every desk in every office in the land is piled with barricades of A4, resisting paperlessness. Nowadays it is not how old a medium might be, but whether or not it serves a purpose better than anything put up to replace it. One invention that passes the test with ease is the mass of printed pages, bound in a portable volume – the book. However, the world of publishing is far from untouched by technology. Computers have changed the way writers organise their words – and their thoughts. The Internet changed the way books are traded. Blogs have changed the way they are reviewed.

Adapted from *The Observer*, 25 May 2008

Activity

2 Read the above case study.

a two or three sentences explaining what the author of the article in the case study is saying.

b How far do you agree with this argument?

Going further

1 Design a **survey** to research the questions in Activity 1 across your whole school/college.

Key terms

Blog: web-based comment by both amateurs and professional writers (from the word 'weblog').

Survey: a research tool, for example, a questionnaire or series of interviews.

Agency of social change: influencing social attitudes and government policy.

Social class: people having the same social status measured by such things as occupation and income.

Ethnicity: the classification of people into groups that share the same culture, history and identity.

AQA Examiner's tip

Sociologists today recognise that individual responses to the media are more complex and open to a variety of influences. Do not fall into the trap of referring to the audience as unthinking and *easily* open to manipulation.

New forms of mass communications technology

Some sociologists have suggested that relatively new forms of communications technology (for example, satellite television and the Internet) have completely swamped people with information. They have become overloaded with ideas and images, to such an extent that the difference between reality and images of reality has begun to break down, creating a form of alternative reality or **hyperreality**. In other words, some people appear to be unable to distinguish between what they see on television and encounter in the virtual world of the Internet, and the everyday world of lived experience. Indeed, for some individuals it is possible that the television and Internet become 'real', more comforting or entertaining perhaps than the harshness and isolation of their day-to-day of lives. This is one explanation for the popularity of 'soap operas' or reality television programmes like *Big Brother*. People who feel **alienated** from others in their day-to-day life begin to place great value on what they see on the television.

Activity

3   Divide into pairs and look at Chart C.

a   How many hours of television does the average person watch per day while doing nothing else?

b   How much do they watch in total?

c   Add up how much TV you watch per week. Do you watch more or less than the people in the survey?

d   Share your findings with the rest of your group.

The Internet can also offer an alternative form of social engagement. Someone can exchange an unsatisfactory reality for the virtual life they aspire to. The web-based **social networking site** 'Second Life' creates an opportunity for individuals to lose themselves in an alternative heightened reality where careers can be built, bodies and sexuality exchanged, even relationships established. For some observers the key element of the latest wave of technological development is the level of interactivity involved. They argue that individuals are no longer passive consumers of the images and ideas presented by the media. Instead they become active members of online communities in an evolving and anarchic virtual world.

An active audience

Sociological thinking about the relationship between the mass media and the audience has developed from early, relatively simple models to increasingly complex theories. One of the earliest attempts to describe this relationship was the hypodermic model. In this, the medium (newspapers, television or the Internet) are the syringe, the media content is the drug and the audience are the patient. This model sees the audience as passive consumers and fails to account for the different ways in which people react to or make use of available media.

Minutes per day per person average viewing

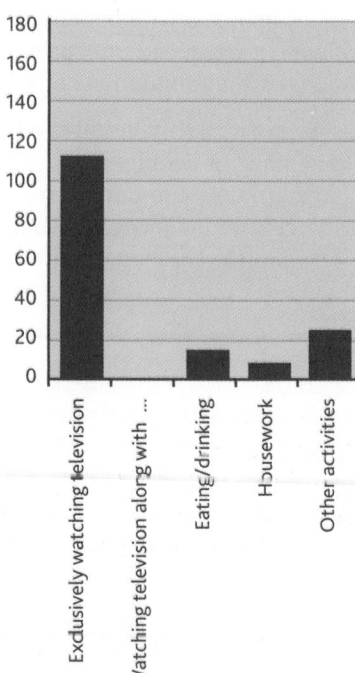

C *Average number of minutes of television watched*

Later attempts to explain the relationship between media and the audience have tried to see the audience in a more active role, interacting with virtual realities on the Internet and creating a new and vibrant **culture of simulation**. However, some sociologists are critical of this idea, suggesting that the development of communication technology has not produced any significant improvements in our society.

Case study

Off The Bus: unofficial web-based journalism

Has the Internet made it more difficult for politicians to manage the flow of information, to 'spin' stories in a particular way? In America in 2008, during the process to select a Democratic nominee for the presidential elections, the *Huffington Post* (a news and comment website) appealed for subscribers to volunteer for an experimental project as unofficial journalists. The project was called 'Off The Bus' (a reference to the official bus provided for accredited journalists). One of these 'unofficial journalists', a 61-year-old grandmother, became famous for breaking stories, for example, that the former President Bill Clinton had described a prominent journalist as 'sleazy, slimy and a scumbag'; while Democratic nominee Barack Obama had referred to working-class voters as people who 'get bitter [and] cling to guns and religion'. Apparently neither man knew that they were talking to an amateur journalist when they made these remarks.

Did you know

Fifteen-year-old New Yorker Christopher Poole developed the social networking site '4chan'. The *Sunday Observer* journalist David Smith marvelled at its contributors' 'ferocious creative force'. He also described the site as a 'lawless Wild West of the web, a place of uninhibited bawdiness and verbal violence'.

Did you know

'Bait-and-switch' is an Internet prank where users are encouraged to visit an 'amazing website'. Some estimates suggest that 18 million people have been 'rickrolled' by linking them to a music video by the performer Rick Astley.

Activities

4   Discuss how far television influences our recognition of particular politicians.

5   Do you think newspapers are more or less influential than TV? Are they more or less influential than the Internet?

6   What part does the Internet play in shaping people's political opinions?

Going further

2   Design a survey to find out how much television per week everyone in your family watches.

AQA Examiner's tip

If you use a term like 'alienation' or 'hyperreality' in your answer to an examination question, make it clear to the examiner that you understand the *meaning* of the term.

Check your understanding

1   List three examples of mass media of communication.

2   Why might the Internet make the idea of a 'mass medium' less relevant?

3   Why do sociologists describe the mass media as an agency of social change?

4   Why do sociologists reject the idea that audiences are unthinking and open to manipulation?

5   What do sociologists mean by the term 'hyperreality'?

Does it matter who owns the mass media?

Some people argue that having newspapers and television studios owned by a variety of different corporations (with some elements paid for by the state out of taxation) is a sign of a healthy democracy at peace with itself. This is called **pluralism**. In Britain the BBC is paid for by a licence fee. This is a form of taxation because all television owners have to pay. Other people argue that too much power can be held in the hands of a few wealthy individuals.

Marxist sociologists believe that the mass media are just one of the many ways in which **elite** groups (the 'ruling classes') control the way that people think and act. For example, if government is seen as keen to introduce polices that are a threat to the profits of 'big business', the owners of newspapers and television stations might wish to ensure that these policies are reported negatively as a 'threat to jobs'.

Income from advertising has also become a vital source of profit for the commercial media. Without the money it provides, many could not survive in their present form. This in turn can give the wealthy businesses that pay for advertising space a great deal of influence over media content.

Are we best served by private enterprise?

Writing in *The Guardian* newspaper in 2007, the writer George Monbiot provided a useful definition of the **world view** that dominates much of what we watch and read in western democracies like Britain. Monbiot described it as the idea that we are best served by allowing the market to have the maximum amount of freedom with the minimum of government control. In this **neo-liberal** (new liberal) view of how the world works, the role of government is simply to defend markets, protect private property and safeguard the nation. Virtually everything else should be left in the hands of private enterprise.

In Britain, television programmes are regulated by an industry code of practice that places limits on what the programme makers can do. However, in America fewer restrictions apply and it is commonplace for television programmes to feature direct links with products that children are actively encouraged to buy.

Key terms

Pluralism: theories about the mass media that see variety and competition as healthy signs of a working democracy.

Marxist: someone who believes in the ideas of Karl Marx and sees the main divisions in society as being based on social class operating in a capitalist system.

Elite: a small dominant group (that may own and control the mass media).

World view: a general view of the way that society works.

Neo-liberalism: a political approach based on the belief that governments should limit their activity to maintaining 'law and order'. In particular, governments should not interfere with market forces in the economy.

Tabloid: popular newspapers generally published in a smaller format than the so called 'quality press'.

Activity

1 Working in groups, discuss these questions:

a Should all the mass media in Britain, including the BBC, be privately owned? Why? Why not?

b Should the government have more control over the programmes that can be shown on television? Why? Why not?

AQA Examiner's tip

If you read a good quality national newspaper and regularly watch television news programmes, you will be much better prepared to answer examination questions. Sociology is not journalism, but the good sociologist needs to be aware of current events.

Case study

1986: Printers and police clash in Wapping

In 1986 violent clashes took place between police and striking print workers at the News International printing plant in Wapping, East London. Their former employer produced some of Britain's best known newspapers, with titles including The Times, The Sunday Times, The Sun and The News of the World. The owner of News International Rupert Murdoch was criticised at the time for his handling of the dispute. The introduction of new technology had deprived the print workers of what had once been a well paid and secure job. When print workers went on strike to protect their jobs and income Murdoch dismissed them and brought in members of another union to keep the print works in operation.

A Press baron Rupert Murdoch

Going further

1 Read the following ditty – there are various versions that exist:

Times readers run the country.

Telegraph readers think they run the country.

Guardian readers wish they ran the country.

Mirror readers would run the country if *Times* readers did not run it already.

Sun readers don't care who runs the country.

2 Design a questionnaire to discover who (or possibly whose parents) in your college/school *regularly* reads a national newspaper. Include questions that will allow you to analyse:

- the social class, gender and age of your respondents
- the use of alternative sources of news, for example, television and the Internet.

3 Use the Internet to find out more about the battle between Rupert Murdoch and the print unions in the 1980s.

Did you know ???????

The daily newspaper with the largest circulation in Britain in 2008 was *The Sun*. Between November 2007 and April 2008 more than 3 million copies of this popular **tabloid** were sold. This compares with sales for *The Times* of less than 623,000 copies. However, *both* newspapers are owned by News International, a corporation controlled by Rupert Murdoch. Murdoch also owns shares in Sky (satellite television), ITV and the publisher HarperCollins.

Did you know ???????

The Guardian newspaper (founded as the Manchester Guardian in 1821) is controlled by the Scott Trust (named after a former editor C. P. Scott). This is designed to prevent the paper from falling under the influence of a single owner.

B There are many different newspapers to choose from

Propaganda and censorship

Individuals and groups in positions of power have tried for a long time to control what we read and watch. Sometimes this is an open attempt to control the media for political ends through **propaganda**, influencing public opinion to support a particular regime. For example in Nazi Germany, Joseph Goebbels who served as Hitler's Minister of Propaganda was completely open about his purpose:

> " We want to work on people until they have capitulated to us, until they grasp ideologically that what is happening in Germany today not only must be accepted but also can be accepted. "
>
> Press conference, March 1933

In the case of Nazi Germany this came to include dictatorship, war and genocide. To this end, Goebbels controlled the content of newspapers, radio and film. His control of national film production is an interesting example of a rather more subtle approach to propaganda. He controlled the content of films that were, to the casual viewer, more to do with entertainment. He encouraged the development of stories that offered a sympathetic view of euthanasia (mercy killing) for those with terminal illnesses or physical disability. He approved the casting of villains who were Jewish, in line with Nazi policies of anti-Semitism that would eventually lead to the mass murder of Jews.

Modern democratic governments including Britain, pride themselves on **freedom of speech** and a 'free press'. However, while open political **censorship** in peace time is unusual, there is plenty of evidence that the mass media are often influenced by politicians and those in positions of power. The mass media frequently reflect a **bias** in favour of powerful interest groups or dominant ideas.

In democratic societies, those who own the media may well decide the general direction of policy, for example, the political party their newspaper supports. They then employ editorial staff to make day-to-day decisions about content. Sociologists often refer to the people who occupy these editorial positions within the media as **gatekeepers**.

Activities

2 In groups, discuss whether you think it is right for a newspaper to support a particular political party.

3 Collect a selection of national newspapers and look for examples of stories that reflect the newspapers' support for a particular political party.

█ Political spin and the media

In democratic societies like Britain, politicians often try to control the media by using **spin**. This means attempting to manage and control the message that the media puts out as news. When Gordon Brown took over the job of Prime Minister, he claimed that under his leadership there would be an end to spin. Within a matter of months, his reputation as an efficient and effective leader had been undermined by stories about indecision and incompetence. In 2007 the acting leader of the Liberal Democrats described him in parliament as 'Mr Bean' in a remark that was widely reported on television, radio and in newspapers. By refusing to spin the news agenda, Prime Minister Brown appeared to lose control of the headlines and of his media **image**.

> **Did you know** ???????
>
> The British Board of Film Censors was established in 1913 by the film industry itself to avoid government censorship.

C *David Cameron arrives at the House of Commons*

Case study

Losing control of the news agenda

Writing in *The Guardian* newspaper, the journalist Polly Toynbee commented on a week when the government of the day failed to make the best of a series of potentially positive stories. For example, a £100 million plan to combat youth crime was reported as being almost entirely about an unpopular plan to take those who used knives to visit their victims in Accident and Emergency Departments. The government failed to 'spin' the story and, by allowing the media to decide what it was about, lost control of the news agenda. Once the story went out, there was no attempt to limit the damage by putting a series of senior ministers in front of the cameras. In Toynbee's view the press and the public had stopped listening to the government and had tuned in to the political opposition.

Activity

4 Politicians often try to choose how they present themselves to the mass media. What image is Photo **B** meant to create of the Conservative Leader David Cameron?

Check your understanding

1 What do sociologists mean by the term 'pluralism'?

2 How do Marxist sociologists interpret the role of the mass media in society?

3 What is the neo-liberal 'world view'?

4 What is political propaganda?

5 Why might governments or interest groups wish to censor the content of the mass media?

6 Why might a newspaper be biased in favour of a particular political party?

7 What do politicians try to do when they 'spin' a news story?

Going further

4 Collect a number of different national newspapers, preferably for the same day's news.

5 Analyse the British *political* news stories that they chose to cover.

6 Design a simple chart to compare the editorial policies of these newspapers.

7 What stories did they decide to cover and how did they report them? For example, is the newspaper clearly supporting a particular political party?

What effect does the mass media have on society?

The mass media as an agency of socialisation

The mass media are one of the secondary agencies of **socialisation**. They are part of the way in which individuals learn about the social world beyond the immediate (primary) influence of the family. The mass media can offer alternative answers to some of the questions that we may ask ourselves beyond the immediate circle of our family and friends. What does it mean to be a man or a woman in the modern world? How should we behave towards others? What can we aspire to achieve?

Obviously our parents, our peer group, our school or college will all have a powerful formative influence on our aspirations and our behaviour. However, above and beyond this the mass media present us with powerful images that dominate our waking moments. Some people argue that the media have a responsibility to represent the social world in such a way that they avoid biased or stereotypical representations of reality. However, it is still the case that much of what we see in the media, particularly on television or in films, relies heavily on **stereotypes** and exaggerated representations of the social world.

∞links

See also Topic 5.4 for more on stereotypes.

Objectives

You will be able to:

- explain the role of the mass media in the socialisation process
- explain the significance of the media for family life and leisure
- outline the characteristics of global culture.

Case study

Different films for different gender groups?

Do men and women react to film differently? Do they want different things from the cinema experience? Read these observations made by a cinema usher working in a multiplex cinema.

'Men always walk out of action and adventure films seeming to walk taller than when they went in. If they are accompanied by their girlfriends they walk out a little way ahead of them almost as if they wished to keep the reality of their relationship separate to the fantasy they have been watching. Similar things happen with a female audience, when you watch them leave after a romantic comedy they often walk out in front of their boyfriends.

Crying is a more common female reaction to films particularly when they are deliberately set up as 'tear-jerkers'; for example love stories with an element of tragedy – especially terminal illness – have their female audiences leaving red eyed with the emotion of it all. When they can persuade their boyfriends to attend the men leave with a slightly embarrassed look.'

Did you know

Released in 1971, the film *A Clockwork Orange* portrayed acts of violence that were blamed in the British press for a series of copycat attacks. The director, Stanley Kubrick, withdrew the film from circulation in Britain (although it remained available in the rest of Europe). It was finally re-released a year after the director's death in 1999. Seen today, it contains little that would really shock a modern adult audience.

AQA Examiner's tip

If you need to discuss the use of stereotypes in the media, have a good selection of examples from your own research that you can use to help make your point.

Activities

1   Use the Internet and your school/college library to do some research. Can you find sociological *evidence* to support the idea that there is a direct link between exposure to violent images and violent behaviour?

2   In groups, discuss whether you think that seeing violence in films and in computer games might make some people more violent themselves.

A world information order

In today's world the mass media are a global phenomenon. Films that originate in Japan are remade in Hollywood. Films made in India find an audience in South London and Liverpool. Computer games produced in Japan are played by people all over the world. British television programmes are remade, adapted and repackaged for an American audience and then sold again to be shown in Asia and Europe. Some sociologists talk about a **world information order** or **global culture**.

However, it is clear that if this global culture exists, it is an unequal one, currently dominated by America. The output of film and television programmes from America swamps the world information market. Young people in Britain and elsewhere imitate the styles of dress, music and behaviour of American youth. Some observers have even taken to referring to this as a form of **media imperialism** with American culture and commercialised values damaging or even replacing local cultural values. This is shown in Photo **A**.

A *Youths in Bhutan show western influence*

Activity

3 Do you agree that American ideas and images tend to dominate the media in the UK?

Going further

1 Work with a group of your fellow students to analyse a typical evening's television by country of origin.

2 Take the television listing for the mainstream terrestrial television channels and then research the country of origin of the programmes on offer.

- How many programmes originate in Britain and how many are imported from abroad?

- How many hours of programming between 5pm and midnight are produced in Britain and how much is imported from America?

3 Take the analysis further by looking for evidence of American commercialised cultural values (that is, the importance of possessions and conspicuous evidence of consumption – buying or owning various items such as clothes, cars and houses).

Did you know ??????

The Lumière brothers are often cited as the fathers of modern film. They first put on a film show in Paris in December 1895. At the time they believed that people would soon tire of paying to see images of reality.

What is mass culture?

In sociology we use the term 'culture' to describe shared behaviours. For example, the language we use to communicate is part of our culture, as is our shared history and national traditions, for example, styles of dress and food. In Britain the mass media play a significant role in reinforcing our sense of national identity and transmitting British cultural values (the **mass culture**).

However, as we have already seen, in a global culture some social scientists question whether distinctive national traditions can be maintained in the face of global communication (particularly American film and television content). Others argue the opposite and say that the enormous variety of media available create opportunities for minorities to find a voice and to preserve their heritage.

How do families use the mass media?

In the middle of the 20th century, some sociologists felt television was replacing traditional family gatherings around the fireside. This was when families would talk about the events of the day and listen to the radio or read a newspaper. There were physical changes in the living rooms of families as they arranged chairs to view the television. The television became a **substitute hearth**.

B *1950s family gathered round the TV*

But is this still true of the 21st century family? The enormous variety of media available to the modern family presents individuals with many choices. We can, for example, use mobile phones for a variety of purposes including texting, listening to music or playing games. We can surf the Internet using high-speed broadband connections. Apparently many of us do this while watching television at the same time. According to research by **Ofcom**, in 2008 young people (aged 16–19) were more likely to say that it was the mobile phone that they could live without rather than the television. Younger people are also more likely to spend time downloading content from the Internet rather than watching scheduled television broadcasts.

Activity

4   In groups, decide which of the following you could *least* do without and which you could *most* do without: mobile phone, Internet, television, newspaper, magazine, i-pod, video recorder, book.

Did you know ??????

One of the first great national television events was the Coronation of Queen Elizabeth in 1953. Over 20 million people are estimated to have watched. Many families did not own a television set and watched gathered around sets owned by neighbours.

Computers are becoming an integral part of family life. In 2004, a Mori survey found that 22 per cent of 15- to 24-year-olds regularly argued with other family members over computer time. In 2008, for the first time, advertisers spent more money on online advertising than on traditional terrestrial television.

Case study

The Middles

Is this a typical middle-class family in 21st century Britain?

The Middles live in the South of England and have three children. Their four-bedroom house contains a television (with a satellite connection) and digital video recorder in the living room and separate televisions in each of the children's rooms. The family has a desktop computer used primarily by the parents. Mr Middle also has a laptop computer and each child has their own laptop computer. The Middles have a fast radio-linked broadband connection to the Internet and Mr Middle has a national daily paper delivered. Every member of the family has a mobile phone. The Middles have an above average income and they are also 'media rich'.

Activity

5   Read the case study on the Middles.

a   Can you think why the possession of all this technology might be an advantage to the Middle children at school and college?

b   Why might families who do not possess this technology be placed at a disadvantage (and not just in educational terms)?

Going further

Use the case study of the Middle family as your starting point.

4   Design a questionnaire to discover how much media access students in your school/college enjoy. You will need to include some of the following ideas:

- The socio-economic class of your respondents (ask them to give their parent's occupation).

- The types of communications media they can access at home, for example, television, computers with Internet access, daily newspapers and mobile phones.

5   Ask your respondents whether they believe that access to communications technology at home gives students an advantage at school/college. Try to get them to explain their answer.

6   Analyse the responses and identify any significant patterns that emerge.

Did you know ??????

One of the first video recorders that could be used in the home was the Sony U-Matic. When it was launched in 1971, it cost £735. In today's money that would be more than £7,000! Right up until 1978, Sony did not really believe that there was much of a market for VCRs in people's homes. The U-Matic was marketed primarily for industrial and educational use.

Check your understanding

1   What do sociologists mean when they refer to the mass media as a secondary agent of socialisation?

2   Is there a clear and provable link between the portrayal of violence in the mass media and actual acts of violence in wider society?

3   Would sociologists agree that the mass media are now a more important agency of socialisation than the family?

4   What is Britain's national media of choice?

5   Why do some sociologists refer to the widespread showing of American television programmes and cinema films as a form of media imperialism?

6   What is global culture?

AQA Examiner's tip

Do not confuse the sociological idea of culture (the total way of life of a society) with the restricted use of the term to describe works of art.

5.4 What are media stereotypes?

Media stereotypes of women

Despite changing social attitudes and media reform, the mass media are still very likely to portray women as a series of familiar stereotypes (**media stereotypes**).

- Women as wives and mothers. Women who are successful homemakers and carers are shown as role models to be admired in advertising and television drama. Negative images are presented of women who neglect their children and homes or who come to regret the decision to place a career above domestic life.

- Women as sex objects. Popular tabloid newspapers and advertisers continue to exploit images of partly clothed women primarily aimed at a white, male working-class readership. Sensational stories regarding the sex lives of celebrities frequently adopt a high moral tone while reinforcing stereotypical sexist interpretations of appropriate behaviour.

- Male authority continues to be represented as 'natural and inevitable' in television dramas. Women who are in positions of power are frequently shown to struggle with their role and emotions.

- Female magazines are dominated by advertising that is concerned with appearance, make-up and hair, developing an 'ideal' body shape through exercise and so remaining 'attractive' to men.

- Women who fail to establish a relationship with a man are still frequently portrayed as failing in life.

These stereotypes can potentially have a significant impact on our idea of how we should live our lives. Social scientists are particularly concerned with the **cumulative effect** they may have on children who are exposed to an enormous amount of media content during their formative years.

Key terms

Media stereotype: simple media image based on prejudice.

Cumulative effect: long periods of exposure to particular media messages.

Lads' magazine: publication aimed at a young male readership often containing images of women as sex objects.

Social construct: patterns of behaviour that are based on society's norms and expectations, for example, masculinity and femininity.

Norms and expectations: generally accepted and expected patterns of behaviour in a particular society.

Case study

Lads' magazines

Michael Grove, the shadow schools secretary, condemns the so-called **lads' magazines** for encouraging men to view women as mere sex objects.

> 66 *Our strategies for dealing with teenage pregnancy need to be focused more on young men and their responsibilities. That's why I believe we need to ask tough questions about the instant-hit hedonism celebrated by the modern men's magazines targeted at younger males. Titles such as Nuts and Zoo paint a picture of women as permanently, lasciviously, uncomplicatedly available.* 99

Adapted from the *Telegraph Online*, August 2008

Activity

1. Working in groups, discuss why Michael Grove links teenage pregnancy to the portrayal of women in 'lads magazines'.

Stereotyping and gender identity

Sociologists see gender as a **social construct**. Society dictates what it is to be a man or woman through the establishment of **norms and expectations**. However, what these norms and expectations are varies over time and between one society and another. The media represent these expectations through stereotypes. These can have a powerful influence on the individual's perception of self as we form our social identity in relation to others. We seek the approval of our parents and our peer group. However, we also look outside these immediate circles as our personalities develop, seeking alternative models of how to behave in society. The media frequently represent different gender groups with the idealised characteristics listed in Table **A**.

The fact that these idealised characteristics may not match with an individual's experience is not what matters. What matters is the fact that they can become aspirations. They are qualities we may seek in a life partner for example, personality traits that we look for in others or try to imitate in our own behaviour towards others.

B *Stereotype or realistic portrayal of a late 20th century family?*

AQA *Examiner's tip*

Read a good quality daily newspaper as often as possible and watch the television news every day. However, do not confuse journalism with social research.

A *Idealised gender characteristics*

Masculine	Feminine
aggressive	affectionate
ambitious	compassionate
assertive	sensitive
leadership	loyal
independence	shy

∞ links

Also see Topic 3.2 for a discussion of gender roles in the stereotypical family.

Did you know ??????

In 2002, the sight of TV personality Jonathan Ross unashamedly weeping in public led to headlines declaring that men were at last free to be openly emotional.

Did you know ??????

In 1958 and again in 1983, advertisers created an imaginary 'Oxo' family. The 1983 family was intended to give a more realistic view of family life, arguments included.

Going further

1. Select a photograph of a woman from a mainstream media publication that illustrates a common media stereotype from the following list:
   - Wife and mother
   - Young and attractive to men
   - Caring and emotional

2. Now select a second photograph that challenges that stereotype from the following list:
   - A single career woman
   - An older woman
   - A woman in a position of power and authority

3. Ask equal numbers of male and female students in your school/college to give their reaction to the pictures, for example, which picture do you prefer and why? Analyse your results and identify any significant patterns.

C Knives collected from a knife amnesty

Group activities

1 According to the British Crime Survey, knives are used in about 8% of violent incidents. This level remained largely the same throughout the decade 1998–2008.

   In groups, discuss whether current media coverage would lead you to believe knife-related crime is increasing or decreasing.

2 In groups, look through some recent newspapers. Do you think Afro-Caribbeans and Muslims are portrayed in the same way as white people?

Other media stereotypes

Ethnic minority groups are frequently portrayed in terms of the 'problem' that they present to the majority population. They are sometimes also portrayed in terms of the 'threat' that they represent to 'our way of life'. By implication, this is due to the **liberal democratic values** of the majority white population. In the 1980s and early 1990s, the issue was Afro-Caribbean youth in inner city areas. The media frequently presented images of young Blacks as violent muggers and in so doing stimulated police crackdowns. In the 21st century, following a series of terrorist incidents, it became Muslim youths who were represented as dangerous fundamentalists and potential terrorists.

The news media claim they are reporting an area of genuine public concern. However, the sheer volume of negative stories and images, together with crude representations in television drama and cinema, reinforce an image of minority groups as different and dangerous.

The process of deviancy amplification

The mass media have a particular and important part to play in the process of defining what is and is not acceptable behaviour. They also help in forming social attitudes towards the punishment of those who break the law or offend against **social conventions**.

The media make frequent use of stereotypes when describing criminal or deviant behaviour. People respond to these stereotypes and use them to form mental images of, for example, murderers, paedophiles, rapists and muggers. Like all stereotypes, these can be at best misleading and at worst they can create an unfounded climate of fear and mistrust. This victimises particular social groups (usually easily identifiable minority groups) and **stigmatises** members of that group as potential criminals.

links

See also Topic 4.4 for more on the increased use of CCTV cameras.

Key terms

Liberal democratic values: the dominant political and social values of western society, for example, freedom of speech and free elections.

Social convention: a generally expected form of social behaviour, for example, politeness and consideration of the needs of others (see Norms and expectations).

Stigmatise: to mark a particular social group or individual as different, disapproved of and even dangerous to others.

Deviancy amplification: the process whereby the mass media can exaggerate the significance of a particular social issue.

News value: the importance attached to a particular news item.

We live in a remarkably safe society and yet media reports emphasise that violent crime is a significant social problem, paedophiles are a serious threat to all young people, the courts are ineffective and the police are incompetent or overwhelmed. Any attempt to place these fears in the context of available statistics on recorded crime, let alone our violent history, receives relatively little attention in the media.

Sociologists often refer to **deviancy amplification** when attempting to describe the impact of the mass media on the public perception of crime and the formation of social policy.

Key terms

Moral panic: when media coverage of an issue leads to exaggerated public concern.

Activity

2   Summarise in three or four sentences what is meant by 'deviancy amplification'.

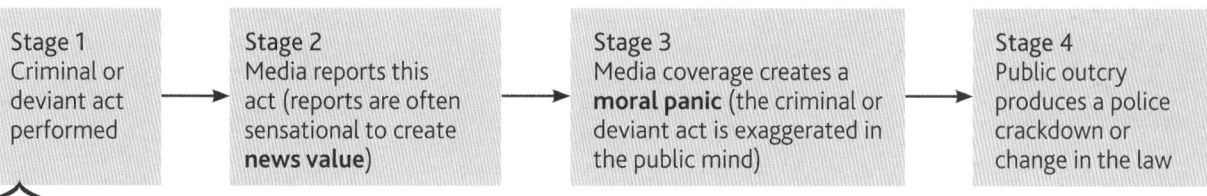

Stage 1
Criminal or deviant act performed

Stage 2
Media reports this act (reports are often sensational to create **news value**)

Stage 3
Media coverage creates a **moral panic** (the criminal or deviant act is exaggerated in the public mind)

Stage 4
Public outcry produces a police crackdown or change in the law

D *Deviancy amplification*

Case study

Gary Glitter

Gary Glitter has been moving around so much – 19 countries have so far said they will refuse him entry – that I don't know where he will be by the time you read this. But he is now said to have reluctantly agreed to get on a plane to London, where he will fall into the arms of up to 35 police officers who have been waiting patiently at Heathrow for his return. That's a lot of police officers deployed at great expense to greet one miserable, perverted, played-out old rock star, but it's proportionate to the hysteria provoked by Glitter's release from a Vietnamese prison, where he served two years and nine months of a three-year sentence for committing 'obscene acts' with two little girls; and it's in line with the seriousness with which the British government is taking the matter. Jacqui Smith, the home secretary, has even framed a new law to make sure that this 'despicable person', as she has publicly called him, will never travel abroad again.

Alexander Chancellor, *The Guardian*, August 2008

Activities

3   How do media stereotypes help to stigmatise certain social groups?

4   What is a social convention?

5   What is moral panic? Include an example in your explanation.

Going further

4   Use the Internet to research examples of news stories that have helped to create a moral panic. Start with one of the following key terms:

- Youth crime
- Hoodies
- Violence in the media
- Gun crime

Use the search facility in the online versions of one or more major national newspapers.

AQA *Examiner's tip*

Use simple diagrams to explain relatively complicated ideas, for example, deviancy amplification.

Check your understanding

1   What are media stereotypes based upon?

2   Can you explain one common media stereotype of women?

3   How do advertisers exploit media stereotypes of women?

4   What do sociologists mean when they say that gender is a social construct?

5   Can you explain one common media stereotype of an ethnic minority group?

6   Why might some people be concerned about the increasing use of CCTV cameras in Britain?

5.5 What is the impact of technological change?

New communication technologies

In the rapidly changing world of communications technology, 'new' means up-to-the minute: the latest version of a device. The latest 'must-have' gadget is tomorrow's electronic junk to be discarded for the next technical fix.

In less than one lifetime, we have gone from computers that filled a large room, used magnetic tape to store data and were programmed using cardboard slips with holes punched in them, to portable devices that can store and process data to an extent not previously dreamed of. We are already living in a world where much of our working lives and leisure time is linked to various forms of computerised communications technology.

A *Early computers were huge, easily filling one or more rooms*

The **Internet** was not designed originally for social and commercial communication. It came into existence to serve a very different purpose. It began in the Cold War as a way of sharing and safeguarding electronic information stored on early **mainframe computers**. The US military commissioned a system that would enable scientists to collaborate while working on military contracts. At the same time, by developing a system that used many linked computers in different places, the military planners were able to protect computer data from the danger of a nuclear attack. It soon became clear to the early software developers that this system also had the potential to communicate messages. So e-mail began almost as an accidental bonus to the original project. Until the 1980s, the Internet consisted of a few hundred computers dedicated to military projects. Then universities began expanding the system and using it for their own purposes. This eventually created an explosion in the number of computers linked to the system and the commercial exploitation of the Internet's potential soon followed.

Objectives

You will be able to:

- identify ways in which people are using the new media
- identify and explain the old media's use of new technology
- identify and explain the implications of the new media for social interaction within society
- identify and explain the political implications of the new media
- explain how the new media have raised social control issues.

Key terms

Internet: a global system of interconnected computers.

Mainframe computer: large, room-sized early computers that stored data using reel-to-reel magnetic tape.

Old media: print media and electronic communications developed during the mid-20th century or earlier.

New media: computerised communications technology.

Activity

1. List all the forms of computerised communications technology that you and your family use. How often do you tend to upgrade these items to the latest version?

Old media, new tricks

Despite all the technical innovation of the computer age, existing **old media** – books, newspapers and magazines, television and radio – continue to exist. This is because they have exploited the potential of new technology. For example, in the middle of the 20th century newspapers were still produced using technology developed in the 19th century that would have been familiar to the earliest developers of the printing press. Today this process is very different. Journalists file their 'copy' electronically and the skilled and relatively highly paid print workers have long been made redundant, replaced by a smaller number of workers with very different skills. Television broadcasts have been employing satellite technology since the 20th century but in the **new media** this brings instant twenty-four hour news, broadcast on new digital channels.

Case study

What future for the Internet?

The Internet could soon be made obsolete. The scientists who pioneered it have now built a lightning-fast replacement capable of downloading entire feature films within seconds.

At speeds about 10,000 times faster than a typical broadband connection, 'the grid' will be able to send the entire Rolling Stones back catalogue from Britain to Japan in less than two seconds.

The latest spin-off from Cern, the particle physics centre that created the web, the grid could also provide the kind of power needed to transmit holographic images; allow instant online gaming with hundreds of thousands of players; and offer high-definition video telephony for the price of a local call.

David Britton, a leading figure in the grid project, believes grid technologies could 'revolutionise' society. 'With this kind of computing power, future generations will have the ability to collaborate and communicate in ways older people like me cannot even imagine,' he said.

Adapted from Jonathan Leake, *The Sunday Times*, 6 April 2008

Going further

1 Interview three or more generations of your family (or the families of friends and neighbours) about their use of communications technology. If possible try to get back to a generation that grew up in the middle of the 20th century.

a Ask them about their experience of using the following:
   - Television
   - Telephones
   - Computers

b Remember to ask about their use of communications technology in their jobs and try to interview equal numbers of men and women.

c Analyse your results and identify any significant patterns that emerge.

d Look for differences between various groups, for example, age, gender and social class.

Did you know ??????

Over 50 years ago the catering company J Lyons introduced the world's first business computer using it to calculate the value of its bakery sales. The company designed and built the computer in-house, and it gave it the name of 'LEO', short for Lyons Electronic Office.

Activity

2 Draw up a table to show the disadvantages and advantages of changing communications technology.

Did you know ??????

In 1949 a New Zealand economist, Bill Phillips, wrote an essay comparing the national economy to a machine pumping coloured water round clear plastic tubes. Then he built just such a machine, selling them to banks and major international companies including Ford. People understood the 'flow of money' around the economy because they could *see* it happen!

Activity

3 Working in groups, find out how much your fellow students use the Internet, and for what purposes.

AQA Examiner's tip

Try to present a *balanced* view of the positive and negative effects of changing communications technology.

Implications for social interaction

We live in a world where people are instantly available and where this instant communication continues 24 hours a day, seven days a week. There is evidence to suggest that we are suffering from **information overload**. In the past, when communication was time-consuming, technically difficult and expensive, people thought carefully before contacting each other. In an age of instant, cheap communication, little thought is required. How many of your mobile telephone conversations or texts are really necessary? With e-mail, how much of your inbox is filled with **SPAM**, cheap advertising for products you probably do not want and do not need?

Many of the concerns we have about the impact of new and cheaper forms of communication technology would be familiar to people living in the 19th and 20th century. The introduction of cheap postal systems and telephones brought with them **junk mail** and **telesales**.

We must not ignore the undoubted benefits of this new technology. In the past, family ties were broken by separation, friends lost contact and news travelled slowly. Today it is much easier to maintain contact with friends and relations living in different parts of the country or the world.

In one sense the technology of electronic communication can be seen as an intrusive burden. We are seldom able to get away from the demands of employers or family. In another more positive sense, we are less likely to be isolated by age or the inability to travel.

> ### Key terms
>
> **Information overload:** the enormous volume of modern electronic communications (sometimes more than an individual can cope with).
>
> **SPAM:** unwanted and unasked for bulk electronic messages accounting for much of the increased volume of e-mail traffic.
>
> **Junk mail:** the postal equivalent of SPAM.
>
> **Telesales:** the selling of goods and services over the telephone.
>
> **Image:** the identity that individuals wish to present to the world, for example, the media image of a particular politician as young and dynamic.

Activity

4   How do you communicate with your friends and family? How many times a day do you phone someone, send a text or e-mail? When did you last write a letter to someone?

Political implications and social control

Nowadays politicians are more exposed to the public than ever before. The **image** that politicians present to the world can be key to a political campaign and to electoral success. New communications technology makes voters more accessible to the messages politicians wish to convey. In 2008, the US Democratic presidential candidate Barack Obama communicated his choice of vice-presidential running mate to journalists and supporters by text message. The text came in at 3am. This was his way of showing his critics that he would not be too inexperienced as a president to deal with an early morning phone call bringing news of a crisis. Politicians 'blog' their opinions and try to smear opponents with Internet broadcasts. Political parties e-mail supporters asking for contributions or alerting them to new policies.

New communications technology is not only capable of conveying a message. It can also be employed to monitor what we do and say. Mobile telephone calls can be intercepted. E-mails are read by security services or journalists hoping to discover some scandal. Nothing we do on a computer is ever completely lost unless the hardware is physically destroyed. Our web searches are stored for future reference, while files that are deleted can be recovered.

B   *Former Prime Minister Margaret Thatcher was said to be a natural when it came to photo-opportunities for journalists*

AQA   Examiner's tip

Be aware of the debate about the use of surveillance in a democracy, for example, the increased use of CCTV and monitoring of e-mail and mobile phone traffic.

Case study

The Internet: danger or opportunity?

- The Internet and video games are very popular with children and young people and offer a range of opportunities for fun, learning and development.

- But there are concerns over potentially inappropriate material, which range from content (for example, violence) through to contact and conduct of children in the digital world.

- There is a generational digital divide which means that parents do not necessarily feel equipped to help their children in this space – which can lead to fear and a sense of helplessness. This can be compounded by a risk-averse culture where we are inclined to keep our children 'indoors' despite their developmental needs to socialise and take risks.

Selected points from the executive summary of
The Byron Review – Children and New Technology, March 2008

Activities

5 Why are people's working lives so closely linked to developing communications technology?

6 What do sociologists mean when they talk about a society that is suffering from information overload?

7 What are the advantages of cheap and easy communication?

8 Why do politicians worry about the image they present to the media?

Activity

9 Read the case study above.

a Do you or your younger brothers and sisters have unsupervised access to the Internet?

b Compare this with the number of younger brothers and sisters who are allowed to play unsupervised in your local neighbourhood.

c Discuss whether there is an inconsistent approach to risk on the part of parents.

Going further

2 In a study by Loughborough University, researchers found that it took people an average of 64 seconds to recover their train of thought after interruption by e-mail. The researchers also found that people tended to respond to e-mail when it arrived. Seventy per cent of those surveyed responded to e-mail within six seconds (roughly the same as three rings on a telephone).

a Design a questionnaire to test the validity of these findings.

b Ask your respondents to spend one day working normally on a computer terminal with access to e-mail.

c Do they agree that e-mail intrudes upon their work and consumes a disproportionate amount of their time?

Did you know ??????

Two million e-mails are sent every minute in the UK. Some office workers can spend up to half their working day going through their inbox.

Check your understanding

1 What was the original purpose of the Internet?

2 How has computerised communications technology changed the way that newspapers are produced?

3 What is 'information overload'?

4 Why do politicians worry about their media image?

5 How can new technology be used to monitor what we do and say?

5.6 What does social research tell us about the mass media in Britain?

Indian cultural heritage and the VHS recorder

In Southall (London) in the 1990s, Marie Gillespie studied the way in which the video cassette recorder was used by parents and grandparents of immigrant families from India as a means of recreating cultural traditions in Britain. During the course of her research, Gillespie visited the homes of Indian families and observed their behaviour. She did this over a number of years whilst all the time building up a rich body of qualitative data.

> 66 *Viewing Hindi films on video are the main, regular, family-centred leisure activity of Indian immigrant families in Southall. The weekend family gathering around the set is a social ritual where notions of togetherness become very important. The weaving of conversation around the film is made easier by the 'episodic structure' of the story which moves the viewer through successive scenes of song, dance and action. The breaks in the story for song and dance provide opportunities for the discussion of issues raised by a member of the family in response to the film. While fathers are generally seen to control access to the main TV screen, when at home, mothers and females in the family more generally, are seen to exert influence over the choice of what is watched. However, female-only viewing sessions which span three or four generations are common. One of the dominant themes of Hindi movies is the 'clash of tradition and **modernity**' in Indian society, which is normally resolved by the triumph of tradition over modernity. Films, or young viewers' interpretation of them, which support modernity against tradition provoke discussion with female elders, who their children often say 'are living in the India which they left twenty years ago', are unwilling to embrace change. British and American films are often viewed by younger members of Indian immigrant families as a symbol of 'breaking away' from parental authority and a rejection of the cultural preferences of their parents' generation. Striking gender differences emerged in the way accounts of the films were framed. Girls often expressed their perceptions of India by drawing out the social and moral values inherent in films through a retelling of the narratives. Boys seemed much more concerned with representational issues, particularly 'negative images', and in many cases rejected Hindi films on that basis. Several male informants saw the films' emphasis on poverty and corruption as offensive.* 99

Adapted from *Television, Ethnicity and Cultural Change*, Routledge, London (1995)

Going further

1. Design a questionnaire to discover how your fellow students experience television programmes in the family home; include questions about ethnicity, gender and social class.

2. Do any of these factors (variables) make a difference?

Check your understanding

1 Among the Indian families in Southall studied by Marie Gillespie, who controlled access to the TV screen?

2 What is Hindi?

3 What does the term 'episodic structure' mean?

4 In Marie Gillespie's study, who chose what film the family would watch?

5 What does Marie Gillespie say that British and American films represented to young Indians in Southall in the 1990s?

6 What does Marie Gillespie identify as one of the dominant themes of Hindi films at this time?

7 What does the term 'cultural tradition' mean? Can you think of any examples of traditions from 'British' culture?

■ Bad news?

The pioneering work of the Glasgow Media Group in the 1970s and 1980s broke new ground in the study of the mass media in British society. This was at a time when 'media studies' was a very new idea and certainly not a common feature of University courses, let alone the school curriculum. Based at Glasgow University, the group chose to focus much of its attention on the way in which television news programmes of the day chose to present certain items of news. They went on to publish a series of books, beginning with *Bad News* (published in 1976), that were very critical of the way in which certain news stories were prepared and broadcast. As a consequence of the structural changes in industry and the economic problems of the day, industrial unrest was very common in the 1970s, and therefore this first book focused on the way in which **industrial disputes** were reported by the television news.

> **Key terms**
>
> **Modernity:** relating to the modern world.
>
> **Industrial disputes:** disagreements between management and workforce, often leading to workers going on strike.

Case study

Reporting a speech by the Prime Minister of the day about striking car workers, BBC2 had a definition of the speech as being about both sides in the dispute. It was introduced as a 'blunt warning to the car industry' and later in the bulletin there was a discussion between an industrial correspondent and the newscaster in which they made it quite clear that the speech was not simply a criticism of the workforce.

BBC2 newscaster:

> 66 *Many of the phrases in the Prime Minister's speech are pointed directly at the unions and the labour force; some are pointed at management, like the need for more efficient working methods. Do the management accept that they have got to do some pretty radical rethinking about production methods and that sort of thing?* 99

BBC2, January 1975

The ITN coverage at no point acknowledged these criticisms. In the introduction the Prime Minister was said to have given 'workers a blunt warning'. In addition to showing excerpts from the speech ITN also had a reporter on the spot who summarised to a camera what he believed it to be about. These summaries again emphasised the speech as an appeal to the workforce.

ITN reporter:

> This was a stern message to come from a Labour Prime Minister, but it was received politely enough by the audience here in a Labour club in his constituency; but the speech was clearly prompted by the growing number of companies going to the government for help and the large sums of public money involved. The Prime Minister clearly expects a greater degree of restraint from the workforce in firms where the government has stepped in to help and he has appealed directly to working people not to rock an already very leaky boat.

ITN, January 1975
Adapted from *Glasgow Media Group Reader Volume 2: Industry, Economy, War and Politics*, Routledge, London (1995)

A *Television has long been a source of news*

Going further

3   Watch a selection of television news programmes for the same day.

4   If possible arrange with a group of fellow students to record the main evening news programme broadcast by all of the major channels.

5   Compare how they report particular domestic news items. Are there any differences in the way in which they present the story (key ideas: interpretation, language and significance)?

Check your understanding

1   What was the subject of the Prime Minister's speech?

2   How did BBC2 report the speech?

3   How did ITN report the speech?

4   How might a sociologist explain the differences between the two reports?

5   Why do you think that the Glasgow Media Group chose this as an example of 'bad' news?

5.7   Exam questions for Mass media

■ Exam question guidance

∞ links

See the Exam question guidance section in Topic 1.8 on page 38 for general advice on answering source-based questions.

Example of a source-based question

> **Item A**
>
> **Growth of the mass media**
>
> Society's use of the media is huge and still growing. In 2004, 55 per cent of adults in the United Kingdom read a daily newspaper and, on average, spent nearly three hours a day watching television. In addition to these well-established communications media, more and more people have access to new media products. For example, in 2007, 79 per cent of households had a DVD and 61 per cent had access to the Internet.
>
> Adapted from *Social Trends 2005 and 2007*, www.statistics.gov.uk
> © Crown Copyright

- **Who?** This source is taken from material published by the Office for National Statistics (government research data).
- **What?** The source reviews the level of access people have to both well-established and new forms of communications media.
- **Why?** Sociologists are interested in people's level of access to various forms of mass media. It has been suggested that some sections of society are media rich. They have easy access to both well-established media and a range of new electronic communications media. However, other sections of society remain media poor with relatively limited access to the new media.

> **a**   From **Item A**, what percentage of households had access to the Internet in 2007?   *(1 mark)*

Answer as briefly as possible. The answer is 61 per cent.

Example of a 4-mark question

> **d**   Explain what sociologists mean by the mass media?   *(4 marks)*

The examiners are expecting you to be able to demonstrate your understanding of a key sociological idea. You should have in mind a working *definition* of the **mass media**. 'Media' refers to a means of communication. 'Mass' implies that this form of communication is capable of reaching a large audience. You should be able to support your definition with *examples*. In this case well-established forms of mass media would include television, radio and newspapers. New media generally refers to electronic forms of mass communication such as the Internet. Also, as the source suggests, it can refer to technologies such as DVD players.

co links

See the Exam question guidance section in Topic 2.7 on page 67 for general advice on answering extended-answer questions.

Example of an extended-answer question

g How far would sociologists agree that the mass media is a more powerful agent of socialisation than the education system? *(12 marks)*

The examiner would expect you to demonstrate your understanding of the role of both the education system *and* the mass media as agents of **secondary socialisation**. They would also expect you to be aware of the distinction between secondary and **primary socialisation**.

The question clearly raises the issue of **extent. How far** would sociologists agree that one agency is more important than the other? There are a number of current issues of debate that you might wish to include in your answer:

- The relationship between the portrayal of violence in the media and the level of violent crime in society. Some social scientists have suggested that there is a clear relationship between the exposure of young people to violent images and subsequent violent behaviour. Others have pointed out that the evidence is controversial and that an individual's response to the mass media forms part of a complex web of social relationships and life experiences. The crude **hypodermic syringe model** of the relationship between audience and media is no longer generally accepted.

- The extent to which some young people reject school and formal education (high levels of truancy, poor results and bad behaviour) can be interpreted as evidence that the school system is not capable of achieving any lasting influence on the behaviour of the young. However, truants and badly behaved students remain a small minority of the total school population. For example, despite the concerns of some commentators, more young people are achieving better results than ever before.

While these debates are important, perhaps the crucial point to include in your answer is that the influence of both the school and the mass media are far less significant than the influence of the **family** and the **peer group**.

Remember to avoid the trap of only referring to the sources in the question. The examiner wants to see evidence that you have studied the sociology of the mass media *and* thought about the issues.

■ Questions to try

What follows are examples of the types of questions you will meet in your exam. The letter in each question matches the letter that will be used for that type of question on your exam paper. The number in brackets is only there to help you and your teacher refer to that particular question in this book.

Item B

Household access to various Information and Communication Technology, January to April 2006.

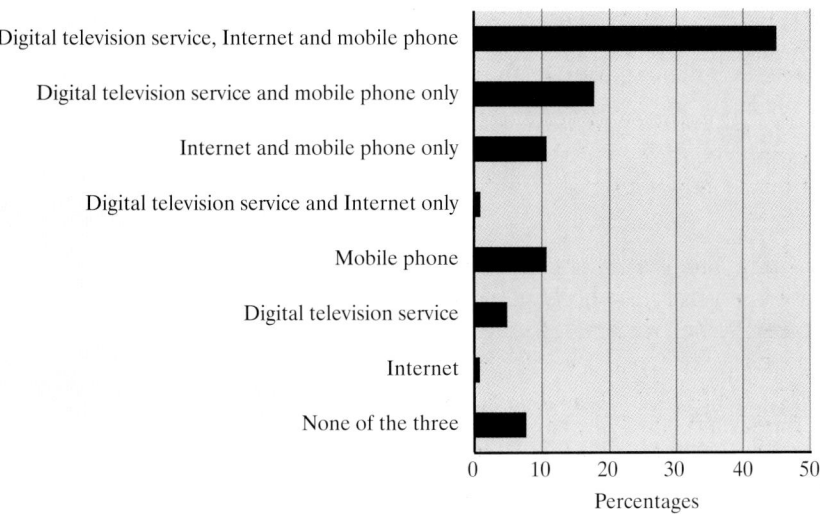

Source: Office for National Statistics

a	From **Item B**, what percentage of households in 2006 did not have access to digital television, the Internet and a mobile phone?	*(1 mark)*
d(1)	Explain what sociologists mean by agenda setting.	*(4 marks)*
d(2)	Explain what sociologists mean by moral panic.	*(4 marks)*
e	Describe **one** way in which recent governments have attempted to regulate the mass media and explain how successful the policy has been.	*(5 marks)*
g(1)	Discuss how far sociologists would agree that our fear of crime is amplified by the mass media.	*(12 marks)*
g(2)	Discuss how far sociologists would agree that the mass media can influence the outcome of a general election.	*(12 marks)*
g(3)	Discuss how far sociologists would agree that the mass media create gender stereotypes.	*(12 marks)*

6.1 How democratic is Britain's political system?

Almost everybody believes that government is necessary to make decisions for society as a whole. Lack of government would lead to chaos. On the other hand, no government can please all members of society all the time. Some will disagree with its decisions. Others will believe that there are individuals better able to govern than those in power. **Democracy** enables a government to govern while allowing critics a chance to replace it with another.

What is democracy?

In a democracy a government is legitimate, that is, entitled to govern, only if it has been chosen by those it governs. The holding of regular elections is, therefore, a requirement. To be 'free and fair' these elections should:

- allow all adults to vote and, if they wish, to stand for election
- treat all voters as equally important, 'one person, one vote'
- allow voters to cast their votes in secret so that others cannot pressure them to vote in a particular way
- be organised so that those who gain a majority of the votes win
- allow voters and candidates to debate issues freely without interference by the government.

Parliamentary democracy

Britain is a parliamentary democracy. At its centre is the House of Commons which has 646 members. Each **Member of Parliament** (MP) is elected by the **'first past the post'** voting system to represent a **constituency**. In this way all citizens have someone to stand up for them when laws are being made and the government is taking decisions.

The importance of political parties

British democracy centres around **political parties**. Almost all candidates for election are party candidates. Voters understand that a vote for a particular candidate is also a vote for the leader of that party to become **Prime Minister**. The party with the largest number of MPs forms a government. The party with the next largest number of MPs becomes the 'official opposition', an alternative to the government.

Objectives

You will be able to:

- outline the characteristics of democracy

- explain the contribution made by elections, the House of Commons and the Opposition, to democracy in Britain

- identify the key conditions of democratic stability and their significance

- explain the importance of human rights for democracy.

A *The little piece of paper at the heart of democracy*

AQA Examiner's tip

Recognise in your discussions the vital importance of the attitudes and beliefs of the citizens of a democracy and those in government for the health and stability of that democracy.

Activity

1. With a partner, consider whether the voting age in Britain should be lowered to 16. One of you should list the reasons *for*; one of you the reasons *against*.

Competition is vital for democracy because the government knows it has a rival to which voters can readily turn at the next election. It has a strong incentive to govern in a way which suits the public. The **Opposition** and other parties will constantly criticise and challenge the government, forcing it to justify its actions. It is as if the government faces a continuous election campaign which ensures it never forgets the opinions and interests of those it governs, the voters.

The 'spirit' of democracy

A democracy sometimes irritates its citizens. 'Look at them squabbling in the House of Commons. Why don't they just get on with governing?' is a frequently expressed viewpoint. If it were possible to be certain that a policy were 'right', arguing against it would be perverse. Democracy, however, recognises that certainties are rare. Fanatics claim to be certain that theirs is the 'right way' and dismiss other opinions. Democrats believe that the more opinions considered the better. They also believe that no one section of society has a monopoly of political wisdom. The views of every citizen deserve respect.

A key democratic value, therefore, is tolerance; tolerance of argument, tolerance of opinions which seem silly or disturbing. Such tolerance, and the discussion which it makes possible, may help a society to prevent disagreement from becoming violent.

B *I may disagree with your opinions, but I will defend forever your right to express them*

Key terms

Democracy: the political system that enables the people to elect periodically those who will govern them.

Member of Parliament (MP): the person elected to represent a constituency in the House of Commons.

'First past the post': the voting system in which the candidate who gains more votes than any of his or her rivals in a constituency is chosen to be the MP.

Constituency: the geographical area which elects a single MP.

Political party: an organisation established to secure the election of its members or supporters into public office.

Prime Minister: the head of the government in Britain. He or she is the leader of the majority party in the House of Commons.

Opposition: the main party that is not in government.

Activity

2 Discuss whether lowering the voting age would strengthen British democracy.

Britain's non-democratic past

Britain has become a democracy only after a long struggle. Remains of our non-democratic past survive. The **monarchy**, for example, has been adapted to meet the needs of democracy. The monarch reigns but does not rule, becoming a unifying symbol of the nation.

Conditions for democracy

Democracy is under constant pressure from powerful sections of society who are trying to get their own way. Britain's democracy is, however, relatively strong because:

- Most **citizens** have sufficient education, free time and financial resources to be informed about politics. Governments know they are being watched.
- Much in the lives of British citizens is beyond the control of governments. As members of families, religious organisations, clubs and societies we think and act independently.
- Democracy is now part of what citizens see and accept as the 'British way'.
- The alternatives offered by the mainstream parties are not radically different. Those voting for losing parties need not fear that their lives will be 'turned upside down'. They have little incentive not to accept defeat. There will be another election within five years.

The threat to democracy

A democracy perhaps faces its greatest challenge when a significant number of citizens feel insecure. In continental Europe during the 1920s and 1930s, for example, recession and mass unemployment created such levels of insecurity that millions of people were prepared to support vicious dictators who promised to restore economic stability and national pride.

Key terms

Monarchy: the political system that has a hereditary Head of State. Britain is a constitutional monarchy in which the monarch's powers are exercised by the Prime Minister.

Citizen: a full, legal member of a nation.

Dictatorship: a political system in which power is concentrated in the hands of an individual or small group who have not been freely and fairly elected.

Did you know ??????

Women did not achieve equal voting rights to men until 1928.

Case study

A threat to academic freedom?

Hicham Yezza, a doctoral student and employee at Nottingham University, was arrested under the Terrorism Act. He was detained by the police for possessing a copy of the al-Qaida training manual that he was printing for a friend who was researching the terrorist group's techniques for his MA. University officials called in the police after a colleague noticed the document on his computer. He and his friend were held for 6 days despite tutors giving statements that the document was directly related to his research. They were finally released without charge.

A growing campaign group of lecturers and students say that the government's anti-terror agenda is putting pressure on universities to spy on their members. Many academics now talk of the pressure they face to become 'police informers' on their students. 'Self-censorship is coming,' said one academic. Another said, 'What worries me is the gradual erosion of our academic freedom.' A third asked 'What does this say about people's right to inform themselves about issues of public concern?'

Adapted from Polly Curtis and Andrea Lipsett, *The Guardian*, 31 May 2008

Activity

3 Working in groups, read the case study and then discuss why academic freedom is vitally important in a democracy but will be attacked by dictators.

It is difficult today to imagine a group overthrowing the British government and establishing a **dictatorship**. However, elected governments may limit, little by little, the long-established rights of British citizens. Permitting the lengthy detention of suspected terrorists without charge, for example, has weakened the restrictions which distinguish policing in a democracy from policing in a dictatorship.

The terrorist threat has two elements. British citizens may be blown up. Also governments may, supported by a majority of public opinion, curtail liberties. If an elected government uses its authority to oppress a minority, democracy can become a 'dictatorship of the majority'. To prevent this, in most modern democracies, citizens are protected by their being given 'human rights'. Respect for these rights limits what the majority believes it is entitled to do. In Britain today the feeling of insecurity is weakening respect for these rights.

C *Destruction caused by terrorism*

D *Victim of terrorism – killed by police who thought he was a terrorist*

Going further

Politicians refer to the need to balance individual liberties and collective security.

Using the Internet, look at the press coverage of the de Menezes killing. What was the atmosphere in London like before the event? With this in mind, write down your views on where the balance between liberty and security should be. Discuss this with the rest of your group.

Check your understanding

1 Identify three characteristics of a 'free and fair' election.

2 Why does a democracy need at least two political parties?

3 Why is political education important in a democracy?

4 Why might it be difficult to establish or maintain democracy in a very poor country?

5 Why are human rights important in a democracy?

How involved are individual citizens in the political process?

In a dictatorship, citizens are not encouraged to express their opinions. Their **political socialisation** emphasises the importance of unquestioning obedience to the ruling group. In a democracy, if public opinion is expressed clearly, the government is able to base policies on it. In Britain a citizen may, for example:

- express an opinion or state a grievance through the media
- request help from their local MP or county councillor
- try to be elected or appointed as a member of a public body, for example, as a school governor
- vote in elections
- join and become active in a political party or **pressure group**.

Why citizens might not participate

- A majority of adults say they know little about politics and lack interest.
- Being politically active can be time-consuming and cost money.
- Some people may worry that they would feel 'out of place' in a political organisation.
- Many people perhaps think that they are not the kind of people to whom the decision makers will pay attention.

Possible consequences of non-participation

The higher social classes and the better educated are more likely to take part in conventional political activity. This could set up a self-fulfilling prophecy as shown in Diagram **A**.

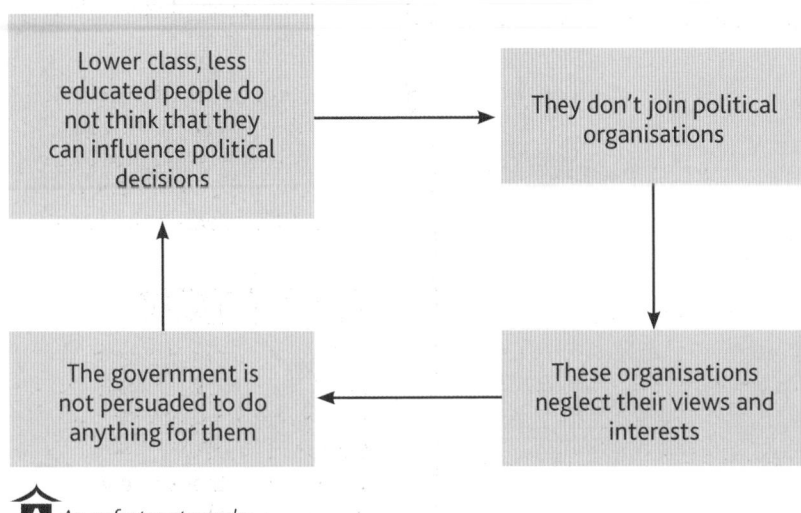

A *An unfortunate cycle*

1 Find out where and when your MP and/or local councillors are available to meet their constituents. When you have done this, report back to the rest of the group on the following questions:

a Would someone with a poor education and/or with limited time be likely to find the necessary information?

b Would it be easy for someone lacking time and/or transport to meet their MP or councillors?

c How genuinely accessible do you think your MP is?

Government concerns

In recent years, political leaders have been concerned that:

- the low turnout in general elections weakens the **authority** of the government
- some of those who feel unable or unwilling to participate in conventional political activities will become angry and frustrated, which may lead to riots or terrorism.

The government response

Governments have tried to encourage constructive participation and limit destructive participation by, for example:

- supporting citizenship education which will help all students to understand and feel part of political life in Britain
- arranging citizenship training, tests and ceremonies, intended to speed the process of integration of immigrants
- sponsoring anti-extremism programmes to prevent some youths from becoming committed to causes encouraging terrorism.

Only 61% of those entitled to vote in the 2005 general election did so.

B *Bradford riots, July 2001*

2 With a partner, look at photograph **B**. Write two or three sentences explaining why the residents of inner city areas might be more likely than others to riot.

3 Read the questions in the case study.

Thinking about people born and raised in the UK, ask yourself how many of these questions they are likely to be able to answer accurately.

Watch the evening TV news broadcasts for a week. Note how much you understand of those items about British politics. Discuss with other students in your group whether on this evidence you know enough to be a constructively active citizen.

Case study

The 'Life in the UK' test

Here are some examples of political and legal questions in the 'Life in the UK' test for new citizens.

What is the Queen's official role and what ceremonial duties does she have?

What is the role of the Prime Minister? Who advises them and what are the main roles in the Cabinet?

What is the Opposition and what is the role of the Leader of the Opposition?

What are MPs? How often are elections held and who forms the government?

Do women have equal rights in voting, education and work, and has this always been the case?

How is political debate reported? Are newspapers free to publish opinions or do they have to remain impartial?

www.lifeintheuktest.gov.uk

Abstaining

Some electors take little interest in elections. Others choose not to vote because, for example:

- There is no candidate of the party they wish to support.
- The constituency is a 'safe seat' in which the same party wins at every election.
- They are disillusioned with party politics.

Voting

In the 1950s and 1960s, sociologists put class at the centre of their explanations, referring to **class alignment**. The middle class voted Conservative and a large majority of the working class voted Labour. During the last 35 years the pattern of voting has changed indicating, it is argued, some **class de-alignment**:

- There are more 'floating voters' prepared to vote for whichever party appears to offer the best deal in a particular election. This suggests that influences that are less permanent than social class have become more significant.
- More voters vote for parties, such as the Liberal Democrats, that are not associated with a particular social class.
- In the 1980s, the Conservative party attracted many working-class voters. In the late 1990s, New Labour attracted many middle-class voters.

Key terms

Class alignment: suggests a connection between voters' class positions and their voting preferences.

Class de-alignment: suggests a weakening of the connection between class position and voting preference.

Did you know ??????

In the 1950s and 1960s, women were more likely than men to vote Conservative. In the 2005 general election, women were more likely than men to vote Labour.

Case study

The 2005 general election

Chart **C** shows that each major party gains a significant percentage of the votes from each class. Also, the higher the social class, the larger is the percentage voting Conservative.

Why might the influence of class have weakened? Here are some possible reasons:

- Class boundaries are now generally less clear. Some manual workers can afford a middle-class lifestyle. Some non-manual workers work in conditions, and for pay, traditionally associated with manual work.
- For many people, gender, ethnicity, sexual orientation or region influence the way in which they see themselves. Their class identity is no longer dominant.
- Labour party leaders wanted to attract the support of 'middle England'. To do this they created New Labour with its classless image.
- Political issues not directly related to class, for example, the environment, have become increasingly significant to voters.
- Communities such as those around coalmines and shipyards have largely disappeared. Previously these maintained a class-based, political sub-culture.
- Differences within social classes have perhaps increased. Sociologists have suggested differences between the 'traditional' and a 'new' working class. Within the middle class, the situation of a teacher, for example, will differ greatly from that of a worker in the financial services sector.

AQA Examiner's tip

When discussing voting behaviour, refer to both middle and working classes.

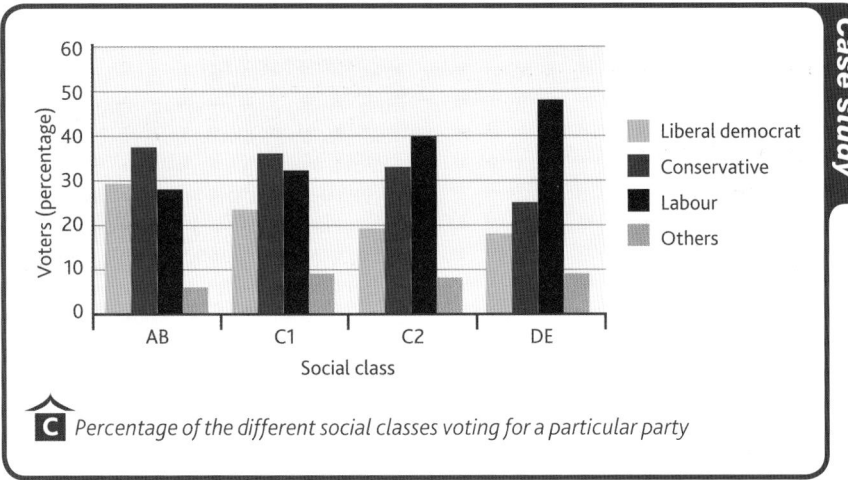

Case study

C *Percentage of the different social classes voting for a particular party*

How do voters choose?

In recent years, sociologists have focused attention on the attitudes of voters and on what they take into account when deciding how to vote. They see voting today as based more on the voter's judgements at election time and less as a habit linked to upbringing and class. Some liken the voter to a customer choosing the best party brand on offer. His or her choice may be influenced by the following:

- A calculation of which party's policies will benefit him or her the most.
- The image of the parties and their leaders seems to matter: whether a party is united or not, well or badly led, competent or not in economic matters, honest or sleazy.
- The 'feel good' factor: if voters feel that things generally have improved and that this is likely to continue, they may be content to vote for the party in power.

For some voters, however, voting remains more than a means to an end. They wish to support the values for which their party stands. They may vote for a party out of family or neighbourhood loyalty.

Check your understanding

1 List three ways in which a British citizen can participate in politics.

2 List three reasons why a poor person may not participate in politics.

3 List three reasons why an 18-year-old woman voting in 2005 might be less likely than an 18-year-old woman voting in 1959 to vote for the same party as her mother.

4 Is the influence of the media on voters likely to have been greater in the elections of the 1950s or the 1980s? Briefly explain your answer.

Activity

4 In the 2005 general election, 75 per cent of 55+-year-olds turned out to vote compared with 37 per cent of 18- to 24-year-olds.

a List three or four reasons for the low turnout of young voters.

b Discuss with others in your group what steps a government could take to encourage young voters to vote.

AQA Examiner's tip

Make your discussions as up to date as possible.

Did you know ???????

Religion can be an important political dividing line.

- In Northern Ireland, Catholics and Protestants vote for different parties.
- In the 2005 general election, many Muslim voters did not vote for Labour because of the invasion of Iraq.

∞links

Also see Topic 5.3 for information about the relationship between the media and the audience.

6.3 What is social reform?

There have always been different opinions about the extent to which governments should intervene in people's lives. Some argue that less intervention means more personal freedom. Others, **socialists**, for example, argue that governments should have a wider responsibility for their citizens' quality of life. Since the 1970s the former view has become more influential in discussions about social reform.

The post-war consensus

In the years following the Second World War, all political parties accepted government intervention and the Welfare State was developed (thanks to **consensus**). Key elements were:

- a National Health Service providing free health care for all (1948)
- financial benefits intended to keep people out of poverty 'from cradle to grave' (1945–1948)
- social services, council housing, free education.

These services and benefits were funded out of taxation.

Approaches to the Welfare State

Conservatives	'Old' Labour
Saw the Welfare State as a practical way of preventing the bad social conditions which lead to social unrest.	Believed in the principle of social equality. The Welfare State would help to redistribute income from the rich to the poor.
Believed that the richer sections of society have a moral duty to improve the conditions of the poorest.	Believed that 'social justice' required society as a whole to ensure that its most vulnerable members enjoyed a decent standard of living.
Placed great value on Britain being 'one nation'. Society would be damaged if the condition of the poor separated them from the rest of society.	

The consensus broken

Under Mrs Thatcher's leadership, the Conservative party, after 1975, adopted **neo-liberal** principles. According to these principles:

- The Welfare State will always be inefficient until those delivering its services face competition. For example, only when patients are able to choose to 'take their custom elsewhere' will doctors have an incentive to give 'value for money'.
- Welfare provided by the state encourages a 'getting something for nothing' attitude. This undermines both social values, such as taking personal responsibility, and institutions, such as the family.

Objectives

You will be able to:

- relate the development of the Welfare State to the post-Second World War consensus
- outline the critical approaches to the Welfare State adopted since the 1970s
- outline recent policies relating to poverty and the ageing population and explain the thinking behind them.

Key terms

Socialists: wish to create a society based on equality.

Consensus: political consensus means that those involved in government, of whatever party, share similar ideas about what governments should do.

Conservatives: see radical change as dangerous and suggest that governments should reform institutions only when a clear need to do so has been established.

'Old' Labour: sees its main aim as protecting the interests of working people. Its approach to politics is based on working-class values such as solidarity.

Neo-liberalism: a political approach based on the belief that governments should limit their activity to maintaining 'law and order'. In particular, governments should not interfere with market forces in the economy.

Did you know ???????

It was a Liberal government between 1906 and 1914 which took the first steps towards creating the Welfare State.

A new consensus?

The 'modernisers' within the Labour party were impressed by the election successes of the Conservative party and the New Labour government elected in 1997 continued the Conservative government's reforms.

Both parties now believe that:

- Government bodies or local councils do not provide services as efficiently as private companies.
- Only competition provides a sufficiently powerful incentive to work hard.
- The 'everybody gets the same' principle of the early Welfare State is no longer appropriate because citizens today expect services tailored to their individual needs.

Reform of the Welfare State

On the basis of these beliefs, much of the organisation of the Welfare State has been reformed:

- Private, profit-making companies now provide a range of services such as refuse collection and running some schools and prisons.
- Where possible, competitive environments have been created for those providing services. For example, schools compete for pupils, hospitals for patients.
- Users of the Welfare State have been encouraged to exercise choice and feel empowered to demand high standards of provision.

A *Cool Britannia*

AQA *Examiner's tip*

Remember, there are different opinions about the Welfare State within the major political parties.

A dissenting view

'Old' Labour

Fear that:

- the cost of services will be greater in the long run because private companies will need to make a profit from providing them
- when schools and hospitals, for example, are run as businesses, teachers and doctors will become mere service providers who lack any special sense of obligation to the public
- the principle that all users should be treated equally will be weakened.

Case study

The 1992 Conservative party attitude towards the Welfare State

This ditty was sung at the conference by the minister in charge of social security.

> 66 *I've got a little list of benefit offenders who I'll soon be rooting out,*
> *And who never would be missed. They never would be missed.*
> *There's those who make up bogus claims in half a dozen names,*
> *And Councillors who draw the dole to run left-wing campaigns.*
> *They never would be missed. They never would be missed.*
> *There's young ladies who get pregnant just to jump the housing queue,*
> *And dads who won't support the kids of the ladies they have kissed,*
> *And I haven't even mentioned all those sponging socialists.*
> *I've got them on my list, and there's none of them be missed.*
> *There's none of them be missed.* 99

Peter Lilley MP

Activity

1 Think about the different 'scroungers' mentioned in the case study.

a Identify three ways in which they damage the Welfare State.

b Identify three ways in which a genuine claimant may be affected by hearing such a ditty on TV.

The approach to poverty

The 1950s was a decade of full employment and two-parent families. By the 1980s, many adults were unemployed and the number of lone parent families was increasing. The suspicion grew that some claimants were choosing to live at the expense of taxpayers. Governments began to emphasise the responsibility of individuals for supporting themselves and their dependants. The Child Support Agency was established to claim money from absent fathers for their children.

While emphasising responsibility, governments accept that citizens are entitled to support. However, funds are limited by the unpopularity of taxation. Lifting the poor out of poverty by raising their benefits is not a possibility. Rather, governments today think that they can best help the poor by removing barriers to their finding and keeping well-paid jobs. The New Labour government set up the Social Exclusion Unit (1997) to advise on this issue.

Welfare to work

- The New Deal offers work experience and training to the young, long-term unemployed and to unemployed lone parents. It also threatens loss of benefit if a claimant makes no effort to get a job.
- Subsidised childcare provision has been expanded to make it easier for parents, particularly lone parents, to have a paid job.
- Tax credits have been introduced for poor working families with children to ensure that their income does not fall below a minimum level.
- The provision of basic literacy and numeracy programmes is intended to reduce the numbers of those held back by low educational qualifications.
- An enforceable minimum wage has helped to raise the income of the low paid.

An ageing population

Britain's population is ageing. Elderly people make a vital contribution to family and community life. However, more financial resources are needed to provide social care, health care and pensions. Balancing spending on the elderly against the demands of other age groups is a delicate issue since the elderly are the age group most likely to vote. Reflecting post-1979 thinking, governments:

- no longer attempt to pay a basic state pension large enough to support a decent standard of living – instead, the poorest pensioners receive a **means tested** pension credit
- encourage and make it easier for people to contribute to personal pension schemes
- have reduced the barriers that made it difficult for the elderly to continue in employment.

Charities and voluntary organisations

For many centuries, charities and voluntary organisations have provided various kinds of welfare for the needy.

Activity

2 In groups of three:

a Find out what the policies of the Conservative, Liberal Democrat and New Labour parties are on reducing child poverty. Each of you should select a different party and obtain the relevant information either by contacting local or national party officers or by consulting the parties' websites. You should seek information particularly about:

- what they see as the causes of child poverty
- what policies they would use to reduce child poverty
- how long they believe it will take to have a serious impact on the problem.

b Compare the answers you gather and identify the similarities and differences between the approaches.

Key terms

Means tested: income and savings assessed to find out if the total is less than a level set by the government.

Many people thought that their significance would diminish with the development of the Welfare State. That a political leader can suggest plausibly that charities should play a crucial role in the 21st century perhaps tells us something significant about the Welfare State.

The role of the voluntary sector

❝ *The social challenges we face today are every bit as serious as the economic challenges Britain faced in 1979...*

'Just as we needed then to realise that the state couldn't run British businesses properly and shouldn't try, today we need to realise that the state can't run British society properly, and shouldn't try. Because in trying to run society from on high, the state takes responsibility away from people, families and communities – and a lack of social responsibility is the fundamental cause of the social breakdown we see all around us.

'...we believe in bottom-up social responsibility...we have a vision of non-state collective provision.

'So we want to see a transformation in the role of community groups, social enterprises and the voluntary sector in helping to build a stronger society for all of us. ❞

Speech by David Cameron MP, 3 June 2008

B   *David Cameron*

Going further

1   Reread the case study 'The role of the voluntary sector'.

2   Think of one or two voluntary organisations with which you are familiar.
   a   What services do they provide?
   b   Could they usefully expand them along the lines suggested by Mr Cameron?

3   Now think more generally about the provision of welfare.
   a   List ways in which, from Mr Cameron's point of view, the provision of welfare by the state weakens society.
   b   List ways in which, from the same point of view, provision of welfare by voluntary organisations strengthens society.

Did you know ??????

In 2006/7, 2.5 million pensioners were in poverty.

Check your understanding

1   Outline two reasons why most Conservatives in the 1950s supported the development of the Welfare State.

2   Outline two reasons why neo-Liberals in the 1970s and 1980s believed that the state benefit system was not giving good value for taxpayer's money.

3   List the features of the current benefit system which reflect the importance of the belief that individuals should take responsibility for themselves and their families.

6.4 Who has the power?

British society is made up of individuals. It is also made up of many sectional interests. Referring to the 'farming interest', for example, recognises that all those engaged in farming share common interests whatever their particular circumstances. We can also refer to the 'business interest' or the 'education interest'.

Interest groups

Some sectional interests are powerful because of the part they play in society. Decisions made by farmers influence the cost of food, for example. However, use of this power may be challenged. The 'farming interest' may be opposed by the 'consumer interest' on the cost of food.

Ensuring that competition between interests does not become a serious conflict is an important task of government. Interests, therefore, must operate within rules set by the government. This leads the interests to set up organisations, **interest groups**, through which they hope to influence the political decisions that might affect them.

Being on the 'inside'

The relationships between decision makers and particular groups and interests can be close and long lasting:

- Some interest groups and wealthy individuals give large sums of money to political parties. The Conservative party has been supported traditionally by business interests and the Labour party by the trade unions.

- Governments need the advice and support of some interests if their policies are to be effective. Running the NHS, for example, requires the cooperation of the 'medical interest'. Governments welcome representatives of such interests on committees that advise ministers. This ensures that the government understands their point of view, giving them an advantage over groups on the 'outside'. Pressure is often exerted more effectively 'behind closed doors'.

- Many MPs and ministers have business or professional backgrounds. They, their friends and relatives mix socially with business people. Through such contacts they come to understand and sympathise with their interests.

Activity

1. What is meant by a 'mandate'? Why is the idea of the 'mandate' central to democracy?

   Divide into groups and discuss the implication for our democracy of the situation outlined in the case study. How do such situations influence the answer to the question 'Who governs Britain?'

Objectives

You will be able to:

- identify significant interests in society

- explain how these interests organise themselves to influence the decision makers

- identify significant changes in the nature and activities of pressure groups

- relate these changes to recent social and technological changes and to globalisation.

Key terms

Interest groups: groups established to protect a sectional interest.

Direct action: political action, sometimes illegal, taken outside the normal political process.

AQA Examiner's tip

Despite the Freedom of Information Act and good investigative journalism, public knowledge of the relationships between some individuals/ groups and the decision makers is limited. You should recognise the significance of what goes on 'behind the scenes'.

Case study

Blackmailing a government

> 66 *I [Labour Prime Minister, Harold Wilson] said that we had now reached the situation where a newly-elected government with a mandate from the people was being told...by international speculators that the policies on which we had fought the election could not be implemented; that the government was to be forced into the adoption of Tory policies to which it was opposed. The Governor (of the Bank of England) confirmed that that was the case. I asked if this meant that it was impossible for any government, whatever its manifesto, to continue, unless it immediately implemented Tory policies. He agreed that this is what his argument meant, because of the sheer compulsion of those who exercised economic power.* 99

Taken from a conversation between the Prime Minister and
the Governor of the Bank of England (1964)
The Labour government 1964 1970: A Personal Record Harold Wilson (1971)

> **Did you know** ??????
>
> More than 33% of the 92 ministers who left government between May 1997 and 2004 became company directors or business consultants.

Being on the 'outside'

Groups outside the decision-making process have to persuade the government that their demands are worth considering. To achieve this they may:

- demonstrate to publicise their views. The groups hope that if they attract public support the government will respond positively to avoid loss of popularity. Governments do not, however, wish to encourage further group activity by appearing to give in.
- try to attract the support of MPs and Lords who can raise the group's concerns in parliament.

A *Stop the War march, London, October 2007*

Groups which believe that they will not be given a fair hearing by government in general or by a particular government may engage in **direct action**. Eco-warriors, for example, may chain themselves to bulldozers to delay building developments. Some animal rights groups may release animals used in experiments from laboratories.

Going further

1. Look on the Internet for examples of direct action and of groups which take it. Focus particularly on the kinds of action. Is it legal? Are people harmed? What are the aims of those participating?

2. Discuss with other members of your group whether direct action which is illegal can ever be justified in a democracy. Can it ever be justified in a dictatorship?

∞ links

Also see Topic 6.2 for a definition of pressure group and a discussion of political participation.

Political change

While much of what was written about pressure groups in the 1960s remains relevant, much has changed. Between 1945 and 1979, governments accepted that they should consult business groups and the trade unions about economic issues. During the 1970s, the Neo-liberals within the Conservative party criticised this 'cosy' partnership. They claimed that it gave the trade unions too much influence. After 1979, the Conservative government pursued policies that weakened the trade unions, making them 'outsiders'. The trade unions had hoped that a Labour government would restore their rights. However, New Labour has hardly done so, being unwilling to antagonise business. Therefore the balance of influence has shifted in favour of business.

Social change

During the 1950s people in Britain became less **deferential** to traditional institutions and ideas. Some sections of society began to believe that their interests were not adequately represented by existing organisations. **New social movements** developed.

The Women's Movement

Women in the 1950s and 1960s were expected to take little interest in politics and public life generally. Even in organisations like trade unions, which stood for social fairness, women were not treated as equals. Many women began to resent the situation and started to organise themselves. Some groups focused on 'women's issues' such as male abuse of women which were neglected by (main) **malestream** organisations. Others wished to make a specifically female contribution to a general cause, for example, women's peace camps. Through such groups women not only participated in political life but grew in confidence.

Other movements

Other 'neglected' sections of society, for example, gays and lesbians and those favouring alternative lifestyles, responded in similar ways. At the same time, established political organisations denied recognition to issues about which people were becoming concerned. The environment, for example, was not on the party political agenda.

Globalisation

Fifty years ago, the British government and parliament made the decisions for the British people. Britain was clearly a **nation state**. Since then, governments have signed treaties transferring some authority to international institutions.

Economic **globalisation** has created huge **transnational companies**. These companies have no particular commitment to the welfare of workers, consumers or the general public in Britain. Their worldwide economic power places them almost beyond the control of any national government.

Key terms

Deferential: an attitude based on the belief that people high on the social scale are superior and should be looked up to.

New social movement: an informal, loosely organised coalition of individuals or groups supporting an interest or cause.

Malestream: a word occasionally used by feminists to mean 'mainstream', thereby drawing attention to the gender bias of much language.

Activity

2 a Over a period of seven days, watch in the media for references to pressure groups. Note such references, paying particular attention to:
  - what they are doing
  - what they want
  - what are the responses of government, other pressure groups, the media and the public in general.

  b At the end of the week, compare notes with the rest of your group. Try to sort the pressure groups into the types mentioned in this topic. Can you see any patterns of activity? For example, do groups of a particular type engage in similar activities?

  c Assess the coverage of the pressure groups by the media. Was any bias apparent?

  d Assess how likely it is that the groups will be successful.

Save the environment

Stop Climate Chaos is a tiny organisation coordinating the biggest public campaign in Britain since Make Poverty History brought hundreds of thousands of people on to the streets.

It is a formidable, broad coalition of campaigning groups representing 4 million to 5 million people, including the Women's Institute, Unicef, Oxfam, many unions, student organisations, Christian and Islamic faith groups, health charities, justice and social networks.

B *Trying to save the world*

But its strength lies in its grassroots appeal. It has galvanised nearly 200 community, student, church and local groups. They range from community cycle, aviation and road groups, to energy, housing, waste and sustainable development organisations.

Adapted from John Vidal, *The Guardian*, 26 September 2007

The new situation has created both problems and opportunities for pressure groups. The British government, for example, may no longer have the power to give a group what it wants. On the other hand, if an international political authority or a transnational company can be persuaded, a group's demands will be implemented in many countries. This is helpful to groups pressing for action on the environment or global poverty.

Technological advances

Many pressure groups have internationalised their activities. They have been helped in this by advanced communication technology. Through the Internet, ideas can be shared and action coordinated across many countries. British pressure groups can now support and be supported by sympathisers across the world.

Key terms

Nation state: an independent state whose inhabitants form a single national community.

Globalisation: a process through which people, organisations and states become increasingly interdependent, both economically and culturally.

Transnational companies: companies, businesses which operate on a global scale, in many countries.

Activity

3   Scientists have for a decade now presented strong evidence about the significance of environmental problems.

Discuss with your group why the government is responding so inadequately that the groups mentioned in the case study feel the need to campaign.

Check your understanding

1   Identify three sectional interests and, for each, list two groups which they have established to influence political decisions.

2   Outline the arguments for believing that the most powerful pressure groups are the ones the public knows least about.

3   Identify one pressure group formed within the last 30 years. Explain why this group did not exist in the 1950s.

4   Identify three ways in which the Internet may be useful to pressure groups.

links

See Topic 5.5 for more examples of the impact of technological change.

Who is in control?

To many people 'power' is what governments have and use. However, for some, power is experienced more immediately and personally. The wife frightened of being beaten by her drunken husband understands abuse of power. Neighbours coming together to rid their estate of drug dealers understand the importance of power.

Power in the home

Privacy is an important freedom in British society. The home is a private space. Activities in the home are not, therefore, subject to direct control by 'the authorities' unless there is clear evidence of gross wrongdoing.

Case study

Domestic abuse

British Crime Survey figures reveal that 28% of women and 18% of men aged 16–59 report that they have been victims of domestic abuse at some point in their lives. A Home Office minister said that family abuse, sexual abuse and stalking shone a light on the violence hidden behind closed doors. A member of the Fawcett Society, which campaigns for gender equality, said, 'Only 60% of victims who go to the police find them very or fairly helpful.'

Adapted from Alan Travis, *The Guardian,* 1 February 2008

Activities

1. List three reasons why women are more likely to be victims of abuse than men.

2. List three reasons why a woman might not inform the police that she or her children are being abused.

3. Why might the police find cases of domestic abuse difficult to deal with?

The distribution of power and authority within any family will be influenced by:

- Family law, which now treats men and women more or less equally and protects the rights of the children.
- Community and religious beliefs, which influence some people's ideas of 'correct' or 'ideal' family relationships.
- Women's entry into paid employment, which limits their partner's 'power of the purse'. Children, however, remain dependent on their parents.
- A member's willingness to use superior physical strength as a source of power. Some feminists see domestic and sexual violence as significant elements of **patriarchy**.

Objectives

You will be able to:

- identify and explain the factors influencing the distribution of power in the home
- explain how the type of neighbourhood influences the distribution of power
- identify and explain the factors influencing the distribution of power in the workplace
- analyse relationships within schools using the concepts of power and authority.

Key terms

Patriarchy: the idea that men dominate society and its institutions.

Community: a set of individuals between whom there is a strong sense of identity. The individuals may or may not live in the same locality.

Group activity

1. Working in groups:

   a. Discuss the possibilities for conducting research into the ways in which you and other group members experience the use of power in the family.

   b. Construct a plan for the research that will satisfy the ethical considerations for investigating such a sensitive, private subject.

links

See Topic 1.6 for the ethical considerations you should bear in mind when conducting research.

- The mental capacity of its members. The young, the elderly and others whose mental capacity is limited are vulnerable to the abuse of power.
- The expectations of family members. Achieving affection and companionship, for example, might be difficult if one of the partners seeks to 'rule' the family.

Power in the neighbourhood

Community

Sociologists have always been interested in relationships within a neighbourhood. **Community** describes a set of people who know each other well, live by similar values and feel attached to each other. People in communities feel they 'belong'. A community can develop norms which members are expected to respect. Community 'leaders' may be given authority to make decisions for the community or settle disputes. Community gives some structure and stability to relationships in the neighbourhood.

Absence of community

Other neighbourhoods are very different. People may not stay long and those living there may not respect their neighbours. In these neighbourhoods, no community authority exists to uphold standards. Those who wish to behave anti-socially have the power to do so because their neighbours fear being beaten up or having their property destroyed. In such situations, order can be established only when the 'respectable' residents challenge their anti-social neighbours. The confidence to do this depends on support by 'outside' authorities, such as the police, who have the power to counter that of the 'neighbours from hell', the 'feral children' and the gangs.

A *It can be difficult to ring for help*

Case study

Life in a rough area

These 3 maladjusted boys are currently attacking one of the houses being renovated. They had previously whacked the occupant over the head with a board. After living in the road for 50 years he left.

No one is safe to walk in the street. They are liable to be verbally attacked and the children are not allowed out by themselves as they are likely to get smacked in the face. The language shouted at passers-by is as foul as it is violently expressed.

A Wirral resident in *Neighbours from Hell* by Frank Field (2003)

Going further

1. How do you explain the higher rates of 'disorder' on council estates and other low income areas?

2. Use the Internet to find out what the government and local authorities have done and are doing to make life better in such areas.

B *Neighbourhood insecurity*

	England and Wales	People living on council estates and other low income areas
Percentage of people recording a high sense of disorder	14	34
Percentage of people experiencing disorder impacting clearly on their quality of life	37	54

Neighbours from Hell by Frank Field (2003)

Power in the workplace

The public expects able-bodied adults to earn their living. The majority will work for an employer. The employer needs work from the employee who needs pay from the employer. Their interests, however, are also opposed. An employer has an interest in keeping costs, including wages, down and getting as much work from the employee as possible. An employee has an interest in increasing his or her wage and working in the most pleasant conditions. To resolve this opposition the two sides negotiate.

Key terms

Alienation: expresses the idea of separation. A sense of powerlessness is part of alienation. At work an employee may have no power to decide how a job will be done or how quickly to work. A citizen may feel powerless to influence the government.

Bargaining power

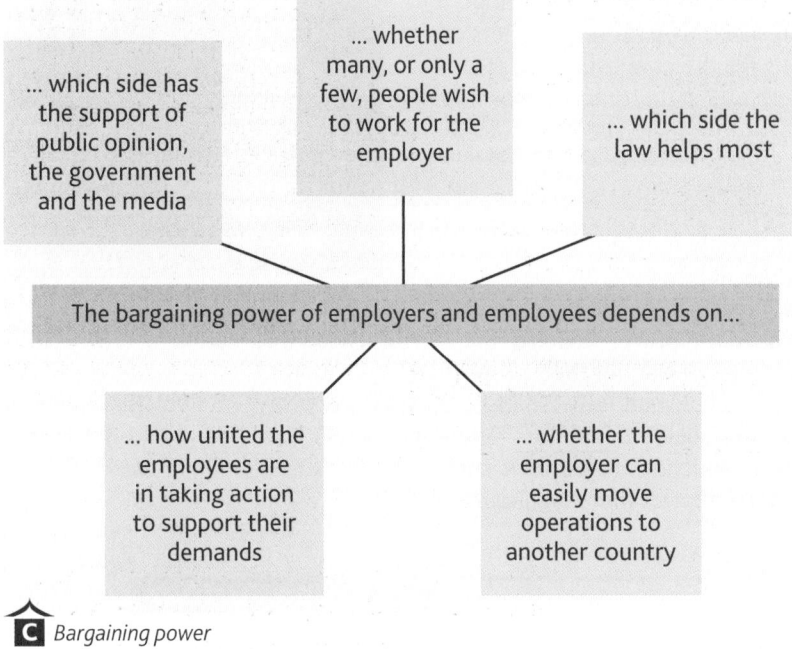

... which side has the support of public opinion, the government and the media

... whether many, or only a few, people wish to work for the employer

... which side the law helps most

The bargaining power of employers and employees depends on...

... how united the employees are in taking action to support their demands

... whether the employer can easily move operations to another country

C *Bargaining power*

Alienation

Employees differ in the extent to which they can exercise some control at work. Contrast the teacher, for example, who hopefully has control in the classroom, with a worker sitting by a conveyor belt performing the same simple, mindless task hundreds of times each working day.

An individual's experience while selling forty or so hours of life each week to an employer can influence their non-work life. Denied power at work an employee may experience **alienation** and may, for example:

- seek power at home through bullying their family or pets
- get out of the habit of thinking and not want to be bothered with politics and other activities requiring intellectual effort
- have little faith in the effectiveness of constructive political activity.

In this way some kinds of work and working environment may not help to produce the confident, thoughtful citizens required by a healthy democracy.

AQA Examiner's tip

Avoid seeing power as if an individual or an institution has a certain quantity of it which can be 'spent' like money. Think rather in terms of 'power relationships' in which the distribution of power will depend on who is involved, the circumstances and the issues, for example.

Power at school

Maintaining order

Schools told to take action on growing menace of gangs

Headteachers will be advised to screen pupils' computer accounts and gather proof, including photographic evidence, if they suspect teenagers, or even primary children, of joining gangs.

It is suggested that:

- headteachers set out emergency plans to deal with sudden outbreaks of weapon-related violence
- teachers should learn to identify signs of gang membership such as pupils wearing certain colours or items of jewellery
- staff should be trained to look out for tags or graffiti in the streets or in notebooks
- schools may monitor students on social networking sites.

A minister said, 'Where there is a culture of fear and uncertainty in a school, it is something that not just the school, but youth services and police have got to grapple with. It is not the schools taking this on alone, but they are in the unique position of being the eyes and ears of the community.'

Adapted from Polly Curtis, *The Guardian,* 22 May 2008

Did you know ???????

According to the Trade Union Congress, business in the United Kingdom loses approximately 18 million working days each year as a result of workplace bullying.

Source: Young Foundation website

Activity

4 Read the case study with the thought that gang members younger than 16 years old belong to families, neighbourhoods and schools. Consider in particular the ways that power is used in the various situations.

a List three or four examples of rules that a family will try to enforce on young people.

b Do the same for neighbourhoods and schools.

c List examples of rewards and punishments that are available to family, neighbourhoods and schools.

d List examples of the rewards and punishments teenage gangs may use to recruit and control members.

e Using these lists, discuss with your classmates how families, neighbourhoods and schools might use their powers to tackle the gang problem effectively.

Check your understanding

1 Describe how decisions would be made in a democratic family.

2 Outline two reasons why there may be less anti-social behaviour in a neighbourhood with a sense of community than in one without.

3 Identify three ways in which globalisation might alter the balance of power between employees and employers.

4 Compare the ways in which the employee at work and the pupil at school experience power. Identify three similarities in their experiences.

What does social research tell us about power in contemporary Britain?

Sociologists are interested in the social backgrounds of those individuals who occupy positions that give them political, economic or cultural power.

How socially representative is Parliament?

A *The background of MPs*

MPs who	Number elected in 2005	Number needed for the House of Commons to reflect their proportion in British society
were educated at Oxford or Cambridge	164	4
were educated at private school	206	45
had worked in a manual job	38	239
had worked in a professional job	242	72

Adapted from Table 1.1 in *Democracy in Britain* by Matt Cole

A British elite?

Sociologists disagree about the distribution of power in Britain. Some point to:

- the opportunities all citizens have to participate in the decision-making process, as individuals, members of political parties or pressure groups
- the competition between parties which enables voters to choose the kind of policies which the government will implement.

Such openness and competition, they suggest, allow any of the different interests and causes in society a fair chance to exercise influence.

Other sociologists suggest that the potential of democracy for distributing power widely remains unrealised. Behind the principle of 'one person, one vote' lies the reality 'one small group, much power'. A significant part of their case is that those occupying senior positions in different powerful institutions:

- come from similar backgrounds
- have similar interests
- use the power their positions give them to defend and advance the interests of their group.

Research by the Sutton Trust concluded that:

We are still to a large extent a society divided by wealth, with future elites groomed at particular schools and universities.

Objectives

You will be able to:

- explore the relationship between research and matters of sociological debate

- explore the relationship between research and matters of political controversy.

Activity

1 Look at Table **A**:

a Which group was most over-represented in comparison with its proportion in British society?

b Which group was most under-represented in comparison with its proportion in British society?

c How do you explain this pattern of over-representation and under-representation?

d Discuss with a partner the possible advantages and disadvantages for a constituent of being represented by someone from a different social class.

Key terms

Elite: a small dominant group.

B   *The educational backgrounds of 500 leading figures in different walks of life, 2007*

	Percentage who attended different types of school		Percentage attending Oxbridge
	Independent school*	State school	
Judges	70	30	78
Politicians	38	62	42
Journalists	54	46	56
Doctors	51	49	15
Chief executives of leading companies	54	46	39

*7% of the total school age population attends independent schools   Sutton Trust website

Activity

2   Look at Table **B**:

a   Which group was most likely to have attended Oxbridge?

b   Which group were most likely to have attended an independent school?

c   Explain why politicians were the group least likely to have attended an independent school.

d   Discuss with others in your group whether the statistics in the table do or do not support the view that an elite exists in modern Britain.

▨ Government – a source of secondary data

Most academic sociologists have limited funding to carry out research. The data derived from research undertaken by private companies or public bodies for their own purposes is, therefore, very useful.

The **National Census**, for example, which the government organises every ten years is a vital source of information about the British population and the ways we live. Few citizens object to filling in the Census forms because:

▨ they know that the personal information they contain is turned into impersonal statistics

▨ they understand that the government is able to formulate effective policies only if it has accurate information on which to base them.

Other data of interest to sociologists is generated by public officials as they 'go about their business'. A police officer, for example, is required to fill in a detailed 'stop and search' form each time he or she carries out that procedure. The form is 'one foot long and takes 25 minutes to complete'. The information thus recorded enables senior officers to monitor use of the 'stop and search' power. Critics, on the other hand, suggest that such 'red tape' is a misuse of valuable police time.

Going further

1   **The Miners' Strike 1984**

Throughout the 20th century, sections of the working class have used strikes to exercise some power and improve their situation. The 1984 miners' strike was a key event in recent British history.

a   By using secondary sources, including media coverage at the time and since, relevant websites and books, discover the ways in which the courts, politicians, media and business responded to the strike. Different people within your group could each investigate a different aspect.

b   Then, as a group, discuss whether what you have found can be used as evidence for or against believing that opposing the miners and their supporters was an elite defending its interests.

Key terms

National Census: a survey conducted on behalf of the government. Data that is collected from every household in the country provides detailed information about our way of life.

Stop and search

The questions on the 'stop and search' form include:

- reason for stop and search, for example, street encounter, drugs, anti-social behaviour, firearms or terrorism
- details of other officers present
- details of first place detained
- location, time, name and address of person searched
- gender, date of birth, height and ethnicity of person searched
- were they on foot, driver or passenger in vehicle?
- was there any injury or force used?
- if arrested, on what offence?
- full description including headgear, hair and tattoos, clothing and footwear, including logos and sizes
- reference to other people stopped
- name of the operation.

C *Policeman completing a 'stop and search' form*

Statistics and political controversy

When using government statistics, sociologists understand the need to be cautious. However, unlike sociologists, governments and the public bodies to which their statistics relate have political agendas. Assembling and publishing statistics has a crucial role in the competition between political parties. Falling hospital waiting lists or improving examination results, for example, can make a government and the public servants involved look good.

Therefore there is always a danger that, when such statistics are constructed, objectivity will be sacrificed so that a favourable image can be presented to the public. Falling unemployment figures, for example, can be achieved in two ways:

- by implementing policies which encourage the creation of jobs
- by changing the definition of unemployment so that fewer of the unemployed are counted in the statistics.

Going further

2 Some politicians and pressure groups which campaign about 'civil liberties' think that Britain is fast becoming a 'surveillance society'.

a Devise a questionnaire to find out the extent to which people are concerned that they may be losing too much of their privacy.

b Find out whether different age groups have different opinions.

Check your understanding

1 List three sets of statistics not mentioned above which are likely to be used in political arguments.

2 For one of these, identify those likely to benefit from the statistics looking favourable.

3 How might the statistics identified be constructed or represented so as to give a more favourable impression than is justified?

Activities

3 Look at the 'Stop and search' Case study and think of the statistics which could be produced from all the completed forms.

a What information about the personal characteristics of the persons searched would not be of interest to sociologists?

b Identify the information that would be of interest to sociologists and explain which issues it would help them to investigate.

c Why has 'stop and search' been a controversial police procedure?

d Which piece of information recorded might be particularly relevant in the debate about 'stop and search'?

4 We expect the police to use their time efficiently in protecting the public. On the other hand, we need them to be accountable for their use of the substantial powers which they are given.

a Discuss with your group how an appropriate balance between efficiency and accountability might be established.

6.7   Exam questions for Power

Exam question guidance

∞ links

See the Exam question guidance section in Topic 1.8 on page 38 for general advice on answering source-based questions.

Example of a source-based question

Item A
People with disabilities protesting outside the gates of Downing Street

Source: Getty images

- **Who?** This source is a picture taken by a photo-journalist. It may even be an image produced by someone who supported the protest and wished to record it. In the photo you can actually see an individual with a camera photographing the event from a different angle.

- **What?** The source demonstrates the level of unhappiness felt at the time by people with disabilities about government changes to the system of disability payments.

- **Why?** Sociologists have long been interested in the relative levels of power and influence enjoyed by different groups within society. They are also interested in the methods used by various interest groups within a democratic society to influence those who hold positions of power (**pressure groups**).

a   From **Item A**, what appears to be the purpose of the demonstration?   *(1 mark)*

Look carefully at the image. In this case the answer is 'to protest against the level of disability benefits' or 'to protest against disability discrimination'. Either answer would gain you the mark, as would 'to gain publicity'.

Example of a 2-mark question

c   Identify **one** advantage and **one** disadvantage of using means tested benefits to reduce the number of people in poverty in Britain.   *(2 marks)*

The examiners expect you to understand the meaning of the term **means tested benefits**. This is essentially the idea that the level of social security payments made to an individual should be determined by an assessment of their needs. Those who support means tested benefits would argue that the advantage of the system is that money can be spent on those who are most in need. A disadvantage is that means testing is frequently complex and can be degrading. This can lead to a significant short-fall in applications. This arises because people who are entitled to benefits either lack the ability to fill in complicated forms or do not wish to be subjected to humiliating interviews or medical assessments.

⊂⊃ **links**

See the Exam question guidance section in Topic 2.7 on page 67 for general advice on answering extended-answer questions.

Example of an extended-answer question

g   Discuss how far sociologists would agree that pressure groups and political parties help to spread power evenly throughout British society.   *(12 marks)*

- The examiner would expect you to be aware of the current debate about our political system and the nature of our democracy. They would expect you to understand how the political system works and how pressure groups function in a democracy.

- The question clearly raises the issue of **extent. How far** would sociologists agree that power is spread evenly throughout British society? Some sociologists would argue that in a **pluralist** democratic society different groups compete for influence in a healthy climate of open debate. This **neo-liberal** view of the social order emphasises that power is exercised for the common good by politicians who are sensitive to the needs of competing interest groups. These politicians also act to decide the best course for the greater good. In a representative democracy, political parties and their leaders are held accountable for their actions at the ballot box. They must seek re-election, usually every five years or so. If the majority of voters believe that the government has done a good job, they will be re-elected.

However, other sociologists particularly **Marxists** are more critical of our unequal society. They point out that power and influence are held disproportionately by wealthy individuals and companies. These people and organisations do not have the welfare of the majority population at heart. Large companies, for example, are often multinational corporations concerned with maximising profits in a **global** economy. Politicians are subject to pressure from these companies because they can often relocate their businesses with relative ease. If one country seeks to regulate or restrict their activities, they can move elsewhere.

To a Marxist sociologist, the activities of small pressure groups in support of environmental issues or the disabled, for example, are relatively insignificant when compared to the influence of global capitalism.

▪ Remember to avoid the trap of only referring to the sources in the question. The examiner wants to see evidence that you have studied the sociology of power *and* thought about the issues.

Questions to try

What follows are examples of the types of questions you will meet in your exam. The letter in each question matches the letter that will be used for that type of question on your exam paper. The number in brackets is only there to help you and your teacher refer to that particular question in this book.

Item B

According to a report from the Equality and Human Rights Commission, professional women who want to reach the top are encountering not so much a glass ceiling as one made from reinforced concrete. The fifth annual Sex and Power report shows a drop in the number of women attaining the top jobs in Britain. They hold just 11% of director-ships in major companies and account for only 19.3% of MPs. The commission says that the most worrying trend is that progress seems to have stalled in some areas and gone into reverse in others. In 12 of the 25 job categories they monitored fewer women held top jobs in 2007 than in the year before; in another five categories the percentage of women was unchanged.

Adapted from The Guardian, September 2008

a   From **Item B**, what is the trend revealed in 12 out of the 25 job categories monitored by the Equality and Human Rights Commission?   *(1 mark)*

d(1)   Explain what sociologists mean by patriarchy.   *(4 marks)*

d(2)   Explain what sociologists mean by the first past the post electoral system.   *(4 marks)*

e   Describe **one** way in which relationships within the family have changed during the last 50 years and explain why this change has made the family more democratic.   *(5 marks)*

g(1)   Discuss how far sociologists would agree that there is no longer a link between social class and voting behaviour.   *(12 marks)*

g(2)   Discuss how far sociologists would agree that relationships between employers and employees have changed since the 1960s.   *(12 marks)*

g(3)   Discuss how far sociologists would agree that pressure groups are able to influence the government.   *(12 marks)*

7.1 What is social stratification?

■ Difference – inequality – stratification

Human beings differ from one another in many ways. Biological differences are inevitable. Difference is not, however, inequality. No one refers to inequality of eye colour. It is society that turns differences into inequalities. For example, centuries ago taller people were maybe better spear throwers. If this helped the tribe, it was 'natural' to consider tall as better than short. A difference became an inequality and inequality became the basis of social organisation. Stratification became a vital characteristic of social structure. The pattern of inequality was passed from one generation to the next.

■ Slavery

Slavery was a form of stratification often linked with the conquest of one society by another. Members of the defeated society were 'strangers' or 'aliens' to the victorious society. They were not protected by those feelings that stop us from treating badly anyone we see as 'like ourselves'. The defeated became possessions of the victorious. The owner could:

- command the slave to perform any task
- allow or forbid the slave's marriage
- sell the slave
- punish the slave as they wished.

There were humane owners but the system denied the slave rights, respect and any control over their life.

Slavery today

Slavery continues to influence people's lives. Although forbidden by international law, slavery exists, even in Britain. People are trafficked, for example, to be used in the sex trade or to undertake hard and menial tasks. Their labour is demanded in return for a debt or forced by intimidation. Others are domestic slaves brought into Britain by the families they serve. Their 'owners' keep the person's passport so that escape is impossible.

A *A Polish labourer searches for cockles on the dangerous sands of Morecambe Bay. In 2004, 21 Chinese labourers died doing the same work.*

Objectives

You will be able to:

- define social stratification
- explain the nature of stratification in slave and caste societies
- identify the significance of slavery and caste in modern Britain
- explain how class societies differ from more traditional forms of stratification
- identify the significance of non-class inequalities for life in modern Britain.

Key terms

Slavery: a form of stratification in which a section of the society has no rights. Individuals in this section of society are items of property which can be bought and sold.

Racism: attitudes to and beliefs about race which usually involve negative stereotypes of another race and lead to discrimination against people of that race.

Caste: a rigid system of stratification in which an individual cannot move from the caste into which he or she was born.

Ascribed status: a position or social standing given to an individual on the basis of inherited characteristics.

Leila, a domestic slave

I was brought to Britain when I was 29 by the family I worked for. I was treated very badly. I had no room of my own and had to sleep in the sitting room where anyone could disturb me. I had to work 16–18 hours every day with no day off for the first two years. I earned £200 per month. I was not allowed to eat with the family and was fed leftovers or onions and potatoes. I was deliberately kept without a visa so I could not run away.

Adapted from the Anti-Slavery International website, June 2008

Activity

1 As you read the case study, think of the normal terms and conditions of employment that British citizens expect.

List the ways in which Leila's situation differs from these.

Going further

1 Some sociologists suggest that the way Afro-Caribbean people are seen, and see themselves today, has been influenced by the experience of slavery.

Look at images of Afro-Caribbean men and women in the media – in films, soap operas and dramas, for example.

■ Are there any aspects of the portrayal of Afro-Caribbean people in the media that could be seen as a legacy of slavery?

■ Could any of the attitudes and beliefs which are part of **racism** have been derived from slavery?

Did you know ??????

The distinctive characteristic of slavery in modern Britain is control of the worker by violence or the threat of violence.

Slavery is more commonly found in domestic work, construction, food production and the sex trade than in other areas of economic activity.

The caste system

The **caste** system remains basic to social life in some parts of India. It is a rigid form of stratification supported by Hindu beliefs. Society is divided into castes. There is no intermarriage between castes and social contact is limited. Caste is an **ascribed status**. Movement from one caste into another is not possible. While each caste is associated with undertaking particular kinds of tasks in society, non-economic distinctions provide the basis of caste. Higher castes are thought to be living a worthier form of life. Any physical contact with the lowest caste is felt to be repulsive and polluting.

> 66 *85% of the respondents felt that Indians actively practise and participate in the caste system. A large proportion of the Dalit (Untouchable) community have experienced caste discrimination in employment, health, politics and education sectors. One of the respondents had a Sikh girlfriend and they had talked about getting married. But when she found out that he was a Dalit she immediately left him.* 99

From the *Dalit Solidarity Network report*, July 2006

Activity

2 Look at the CasteWatchUK website **www.castewatchuk.org** and find information about caste in Britain.

Discuss with your group how different life in your school/college would be if all students were divided into different 'castes' of one sort or another. What problems would there be?

Class societies

Societies tend to generate forms of stratification which enable them to function efficiently. Modern industrial societies tend to be class societies because:

- The social upheavals accompanying industrialisation weaken the non-economic distinctions significant in pre-industrial societies.

- Modern industrial societies are constantly changing. They need to be able to adapt to the economic and social developments stimulated by advances in technology. They need to be 'open societies', able to reward success with high **achieved status**.

Characteristics

Class stratification is based on economic inequality. In a class society:

- An individual's position in the system of stratification depends only on his or her economic situation. Whether a factory worker is male or female, black or white, Catholic or Hindu, cockney or Geordie, *Guardian* or *Sun* reader is irrelevant. He or she is a factory worker.

- There are no legal or other formal restrictions on marriage between members of different classes.

- All citizens have equal rights whatever their class position. A rich man will have more money than a poor man to spend on legal help. However, both are equal before the law.

- There are no clear or official distinctions between classes. People in one class may not see any differences between themselves and those in another class.

- **Social mobility** is possible and occurs. Luck, talent and/or hard work, for example, may enable an individual to climb from one class into a higher class.

The openness of a class system enables talent and hard work to be rewarded. The society benefits from individuals born into a lower class having an incentive to develop and use their talent.

Non-class inequalities

Although Britain is a class society, non-economic inequalities can be significant.

Class has not completely replaced the system of stratification which preceded it. A hierarchy of distinction symbolised, for example, by titles, curtseying, the House of Lords, smart accents and antique regalia continues to be important. While birth is at the heart of this system, it is possible to achieve 'honour'.

A more contemporary hierarchy is based on celebrity. With the media playing such a crucial part in people's lives, 'being known' has become desirable and a source of respect and influence. Celebrities become role models.

The beliefs and attitudes that supported inequalities based on gender and ethnicity in previous centuries have not disappeared. Despite anti-discrimination laws, sexism and racism continue to influence the ways in which many people decide who to respect.

Key terms

Achieved status: a social position which individuals are able to gain through, for example, hard work and/or educational qualifications.

Social mobility: movement of individuals up or down a social scale.

∞ links

See Topic 1.3 for an outline of the ways in which sociologists decide to which class an individual belongs.

B *Some positions depend on birth not talent*

Activity

3 Obtain a copy of a recent Queen's Birthday or New Year Honours List. The broadsheet newspapers publish these in full or you can look on The UK Honours System website: www.honours.gov.uk

a Find out:

■ what kind of contributions to society are likely to be honoured at the different levels

■ whether there is a pattern to what kinds of activity are valued more or less highly.

b Discuss with your group whether the highest awards are made to those people who, in your view, make the most useful contributions to our society's wellbeing.

Looking after your own

A pessimist might suggest that in any society which boasts that position is based on achievement lurks a society pushing for position to be based on birth. Family loyalty will lead successful men and women to do all they can to pass on their high positions to their children. They often succeed, even in a new and supposedly 'open' profession like journalism.

Activity

4 List as many family connections in journalism as you can.

> 66 Family ties remain a powerful force in the newsroom. There are countless examples of sons and daughters, brothers and sisters, partners and former partners who have followed in the footsteps of relatives in pursuing successful careers in journalism. 99
>
> Sutton Trust, 2007

Going further

2 Nepotism is the process by which 'well-placed' individuals use their positions to obtain 'good' positions for family members.

a Find statistics showing the occupational and class backgrounds of those in the medical and legal professions.

b How 'open' does the recruitment process appear to be?

AQA Examiner's tip

Remember that sociologists use 'social status' in two ways:

■ It can mean social position.

■ It can also refer to the social standing or honour attached to a position.

Check your understanding

1 Explain, using an example, what sociologists mean by 'social stratification'.

2 Outline one way in which slavery may be an issue in modern Britain.

3 Identify three differences between caste and class societies.

4 Outline two ways in which the 'openness' of modern British society is limited.

People's lives are influenced by factors beyond their own, or any one person's, control. The concept of **life chances** recognises this. The likelihood of avoiding a heart attack, attending university, or owning a house, for example, is linked to social position. By calculating and comparing the life chances of different sections of society, sociologists can map the pattern of inequality.

A *Children's dental health*

	Percentage with obvious decay in primary teeth		Percentage with obvious decay in permanent teeth	
	Age = 5 years	Age = 8 years	Age = 12 years	Age = 15 years
In 'deprived' schools	60	70	55	72
In 'non-deprived' schools	40	55	42	55

National Statistics online

Activity

1   Looking at Table **A**, what trend is apparent in the figures?

Identify as many factors as you can that might be related to children's chances of having good teeth at the ages shown. You might consider them under the headings:

- the culture of the area or the family
- the resources of the family
- the condition of and the facilities in the area.

Objectives

You will be able to:

- define life chances
- give examples of inequality in life chances
- explain the unequal distribution of life chances
- relate the distribution of life chances to the development of social classes
- explain how social class may influence life in society.

Key terms

Life chances: the chances that sections of society have of achieving the 'things' which are valued by their society.

■ Why are life chances distributed unequally?

Some sociologists see inequality as inevitable in any competitive, free market society. In such societies, economic and social processes are constantly generating inequality. In modern British society, competition creates positions for winners and losers. Some people have higher life chances than others, therefore, because society is organised to give much to some and little to others.

Other sociologists suggest that, whatever the level of resources available, individuals can improve their life chances if they so choose. Welfare benefits and free education offer opportunities for all. Hard work and a sensible lifestyle can turn these opportunities into better life chances.

AQA Examiner's tip

Remember that life chances are statistical averages.

Case study

Smoking and class

Today, smoking is connected to disadvantage. Those from lower socio-economic groups find it much harder to give up, despite the fact that they want to and try to at the same rate as other smokers. Studies have shown that these groups assess the risks differently. It is only when you have an optimistic view of the future that you are minded to make an investment in a future health gain that may well prove difficult and unpleasant in the short term. If your priority is putting food on the table rather than living to 73, the immediate gratification that smoking brings – be that satisfaction of a physical addiction or the psychological boost of being able to afford a small luxury – makes more sense.

Adapted from Libby Brooks, *The Guardian*, 1 July 2008

Activity

2 Looking at the case study:

a Why does an 'optimistic view of the future' make it easier to make sacrifices in the present for a future gain?

b What factors are likely to influence whether people take an optimistic or pessimistic view of the future?

c Discuss with your group whether the lower life expectancy of the people in the extract is more realistically explained by a lack of resources or lack of personal determination.

Did you know ???????

Men in Kensington live on average 10 years longer than men in Manchester.

Women in Kensington live on average 9 years longer than women in Liverpool.

Inequality versus equality

Over the centuries, unequal societies have been challenged as being unfair. In the past, they have been defended on the grounds that inequality was God's will. Today, inequality is defended by some sociologists as being necessary to encourage capable people to fill the more socially useful positions in society. However, other sociologists and social psychologists, making comparisons between people living in less equal societies and more equal societies, conclude that those in living in less equal societies:

- feel less secure
- suffer worse health
- experience greater violence
- experience less satisfactory social relationships.

AQA Examiner's tip

Sociology studies many topics about which people disagree passionately. Always remember that sociologists are expected to favour the point of view which is supported by the strongest evidence.

What is class?

Class can refer to a section of society made up of individuals who have similar life chances. It exists statistically, on paper, as an idea which helps sociologists to describe the patterns of inequality they discover. Class can also become a reality to ordinary people when similar life chances lead them to similar experiences. Class in this sense has long been a subject for films, plays and soap operas. Class has long been a topic of public debate.

Group activity

Discuss with your group the advantages and disadvantages of inequality in society.

Class in people's lives

Class can be a source of identity. In the middle of the 20th century, the **lifestyles** of different sections of society reflected the underlying inequalities in obvious ways. The majority of people clearly saw themselves as belonging to a class, their **subjective class** generally being that to which a sociologist would allocate them.

For most people, lifestyles in modern Britain indicate life chances less clearly than in the past. Also, gender, ethnicity, sexuality and age have become significant sources of identity. As a result, while people continue to acknowledge that they belong to a class, they do so with less accuracy and certainty.

B *Leaving the factory*

C *Terraced housing*

Activities

3 List five ways in which the people in Photo **B** would have seen that they had similar life chances.

4 List five activities which the adults living in a neighbourhood such as in Photo **C** would have been likely to do together.

Class rules

> ❝ *Among the middle-class professionals questioned, a third thought that they were **working class** and nearly a third of manual workers believed themselves to be **middle class**.*
>
> *An experienced researcher said, 'Fifty years ago there was an almost official and agreed class ranking, and everyone knew where they were located. That has completely gone now. Whereas once it would have been straightforwardly, objectively wrong for someone in a middle-class profession to think of themselves as working class, that's not necessarily true now. These aren't terms that have an agreed meaning any more.'* ❞

Adapted from Decca Aitkenhead, *The Guardian*, 20 October 2007

AQA Examiner's tip

Don't worry if you find the idea of class confusing – so do many journalists, politicians and sociologists. Different sociologists have given it slightly different meanings. Remember, however, that the basis of all of its meanings is something economic.

Activity

5 Read the extract 'Class rules' and then answer the following questions.

a What proportion of professionals thought they were working class?

b What does 'objectively wrong' mean?

c Look at Photo **B** and Photo **C** again and compare the Britain they portray with the Britain we experience today. In what ways has it changed?

d Discuss with your group whether these changes help to explain the lack of clarity and uncertainty in people's views about class today.

Class can become the basis of a sub-culture. Many sociological studies in the 1950s and 1960s described the ways in which working-class communities had developed a distinctive sub-culture which enabled them to cope with the particular circumstances in which they lived. A high value was placed on solidarity, and collective action underpinned this way of life. **Trade unions**, the Co-op, working men's clubs, choirs, May day walks, galas, the local rugby league or football team all played a part in making life as pleasant as possible and allowed the community to express and feel proud of itself.

Although you have reached this topic towards the end of this book, you have been studying life chances and the effects of class since the beginning. Class, with its associated inequalities, continues to structure life in Britain today.

∞ links

See Topics 2.4, 3.6 and 4.5 for examples of the significance of class for family, educational achievement, crime and deviance.

Going further

1 Watch the film *Brassed Off*.

2 Keep a diary for a week or two, recording references to class in the media.

3 Compare notes with others in your group. Sort the references according to whether they refer to the middle, working or other classes. How often do the references suggest approval or disapproval of what is described?

4 Discuss with your group the explanation and significance of any pattern which emerges.

Check your understanding

1 Identify three examples of unequal life chances that sociologists may see as particularly significant.

2 Identify three reasons why individuals in some sections of society are likely to live for longer than individuals in other sections of society.

3 Outline briefly why inequalities in life chances may lead people to see themselves as members of a class.

4 Outline two reasons for believing that class today is only a weak influence on the lives of British people and two reasons for believing that it continues to be an important influence.

In 20th century Britain, several significant sections of society were denied equality of opportunity. They faced powerful barriers created by stereotypes and prejudices firmly established in our culture. Parents, teachers and employers were influenced by ideas and beliefs which linked aptitude with gender, ethnicity, age and physical capacity. Girls, the children of some **ethnic minorities** and the physically disabled grew up with limited expectations of themselves.

▮ Gender barriers

Case study

Girlification destroys the hope of feminists

❝ *Little girls quickly learn where they belong. The pink disease is far worse than 20 years ago. 'Princess on board' read the yukky signs in family cars. It's almost impossible to buy toys now that are not putridly pink branded or aggressively superhero male. Barbie and Bratz, pink, pink, everywhere. That's before you start on thongs for seven-year-olds and sexy slogans on three-year-olds' T-shirts.*

One study showed how anxiety about appearance harms brain function. Girls were asked to try on a swimsuit or a sweater in a private room, supposedly to give their opinion. While waiting they did a maths test. The girls given swimsuits did much worse than the others as thinking about their bodies undermined their intellectual self-confidence.

At ever younger ages, girls are judged by their appearance. Girlification is worse than it ever was. ❞

Adapted from Polly Toynbee, *The Guardian*, 15 April 2008

Activity

1 Read the case study 'Girlification destroys the hope of feminists'.

a What do you understand by 'girlification'?

b Which agents of socialisation are responsible for subjecting little girls to the 'pink disease'?

c How might playing with her Barbie doll and wearing a 'sexy T-shirt' influence a young girl's view of herself and the world?

d What sort of environment might encourage the development of a less 'girly' femininity?

e Discuss the possible explanations for parents treating their daughters in this way.

Going further

1 Undertake a small-scale piece of research to find out what aspirations young parents have for their children and whether these aspirations differ according to the gender of the child.

Barriers can be created by deliberate favouritism on the part of those able to influence the achievements of others. Such favouritism may result from simple **sexism**, **racism** or **ageism**. It may result from more complicated attitudes and beliefs about what roles are appropriate for women, people in ethnic minorities or old people.

Racist barriers

Case study

Police accused of discrimination against Muslim officers

66 *Chief Constables are accused of blocking an inquiry into discrimination against Muslim officers.*

A letter sent by the National Association of Muslim Police to the Home Secretary says, 'If the police are serious about ensuring that Muslim officers are able to rise through the ranks at the same speed as white officers, and ensuring that Muslims are deployed to counter-terrorism duties we must have reliable data to track progress and measure success…Muslim officers are being overlooked for promotion and are not receiving the training and personal development needed for them to rise through the ranks.'

Some forces do not have a single Muslim working in counter-terrorism or Special Branch and only 32 out of 1600 Superintendents are black or Asian. 99

Adapted from Mark Townsend, *The Observer*, 29 June 2008

Did you know ??????

- In 2007, approximately 31% (1,500,000 individuals) of disabled adults aged between 25 years and retirement age were living in poverty.
- A disabled adult is twice as likely to be living in poverty as a non-disabled adult.

Male graduates earn £1,000 more per annum than female graduates within three years of leaving university.

Activity

2 Read the case study about discrimination against Muslim police officers.

  a What stereotype is likely to have influenced decisions not to appoint Muslim officers to counter-terrorism posts?

  b Why might a candidate from a similar background to those making the appointment have an advantage when applying for a job? Is it possible to ensure that all applicants for a job are treated fairly?

  c What sort of data would be necessary to find the extent to which the police force is racist?

Barriers against people with disabilities

Unsympathetically designed buildings and lack of facilities make it difficult if not impossible for people with disabilities to develop their potential through education and at work.

Activities

3 How accessible for disabled people are the libraries, museums and theatres in your local area?

4 Ask various people how easy it would be, or is, for a physically disabled person to be employed at their place of work.

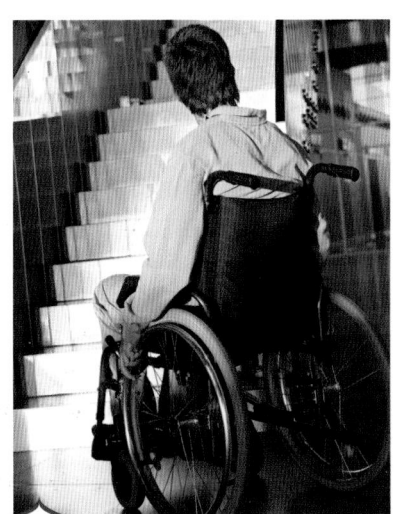

A *No access here for wheelchair users*

Towards equality of opportunity

Government action

Political parties have agreed for many years now that British society should offer equal opportunities to its citizens. Not to do so would be unfair and would waste talent. Governments have, therefore, attempted to remove the barriers limiting achievement:

- The law now forbids decisions relating to the recruitment, promotion and pay of employees to be taken on a sexist or a racist basis.
- Abuse or harassment on the basis of sexuality, gender or ethnicity is now outlawed.
- Educational reforms have been introduced to create a school system that enables children to develop their talents irrespective of gender, ethnicity, physical or mental capacity.
- Programmes have been introduced to help children from families suffering substantial material and cultural deprivation.

Non-governmental action

Dissatisfaction has led those experiencing barriers to create groups through which they can campaign for equality of opportunity and encourage self-confidence and high expectations.

Partly as a result of pressure from campaigners, media images of women, ethnic minorities, the elderly and the disabled have to some extent changed.

The limited effect of the changes

Despite these efforts, equality of opportunity has not been achieved in all areas for the following reasons:

- Governments, not wishing to offend the business interest, are reluctant to impose and enforce strict regulations, which employers attack as being 'red tape'. Many companies who wish to discriminate still do so.
- Women who want to have a family and a job are not always treated fairly by employers. A **glass ceiling** still exists.

Key terms

Glass ceiling: the informal barrier that makes it difficult for women to achieve high-level positions at work.

Gender discrimination: treating people unfairly because of their gender.

Racial discrimination: treating people unfairly because of their ethnicity.

Institutional racism: occurs when the everyday practices and procedures of an organisation, for example, the police, lead to discrimination against ethnic groups either intentionally or unintentionally.

Case study

Gender discrimination

66 *Women managers wishing to work part-time after a baby are seeing their talents and qualifications wasted because they can only find employment well below their skill level. A report suggested 'This loss of career status with part-time work is a stark failure among other encouraging trends for women's advancement. Girls and young women are outperforming males at all educational levels. They are moving into an expanding range of occupations and building successful careers. The gender pay gap is narrowing. But for many this comes to an abrupt halt when children claim part of the working week.'* 99

Adapted from *The Guardian*, 27 February 2008

AQA Examiner's tip

Attitudes and behaviour patterns do not necessarily change very quickly after a law has been passed. Making discrimination illegal, for example, does not immediately end discrimination.

B *Working women: split between full-time and part-time employment*

Status of woman	Percentage full-time	Percentage part-time
Before having children	85	15
With preschool children	34	66
Youngest child at school	41	59
Children no longer dependent	58	42

Economic Journal; NES; LFS

As action is taken to increase the opportunities of some sections of society, the disadvantages of others become more apparent.

Racial discrimination

Case study

66 *Poor white boys are victims too*

*The problems of **racial discrimination** against minorities haven't gone away – black and Asian young men are still up to seven times more likely to be arrested; Pakistani men will earn over a quarter of a million pounds less than their white equivalents over a lifetime; young Bangladeshi women have to settle for jobs for which they are overqualified.*

*But we are confronting for the first time an equality deficit not much mentioned in Parliament – the growing underclass of poor white boys, a forgotten group who face a kind of **institutional racism**.* 99

Adapted from Trevor Phillips, *The Sunday Times*, 27 April 2008

Activity

5 Read the Case study 'Gender discrimination'.

a Which women are most likely to be in part-time work?

b What trends in women's advancement are identified?

c Explain why the job status of many women falls when they become mothers.

d Discuss with your group whether the fact that it is women who give birth will always put them at a disadvantage in the world of work.

Activity

6 Read the Case study 'Racial discrimination'.

a Think of ways in which poor, white boys may be discriminated against.

b List points for and against thinking that poor, white boys suffer 'institutional racism'.

c Explain why the authorities are being slow to recognise the problems faced by poor, white boys.

d Discuss with your group the possible economic, social and political consequences of the underachievement of poor, white boys.

Check your understanding

1 List five ways in which early socialisation might restrict the development of an individual's potential. Use examples relating to gender, ethnicity and physical capacity.

2 Outline three reasons why a disabled adult is more likely than a non-disabled adult to be living in poverty.

3 How does 'social equality' differ from 'equality of opportunity'?

4 Explain briefly why laws promoting equality of opportunity may have a limited effect.

Going further

2 Look at government websites to find out why an Equality Bill (2008) was thought necessary.

3 Look at the website of the Equality and Human Rights Commission to view research findings on unequal opportunities.

4 Discuss with your group whether the present social, political and economic inequalities in British society make the achievement of equality of opportunity impossible.

How is wealth distributed in Britain today?

Wealth distribution

Wealth is distributed very unequally in Britain because:

- Long established inequalities of wealth have never been successfully challenged. Loopholes enable the very rich to avoid taxation.
- Over time, houses, land, shares and fine art tend to increase in value. The gap between those owning such property and those without thus widens.
- In recent years, globalisation has led super-rich non-natives to live in Britain.
- The rewards available in modern sport, entertainment and the financial services industries have led some to accumulate fortunes.

Objectives

You will be able to:

- outline the distribution of income and wealth in Britain
- explain the pattern of distribution
- outline the class structure of modern Britain
- relate the class structure to the pattern of inequality.

Case study

The mega-wealthy in modern Britain

> ❝ *The mega rich have been accumulating fortunes on a scale and at a pace not seen for almost a century. The parties and yachts are ever more lavish: premiership football clubs are being used as toys of the global super-wealthy.*
>
> *Not so long ago a soaring wealth gap would have proved politically unacceptable. But today's wealth explosion has been welcomed across the political spectrum. Tony Blair applauded the rise of the super rich. The wealth boom is defended as a sign of a more entrepreneurial Britain.*
>
> *Twenty years ago the typical Chief Executive of a FTSE 100 company earned some 25 times the pay of the average worker; today it is close to 120 times.*
>
> *Successive attempts to encourage a new enterprise culture would, we were promised, lead to a process of 'trickle down' and, ultimately benefit us all. In fact, the richest 1% have been taking an increasingly disproportionate share of the nation's wealth: 23% today compared with 17% at the end of the 1980s. In contrast, the share going to the bottom half of the population has fallen from 10% to 6%. This is more 'trickle up' than 'trickle down'.* ❞

Adapted from Stewart Lansley, *The Guardian*, 1 April 2006

Key terms

Wealth: the assets owned by an individual, for example, house, savings, a business.

Income: the money received by an individual in a period of time, for example, wages, interest on savings.

A *A day out at Henley Royal Regatta*

Going further

1. Look at the websites of the major political parties. What are their approaches to taxation and the distribution of wealth?

2. Discuss with your group why these parties do not promise to close the 'wealth gap' by setting an upper limit to the wealth that any individual may possess.

Activity

1. Read the case study about wealth in modern Britain.

   a. Why would an increasing 'wealth gap' have been politically unacceptable in the past?

   b. How might 'globalisation' have influenced the approach of politicians to the 'wealth gap'?

   c. What does 'trickle down' mean in the context of the passage?

The distribution of income

Income is distributed unequally in Britain because:

- Wealth is distributed unequally and therefore the income from savings and investments will be distributed unequally.
- Occupations do not offer the same level of income for the following reasons.
  - 'Market forces' operate. Those who have a skill for which there is a high demand are in a strong bargaining position. Those lacking skills or whose skills are not in demand are in a weak bargaining position.
  - Different principles apply to senior executives and to ordinary employees. The pay of the former must be high 'to attract the best talent'. The pay of the latter must be low so that the workers 'do not price themselves out of a job'.
  - The high status and power of some occupations, such as doctors, gives them an advantage when bargaining for pay.
- Some people are dependent on benefits paid by the state. These benefits tend to be low.

British society thus has positions available to its members at many different levels of wealth and income. How individuals are allocated to these positions is of great interest to sociologists.

The family and inequality

Some families have wealth which can:

- be inherited directly by the children
- purchase high quality schooling, either directly by paying fees or by buying a house in the catchment area of a good state school
- fund social activities for their children which allow them to meet with the 'right kind of people'.

Many of the children of wealthy parents thus grow up to occupy the privileged positions which their parents held. The less wealthy a family, the less it is able to insulate their children's future from the effects of external circumstances. These include the lack of appropriate job opportunities for people with less good qualifications.

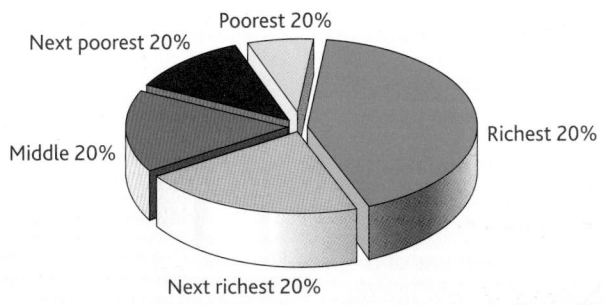

B *Share of national income, 2006/7*

Poorest 20%
Next poorest 20%
Middle 20%
Next richest 20%
Richest 20%

Source: Department of Work and Pensions

links

Also see Topic 2.4 for an outline of the ways in which family circumstances influence educational achievements.

Changes in the class structure

While the gap between rich and poor has increased and people are generally 'better off', the overall pattern of economic inequality in Britain has remained fairly stable during the last 50 years. Some changes have, however, stimulated sociological debate.

Have the working classes changed?

In the late 1950s, some manual workers became able to afford what was seen as a middle-class lifestyle and seemed to be changing their attitudes. Some sociologists claimed that **embourgeoisement** was occurring, creating a manual middle class. Other sociologists demonstrated that the social and political attitudes of these workers differed from those of the traditional middle class. Also, they neither thought of themselves as middle class nor were they thought of as middle class by the middle class. This was a 'new' working class and it is now widely assumed that there exist at least two working classes:

- A 'traditional', largely northern working class employed in old industries and living in working-class communities. This group belongs to trade unions and could be considered 'core' or 'heartland' supporters of the Labour party until 'New' Labour replaced it.

- A 'new', more prosperous, often self-employed, southern, home-owning working class. This group, characterised by journalists as 'Essex' or 'Mondeo' man, lacks deep sentiments of class solidarity and has been prepared to vote Conservative.

Have the middle classes changed?

Some sociologists refer to the **proletarianisation** of a part of the middle class. They suggest that some non-manual jobs created in recent decades have much in common with manual jobs. Call centre workers, for example, work in highly supervised, 'factory-like' conditions and are not superior to manual workers in social status or pay. Differences between the situations of public sector professionals, such as teachers or nurses, and private sector managerial staff are further examples of diversity within the middle class.

> 66 *Up to age 24, the average working-class income is 16 per cent higher than the average middle class income. After age 45, middle class workers earn 54 per cent more than their working-class equivalents.* 99
> *New Middle Britain Report*, research by the Future Foundation for the Liverpool Victoria Friendly Society

The underclass

The existence of a British **underclass** is now taken for granted, although there are disagreements about what it involves. To some, the increase in lone parent families, crime and long-term reliance on state benefits in many deprived areas indicates the development of a 'new rabble' of idlers, content to base their disorganised way of life on welfare dependency.

Did you know ??????

In 1971, 49% of houses were owner occupied; 51% were rented. In 2004, 70% of houses were owner occupied; 30% were rented.

Activities

2 List three reasons why the average working-class income is higher than that of the middle class for the under 24s.

3 List three reasons why the middle-class worker earns more than the average working-class worker after age 45.

Case study

Gang culture

" Britain, where gangs are the only family

An underclass now exists and at its heart gang culture prevails. Because of the collapse of normal household structures among this underclass, the gangs have become an alternative form of family for young members. They live with a string of unreliable and violent stepfathers. Drug taking, alcohol abuse and violence is the norm. The boys have no male role models to display the traditional virtues of stability, fidelity and the work ethic. For many, the gang leader becomes the inspiration, assuming the role of a father figure but with a brutal code. In the midst of this sits rap music, celebrating and exciting the same values. British poverty is not just financial. The poverty is one of spirit, caused by the erosion of all essential standards and structures. **"**

Adapted from an article by Ian Duncan Smith 'Britain, where gangs are the only family',
Daily Mail online

C *Going nowhere*

Activity

4 Read the Case study 'Gang culture'.

a According to the case study, what are the main reasons for the development of this underclass?

b List the elements of the underclass culture mentioned in the extract.

c Explain why teenagers living in the circumstances described are likely to remain members of the underclass.

d Look back at the references to working-class sub-culture in Topic 7.2, page 187. List the ways in which that sub-culture differs from the sub-culture described here.

An alternative approach to the underclass focuses on the disadvantages suffered by particular sections of the working class. Being non-white in a racist society in addition to being working class, for example, can make it difficult to achieve secure, well-paid employment with prospects. Unfamiliarity with British laws and customs makes many recently arrived immigrants vulnerable to exploitation by unscrupulous employers. Some sociologists focus generally on the way in which poor facilities, social attitudes and local scarcity of suitable jobs can effectively exclude some people from society.

Check your understanding

1 Outline three reasons why wealth is distributed unequally in Britain.

2 Explain why skilled workers are likely to earn more money during their working lives than unskilled workers.

3 Outline two reasons for and two reasons against thinking that it is more realistic to refer to 'the working classes' rather than 'the working class' in modern Britain.

4 Outline one reason for seeing the 'underclass' as part of the working class and one reason for seeing it as a section of society distinct from the working class.

Going further

3 By using the Internet, look out for references to the underclass in the media in recent years. Take note in particular of:

■ what kind of people are said to belong to the underclass

■ explanations of the growth of the underclass

■ the ways in which the underclass is seen as a problem

■ the ways in which the problem should be tackled, according to the media

■ the tone of the coverage by the media.

4 Discuss with your group whether British society is having a moral panic over the underclass.

What does it mean to be poor in Britain today?

Absolute poverty

The British public recognise the emaciated African child as suffering poverty (**absolute poverty**). They have often found it more difficult to accept that there is much 'real' poverty in modern Britain. To them the homeless in their cardboard boxes and the elderly forced to choose between eating and keeping warm seem exceptions, the result of particular circumstances.

Relative poverty

Poverty is a useful idea to sociologists because it draws attention to the great material inequality in our society and to the differences between the lifestyles of its richer and poorer members. **Relative poverty** recognises the deprivation and suffering associated with **social exclusion**. Members of human societies are not mere biological machines. They have social needs. Being unable to do and have those things which constitute a 'normal' life is a source of deprivation. For the grandfather who goes without food to afford a little toy for his granddaughter's birthday, the pain of hunger is less than that of not being able to do what granddads do.

How to draw the poverty line

It is not easy to measure relative poverty. One method, often used to make official estimates, is to draw the line at 60 per cent of the national average income. This figure is, however, arbitrary: why not 55 per cent or 65 per cent?

A more sociological method is to identify what people generally consider to be the essentials of a 'normal' life in Britain today. The cost of purchasing these agreed essentials can be used as the poverty line.

Case study

The Minimum Income Standard

In 2008 the Joseph Rowntree Foundation published the results of a major research project designed to establish such a line. The study investigated the opinions of a wide sample of the British public, including members from all types of household and different income backgrounds. They were asked to identify the minimum that people need 'in order to have the opportunities and choices necessary to participate in society' today. The findings indicated that 'most families with one person working full time but relying only on the minimum wage would be unable to reach the minimum acceptable standard of living'.

Household type	pensioner couple	lone parent + child
Amount received	105%	68%

Joseph Rowntree Foundation

A *Amount received in income support and pension credit as a percentage of the Minimum Income Standard*

Objectives

You will be able to:

- define poverty
- outline ways in which poverty is measured
- identify different types of deprivation
- explain the contexts in which poverty is experienced
- explain the significance of poverty for those experiencing it.

Key terms

Absolute poverty: a situation in which someone lacks the money to pay for the food, clothing and housing necessary to maintain a healthy way of life.

Relative poverty: a situation in which someone cannot afford to possess the kind of things and participate in the kind of activities considered by members of their society to be a normal part of life.

Social exclusion: when people are unable, or feel unable, to play a full part in society. This may be owing to lack of material resources, discrimination by others and/or a sense that the rest of society neither wants nor respects them.

Environmental poverty: deprivation experienced in neighbourhoods that are ugly, dirty, unsafe and which lack adequate services and amenities.

Relative deprivation: felt when people compare their own situation to that of others whom they believe to be unfairly better off.

Activities

1. Does income support enable the lone parent with one child to reach the Minimum Income Standard?

2. What is the difference between a social 'need' and a 'want'?

Going further

1. Think of how ordinary people live in Britain today.
   - What possessions do they have?
   - What do they eat and drink?
   - What facilities do their houses have?
   - What do they do in their free time?
   - What spending is involved in their social relationships?

2. Make a list of 25 'things' that an individual needs to have or do to be part of this lifestyle.

3. Compare your list with others in your group. What level of agreement is there?

4. Look at the Joseph Rowntree Foundation website and compare their findings with those of your group.

B *Making the best of it*

▨ Other poverties

'Poverty' is used in various contexts to indicate 'lack of'. Some people, for example, have claimed that modern secular, consumer societies suffer from 'spiritual poverty'. Others have suggested that people who rely on the mass media for information and entertainment suffer from 'cultural poverty'.

Sociologists have drawn attention to the significance of the quality of the environment for people's sense of wellbeing. All but the housebound spend time in public spaces, meeting friends, taking children to the playground, shopping and so on. **Environmental poverty** suggests public spaces that are ugly, inconvenient and unsafe. Many poor people suffer the discomfort of living in neighbourhoods with such characteristics.

Subjective poverty

Whether an individual feels deprived does not depend simply on his or her level of income. People compare their situation with that of others. Despite being 'well off', an individual can feel deprived if he or she identifies with a group, most of whom are even better off. A poor person may not feel deprived when looking at a photograph of his or her parents who were even poorer. Sociologists recognise this in the concept of **relative deprivation**. The ways in which the poor view their poverty is complex. An individual may or may not believe his or her poverty is deserved, may or may not be angry about the poverty, may or may not try to escape it.

> **Did you know** ???????
>
> In 2006/7, approximately 40% of pensioner households (1,500,000 people) entitled to pension credit did not claim it.

The experience of poverty in Britain today

The experience of poverty will be influenced by:

- **Its duration**

  Being poor for a long time adds the problems of being poor to those which led the individuals or families into poverty in the first place. Illness, separation from people not in poverty, the **poverty trap** and loss of self-confidence are all likely consequences.

- **Its location**

  People can be poor in a city or in a village. The problems and advantages of living among other poor people on a city estate can be quite different from those experienced by the only poor family in a village.

- **The attitude of the non-poor**

  Some of the poor are seen as victims of circumstance and attract public sympathy. Many are seen as **welfare scroungers**.

> 66 *David Cameron tells the fat and the poor: take responsibility*
>
> *David Cameron declared that some people who are poor, fat or addicted to alcohol have only themselves to blame. He said that society had been too sensitive in failing to judge the behaviour of others as good or bad, right or wrong, and that it was time for him to speak out against 'moral neutrality'. 'We talk about people being "at risk of obesity" instead of talking about people who eat too much and take too little exercise,' he said. 'We talk about people being at risk of poverty. It's as if these things are purely external events like a plague or bad weather. Of course, where you were born, your neighbourhood, your school and the choices your parents make have a huge impact. But social problems are often the consequence of the choices people make.* 99
>
> Adapted from David Cameron, *The Times*, 8 July 2008

C *Where are people more likely to feel their poverty most?*

Activities

3 What factors does David Cameron point to as having a bearing on whether people are poor or not?

4 What is meant by 'moral neutrality'?

5 Outline the arguments for and against sociologists being 'morally neutral' when they discuss issues such as poverty.

Did you know ??????

In 2007, in 60 neighbourhoods in Britain, over half of the adults were unemployed and receiving benefits.

Although sociologists often present impersonal statistics, they recognise that each poor person has a unique history which makes his or her experience of poverty different from that of everyone else.

Did you know ??????

In 2005/6:

- 1 in 6 people in rural districts lived in poverty
- 1 in 4 people in urban districts lived in poverty.

Case study

Poverty among the young and the old

The young

Jodie and her two daughters live on income support and find it difficult. 'It feels like I'm living on the breadline. It feels like I'm not giving my children what I had. I don't struggle getting enough food on their plates – but I can't take them to nice places like the zoo.'

Jodie is dreading the girls going to school. 'I am thinking of school uniforms, shoes, school meals. I am scared of them seeing all the other kids whose parents have got more and feeling left out. My Nan helps with their clothes. If not I go to places like Primark where it's cheap.'

The old

Pensioners Sylvia, Dorothy and Jean agree that rises in the cost of heating, fruit and veg, and presents for their grandchildren and great-grandchildren have started to wreck their frail finances.

'I've saved a bit but that'll disappear quickly at this rate' says Sylvia. 'It's lucky for me I learned how to scrimp and save and make do in the war.'

'What do you do when everything is going up except our pensions?' says Jean.

All three women survive through an unofficial economy – the unpaid, unstinting work of their families. 'What would it be like if we didn't have them to help?' wonders Sylvia, 'or people like Bramley Elderly Action.

Both extracts adapted from Audrey Gillan, *The Guardian*, 11 June 2008

AQA *Examiner's tip*

Recognise that the situation of the poor may be influenced by general changes in the British economy. A rise in fuel or food prices, for example, may have a more damaging impact on the poor than on other people.

Activity

6   Read both extracts in the case study.

a   In the first extract, what indicates that Jodie and her children are not suffering absolute poverty?

b   What two comparisons does Jodie make when talking about her poverty?

c   In the second extract, what past experience helps Sylvia to cope with life on a limited income?

Jodie's poverty links her to other poor people in other parts of the world:

" *Primark sacked 3 of its suppliers after an investigation uncovered children in Indian refugee camps producing some of its cheapest garments.* "

The Observer, 22 June 2008

Check your understanding

1   Outline one way of drawing a relative poverty line.

2   Explain briefly why an individual with an income above the poverty line may feel relatively deprived.

3   Outline three ways in which the experience of being poor in a city may differ from being poor in a village.

4   Outline three ways in which the issues raised by being poor are likely to be different and three ways likely to be similar for an 80-year-old single man and a 20-year-old single mother.

Going further

5   View the websites of voluntary organisations that help vulnerable groups at risk of poverty, for example, ex-offenders, the mentally ill, lone parents, the physically disabled, illegally trafficked workers.

6   Record any case studies that show how individuals fall into and experience poverty.

7   Compare notes with others in your group.

What does social research tell us about social stratification in contemporary Britain?

Sociologists often debate the process by which those born into a poor family become and remain poor adults. This is the **cycle of deprivation**.

 ## Language and disadvantage

A key ingredient in determining future class is language.

Meaningful Differences in the Everyday Experiences of Young American Children is one of the most thorough studies ever conducted. Three groups of children were tape recorded throughout their first years –welfare families, working-class families and professional families. With painstaking care, researchers counted then extrapolated all the words a child would hear and speak in every encounter with its parent or caregiver. When they analysed the hours of recordings, the sharp class differences were startling.

By the age of four, a professional's child will have had 50 million words addressed to it, a working-class child 30 million and a welfare child just 12 million. The professional child at the age of three had a bigger vocabulary than the parent of the welfare child. The way children were spoken to was also measured, how much they were listened to, explained things, given choices and in what tone of voice. At the age of three the professional child has had 700,000 encouragements addressed to it and only some 80,000 discouragements. But the welfare child will only ever have been encouraged 60,000 times in its life, suffering twice as many discouragements. The working-class child is between the two.

When the children in the study were measured at aged nine to ten, the authors conclude: 'We were awestruck at how well our measures of accomplishments at three predicted language skill at nine to ten'. In other words school had added little value after the age of three: it was already too late.

Adapted from Polly Toynbee, *The Guardian*, 2 January 2004

Check your understanding

1 To what extent is research undertaken in the USA on this kind of topic likely to be relevant in Britain?

2 What does 'the researchers counted then extrapolated all the words' mean? Explain why they did this.

3 Under what kind of conditions is research into children under three years old ethical?

Education and social mobility

Class and social mobility are issues for politicians. They like to think that government action on education and the Welfare State, for example, has helped to create a modern society in which opportunities are equal for all and that talent is not wasted.

The education boom has proved a curse for the poor

'I want to see a Britain that is far more upwardly mobile', said Gordon Brown. On the day he spoke, the nation's social mobility experts assembled at the London School of Economics. Top economists and sociologists arrived at the same devastating conclusion: education has done virtually nothing to improve social mobility. Worse still, as a greater number of people gain more qualifications the less socially mobile the country has become.

This is not what most people might expect. Education, however, is not, and never was, the prime motor for upward mobility. The only time there was a burst of people moving from working-class backgrounds to middle-class employment was in the 1950s and 60s with a sudden increase in **white collar** jobs. Educated or not – most left school with no qualifications – people were sucked upwards by a changed labour market. A third of children from working-class backgrounds joined the home-owning white-collar classes.

And then it stopped. Worse still, the shrinking of many traditional industries in the 1980s brought the catastrophic downward mobility of the skilled working class, their de-skilled children destined to earn far less. Meanwhile, the great growth in universities has become an agent to fix children of the big new middle class into their parents' status more securely than before, while only a few more working-class children get degrees. In the 1960s bright school leavers at 16 could work their way up. Now lack of qualifications keeps them in their place as graduates from better backgrounds seize that job instead. Of course nothing is certain, some make it against the odds.

The countries with the most social mobility also have most income and wealth equality, but they never set out to pursue social mobility; fairness is their aim, and mobility a result over many years. Good education is a channel of mobility, but its source is a fairer share in the first place. If education is the prime motor, why hasn't social mobility risen in these decades of vastly increased qualifications?

Adapted from Polly Toynbee, *The Guardian*, 5 July 2008

Check your understanding

1   What is meant by social mobility?

2   What led to the 'burst' of social mobility in the 1950s and 1960s?

3   Why did the industrial decline of the 1980s lead to downward mobility of the skilled working class?

4   Which social class has benefited most from the expansion of university education?

5   Explain why the expansion of university education might reduce the chances of upward mobility for working-class children?

Key terms

White collar: clerical, routine middle class.

AQA Examiner's tip

Remember to mention downward social mobility when discussing 'equality of opportunity'. It is a better measure of the 'openness' of British society than is upward mobility.

Going further

Conduct a simple piece of research with other members of your group to get a general idea of how much social mobility has occurred in recent years.

4   Each member of the group should find out, where possible, what were the occupations of their relatives at age 35. Try to find this out for each of the following: mother, father, grandmother, grandfather, great-grandmother and great-grandfather.

5   Discuss which occupational scale you should use to rank the occupations, and then measure the mobility that has taken place.

6   Put the results for the whole group together and discuss whether any general conclusions can be drawn from any resulting pattern.

Exam question guidance

Example of a source-based question

∞ links
See the Exam question guidance section in Topic 1.8 on page 38 for general advice on answering source-based questions.

Item A

Child poverty

In order to measure the extent of child poverty in the United Kingdom, the term 'poverty' must be defined. Children are said to be in poverty when they live in households with less than 60% of average household income. In 1998, there were 4.1 million children living in poverty; by 2005 the number was 3.6 million.

Adapted from an article in *The Guardian*, 3 March 2008

- **Who?** This source is taken from a newspaper article published in *The Guardian* newspaper, a liberal broadsheet with a long tradition of championing social reform.
- **What?** The level of child poverty has been of particular concern to recent New Labour governments. They have introduced a number of policies designed to reduce the level of child poverty and while these have enjoyed some success, the level of child poverty remains distressingly high.
- **Why?** Sociologists are interested in the ways in which poverty can be defined and measured. They are also concerned with the underlying structural causes of poverty in our society. The source suggests a definition of poverty based on a household's average annual income. It also quotes a number of statistics, presumably based on government data.

a   From **Item A**, how many children were living in poverty in the UK in 2005?   *(1 mark)*

Answer as briefly as possible. In this case the answer is 3.6 million.

Example of a 2-mark question

c   Identify **two** ways in which governments have attempted to reduce inequalities between men and women in Britain during the last 50 years.   *(2 marks)*

The examiners want you to demonstrate your knowledge of equal opportunities laws dating back to the 1970s, and/or some of the subsequent changes in social policy, for example, laws that have promoted equal pay and equal opportunities. The time frame is a catch-all. You are not expected to write a history of women's fight for equality. Also the examiner does not expect you to go back beyond the time frame and discuss suffragettes who fought to gain the vote for women.

co links

See the Exam question guidance
section in Topic 2.7 on page 67
for general advice on answering
extended-answer questions.

Extended answer questions

g   Discuss how far would sociologists agree that children born into poverty will grow
       up to be poor throughout their lives?   *(12 marks)*

The examiner would expect you to be aware of current debates about
welfare reform and social provision. You would not be expected to
have a detailed knowledge of the social security system or changes in
the law. However, you will be expected to have an overview of social
policy and of attempts to reduce the level of child poverty in the UK.
You will also be expected to have an understanding of some of the key
sociological ideas about poverty.

The question clearly raises the issue of **extent. How far** would
sociologists agree that a child born into poverty is destined to remain
poor? There are a number of important sociological ideas that are
relevant to your answer:

- the **cycle of poverty.** This is the idea that poverty can be inherited
  from one generation to the next. The basic idea is that the child
  of poor parents will grow up with a number of disadvantages
  that might, for example, prevent them from achieving good
  qualifications at school. This lack of qualifications would then
  condemn the child to an adult life of low paid and insecure
  employment. It is likely that they will marry someone from a similar
  social background and when they have children the pattern of the
  parents' lives will be repeated.

- the **culture of poverty.** This is the idea that people who grow up
  in poverty come to accept their lot in life. They are less likely to
  become politically involved, to join a trade union or to seek to
  better themselves through adult education. This is because they lack
  the motivation to do so. Life is hard and short and they accept that
  it will be so. They live for the moment and transmit these values
  to their children (a link with the cycle of poverty). This idea is
  sometimes used to blame the poor for their poverty. The argument
  is made that if only poor people were less apathetic they could
  better themselves through hard work.

To break the cycle of poverty it is necessary to ensure that the children
of poor families are not disadvantaged at school or in further or higher
education. Recent government initiatives to increase educational
opportunities and to support poor families have had a positive effect on
individual lives. However, the continuing high levels of child poverty
would seem to indicate that the causes are deeper rooted. The causes
of poverty cannot be easily resolved by simply reforming the education
system or updating the welfare system.

Remember to avoid the trap of only referring to the sources in the
question. The examiner wants to see evidence that you have studied
the sociology of inequality *and* thought about the issues.

■ Questions to try

What follows are examples of the types of questions you will meet in your exam. The letter in each question matches the letter that will be used for that type of question on your exam paper. The number in brackets is only there to help you and your teacher refer to that particular question in this book.

Item B

Researchers from Warwick University have uncovered evidence that teachers are routinely underestimating the abilities of some black Caribbean pupils, suggesting that assumptions about behavioural problems are overshadowing their academic talents. The findings are based on a survey that tracked 15,000 pupils through their education. The research examined the profile of pupils entered by teachers to take higher tier test papers in Maths and Science tests at 14. White pupils are significantly more likely to be entered for the higher tier papers than their black Caribbean, Pakistani and black African and Bangladeshi classmates. Most of the differences are explained by previous results or other factors which might have put them at a disadvantage. But for a significant proportion of black Caribbean pupils there was no academic explanation.

Adapted from *The Guardian*, September 2008

a	From **Item B**, which group of pupils are most likely to be entered for higher tier test papers at 14?	*(1 mark)*
d(1)	Explain what sociologists mean by relative poverty.	*(4 marks)*
d(2)	Explain what sociologists mean by the glass ceiling.	*(4 marks)*
d(3)	Explain what sociologists mean by ageism.	*(4 marks)*
e	Describe **one** way in which sociologists have tried to measure poverty and explain why this method might not be accurate.	*(5 marks)*
g(1)	Discuss how far sociologists would agree that social mobility has become less common in Britain.	*(12 marks)*
g(2)	Discuss how far sociologists would agree that the Welfare State has been successful in reducing poverty in Britain.	*(12 marks)*

■ Revision Advice – Full Course

AQA GCSE Sociology is divided into two elements: the first is the **Short Course** (Paper 1) as detailed earlier and the second is the **Full Course** (Paper 2):

Written paper – 1 hour 30 minutes

Covers 50 per cent of Full Course

90 marks available

In order to complete the **full** GCSE course, you must answer questions based on **three** out of the **four** remaining modules in Unit 2: Crime and Deviance, Mass Media, Power, Social Inequality. However, you are strongly advised to cover **all** the subject content. The key ideas in sociology are linked and if you fail to cover one of the remaining modules you may find yourself confronted by a question you are not well prepared for.

The examiner wants you to demonstrate your understanding of the 'big picture'. For example, in Unit 1 you will have been introduced to the various approaches that sociologists have used in their attempt to understand our society. You will have studied aspects of family life and the education system. That does not mean that you can now forget about methodological issues or dismiss these social structures and processes and move on. A question on crime and deviance, power or social inequality may well make demands on your understanding of the education system or of the dynamics of family life, while a question on the mass media might raise issues about social research.

You will already have met a very similar pattern of questions in the Short Course: source material, short answer questions, paragraph answer questions and extended answer (essay style) questions.

Use a copy of the specification as a revision **check list** and follow the general principles established in the Short Course revision advice. Depending on your understanding highlight the content red, orange or green. The red list is your priority for revision.

Top tips:

▯ When the specification says that 'candidates should be aware' it means that you should know something about these issues *and* be prepared to **discuss** them in your answers.

▯ When the specification says that that 'candidates should be able to distinguish' it means that you should know the **difference** between one thing and another.

You must revise the key ideas contained in this book **well before** you enter the examination room. Be **active**, make lists, draw up spider diagrams that show how ideas link up and use the examination style questions at the end of each chapter to practise writing answers. Compare your work with that of other students. Make constructive and helpful comment on the strengths and weaknesses of fellow students' answers and they should do the same for you.

Recommended websites

Website addresses change and websites come and go. If all else fails simply type 'GCSE Sociology revision' into the search engine of your choice and see what comes up! However, the following sites may be useful to you:

A web portal hosted by the University of Leicester with lots of useful links:

www.le.ac.uk/education/centres/ATSS/sites.html

A website hosted by the University of Hull with information on how to construct spider diagrams.

www.hull.ac.uk/disability/downloads/dysnotehowtomindmap.pdf

The principles of drawing a spider diagram are very simple: start with a strong central idea and see where it takes you. Like most things, the more you practise the better you get.

Glossary

A

Absolute poverty: a situation in which someone lacks the money to pay for the food, clothing and housing necessary to maintain a healthy way of life.

Achieved status: a social position which individuals are able to gain through, for example, hard work and/or educational qualifications.

Ageism: being prejudiced against people because of their age.

Agency of social change: influencing social attitudes and government policy.

Agent of social control: individual or group that is responsible for ensuring members of society conform to socially acceptable behaviour.

Alienated: lacking connection with the social world.

Alienation: expresses the idea of separation. A sense of powerlessness is part of alienation. At work an employee may have no power to decide how a job will be done or how quickly to work. A citizen may feel powerless to influence the government.

Anomie: a situation where large numbers of people fail to follow generally accepted values, instead adopting various deviant forms of behaviour, such as theft.

Anonymity: making sure that no names are mentioned in your finished report or in the data collection process.

Anti-school sub-culture: these are formed because pupils feel that they are not valued by the school or because they do not identify with the value system and the goals of the school.

Arranged marriage: a marriage in which the parents have a say in the choice of a bride or bridegroom for their son or daughter.

ASBO (Anti-Social Behaviour Order): an order made by the courts against a person who has been shown to have engaged in anti social behaviour, for example, drinking on·the streets.

Ascribed status: a position or social standing given to an individual on the basis of inherited characteristics.

Authority: the power of those entitled to use it.

B

Bias: not taking a neutral view but favouring one side of an argument or debate.

Bigamy: the illegal practice in a monogamous society of having more than one spouse.

Blog: web-based comment by both amateurs and professional writers (from the word 'weblog').

Breadwinner: the person in the household who is the main income earner.

British Crime Survey (BCS): a victim survey conducted annually by a team of researchers at the Home Office. The BCS measures the amount of crime in England and Wales by asking people about crimes they have experienced in the last year.

C

Canalisation: being channelled in a particular direction.

Capitalism: industry and services are owned by private individuals who gain their profits from the labour power of their workers.

Capitalist society: an economic system where the production of goods is organised for profit and sold to a free market.

Caste: a rigid system of stratification in which an individual cannot move from the caste into which he or she was born.

CCTV (Closed-circuit television): a television system often used for surveillance.

Censorship: preventing certain information from becoming public knowledge.

Census: a survey of all people and households in the country, held every 10 years (UK).

Cereal packet family: the traditional image of the nuclear family presented through the media involving clearly defined male and female roles.

Chivalry thesis: the belief that the police and courts, because they are male dominated, are easier on women.

Chronic: a continuous problem that extends over a period of time.

Citizen: a full, legal member of a nation.

Class alignment: suggests a connection between voters' class positions and their voting preferences.

Class de-alignment: suggests a weakening of the connection between class position and voting preference.

Cohabiting: partners living together without being married.

Commune: a small community whose members share in the ownership of property and the division of labour.

Community service: a service that a person performs for the benefit of his or her local community in place of a prison sentence.

Community: a set of individuals between whom there is a strong sense of identity. The individuals may or may not live in the same locality.

Confidentiality: keeping personal details between you and the respondent.

Conflict: a general state of disagreement between opposing groups.

Conformity: doing what is expected and behaving in a way that is in agreement with norms.

Conjugal bond: the attachment that exists between marriage partners.

Consensus (non-political): a general state of agreement between individuals or groups.

Consensus (political): a situation in which those involved in government, of whatever party, share similar ideas about what governments should do.

Conservatives: see radical change as dangerous and suggest that governments should reform institutions only when a clear need to do so has been established.

Constituency: the geographical area which elects a single MP.

Constraint: not being able to do what you want; being restricted or limited.

Covert observation: the researcher is 'undercover' and the group is not aware of the fact they are being observed.

Crime: behaviour that breaks the law.

Crisis of masculinity: the idea that men's perception of what a man is and how he ought to behave has been undermined by social and economic changes.

Cultural capital: the desired skills, for example, language which middle classes pass on to their children.

Culture of simulation: a virtual world that becomes more important to the individual than their day-to-day lived experience (see Hyperreality).

Culture: the whole way of life of a group of people passed from one generation to the next.

Cumulative effect: long periods of exposure to particular media messages.

Cycle of deprivation: a social process which may lead the children of poor parents to suffer poverty when adults. The factors identified as driving the process will depend on the perspective of the sociologist outlining the cycle.

D

Dark figure of crime: a large amount of criminal activity never appears in the crime statistics.

Decree absolute: this is the legal ending of the marriage. Once this has been granted, your marriage has been dissolved and you are legally single.

Deferential: an attitude based on the belief that people high on the social scale are superior and should be looked up to.

Democracy: the political system that enables the people to elect periodically those who will govern them.

Dependent child: a person living in the household who is under 16 years of age or aged between 16 and 18 but in full-time education.

De-schooling: the idea that schools should be abolished because the compulsory nature of schools hinders the learning process.

Deviance: behaviour that does not conform to the dominant norms of a specific society.

Deviancy amplification: the process whereby the mass media can exaggerate the significance of a particular social issue.

Dictatorship: a political system in which power is concentrated in the hands of an individual or small group who have not been freely and fairly elected.

Diploma: qualification for 14–19-year-olds introduced as a pilot in 2008 with up to 10 subjects to choose from.

Direct action: political action, sometimes illegal, taken outside the normal political process.

Divorce: the legal ending of a marriage.

Divorce petition: the formal request to start divorce proceedings.

Domestic division of labour: how household tasks are divided between family members.

E

Education Action Zones (EAZs): are built around groups of schools that are determined to raise educational standards in the most challenging areas in the UK.

Educational Maintenance Allowance (EMA): money paid directly to students who stay on in education after the age of 16. The amount received depends on parents' income.

Egalitarian: the idea that all are equal.

Eleven plus: a type of intelligence test taken at age 11 to determine whether a child should attend a grammar school, a technical school or a secondary modern.

Elite: a small dominant group (that may own and control the mass media).

Embourgeoisement: the proposition that members of the working class develop middle-class attitudes and patterns of behaviour as they become more affluent.

Empty shell marriage: when a couple are still married and live in the same house but lead separate lives.

Environmental poverty: deprivation experienced in neighbourhoods that are ugly, dirty, unsafe and which lack adequate services and amenities.

Ethical considerations: making sure that your research is not offending or harming anyone – that you are doing the right thing.

Ethnicity: the classification of people into groups that share the same culture, history and identity.

Ethnic minority: an identifiable section of society with a distinct culture which constitutes a relatively small proportion of the population.

Ethnocentric curriculum: schools are structured in a particular way including such aspects as school assemblies, history and language which reflect the culture of the majority.

Ethnography: looking at the whole way of life of a group, usually by using a variety of methods of data collection.

Excellence in Cities (EiC): the Excellence in Cities programme, launched in March 1999, made a unique contribution to the raising of attainment of disadvantaged pupils in our most deprived cities, towns, and rural areas.

Extended family: a family composed of the nuclear family and other relatives.

F

Family: a group of two or more persons associated by birth, cohabitation, marriage, or adoption.

Family diversity: the idea that there are many different types of family structure.

Female infanticide: the intentional killing of baby girls due to the preference for male babies.

Feminist: someone who believes that women should have the same status and opportunities as men.

Financial dependency: relying upon someone else for money.

'First past the post': the voting system in which the candidate who gains more votes than any of his or her rivals in a constituency is chosen to be the MP.

Focus group: opinions of a small group are recorded and taken into account when decisions are made.

Formal curriculum: what students learn in their timetabled lessons, for example, maths and English.

Formal education: learning particular subjects, for example, maths, English, in organised institutions (schools).

Freedom of speech: the democratic principle that protects legitimate comment regarding the actions of the government or matters of public interest.

Functionalism: an approach in sociology that seeks to explain the existence of social structures by the role they perform for society as a whole.

Functionalists: argue that the function of institutions such as education is to reproduce culture by socialising individuals into the key values and roles required for social stability.

G

Gatekeeper (media): one who has editorial control over media content.

Gatekeeper (research): someone who gives permission for others to be involved in your research.

GCSE (General Certificate in Secondary Education): national examinations taken at the age of 16.

Gender: the social and cultural differences between the sexes – between femininity and masculinity.

Gender discrimination: treating people unfairly because of their gender.

Generalisations: feeling confident that your findings will reflect the views of everyone else who could have been asked.

Generation: a group of people who live during the same time period.

Geographical proximity: not being far away.

Glass ceiling: the informal barrier that makes it difficult for women to achieve high-level positions at work.

Global culture: the idea that many cultural values (generally Western and often American) are now shared by people across the world.

Globalisation: a process through which people, organisations and states become increasingly interdependent, both economically and culturally.

Grounds for divorce: the legal reasons given for wanting a divorce.

H

Hidden curriculum: the ways in which the organisation of teaching, school regulations and routines shape pupil attitude and behaviour, that is, what students learn at school that is not taught in lessons.

Household: all the people living together in a domestic dwelling.

Hyperreality: an alternative reality based on the individual's experience of the mass media – particularly television and the Internet.

I

Identity theft: the misappropriation of the identity (such as the name, date of birth, current address or previous addresses) of another person, without their knowledge or consent. These identity details are then used to obtain goods and services in that person's name.

Image: the identity that individuals wish to present to the world, for example, the media image of a particular politician as young and dynamic.

Income: the money received by an individual in a period of time, for example, wages, interest on savings.

Indictable offences: serious crimes, generally those for which an accused person may be sent to prison if found guilty.

Industrial disputes: disagreements between management and workforce, often leading to workers going on strike.

Informal education: occurs through observing what goes on around us, through experiences of life.

Information overload: the enormous volume of modern electronic communications (sometimes more than an individual can cope with).

Informed consent: making sure that your respondents know what you are doing and agree to participate.

Injustice: when a person is accused of a crime of which they are not guilty.

Institutional racism: occurs when the everyday practices and procedures of an organisation, for example, the police, lead to discrimination against ethnic groups either intentionally or unintentionally.

Integrated conjugal roles: husband and wife perform similar tasks and have a number of common interests and activities.

Interest groups: groups established to protect a sectional interest.

Intergenerational: between or across generations.

Internet: a global system of interconnected computers.

J

Judiciary: the section of the government that has the power to apply the law, that is, the court system including judges.

Junk mail: the postal equivalent of SPAM.

K

Kibbutz: a collective community in Israel (plural Kibbutzim).

L

Labelling: names/labels given to individuals by teachers (and others, for example, police) which then influences the behaviour of those individuals and also influences the way others respond to those individuals.

Ladette: young woman who behaves in a boisterously assertive or crude manner and engages in heavy drinking sessions.

Lads' magazine: publication aimed at a young male readership often containing images of women as sex objects.

Law: a set of written rules regulating what may or may not be done by members of a society.

League tables: lists produced by the government indicating the position of each school in comparison to others depending on their exam performance.

Legislature: the section of the government that is responsible for making laws.

Liberal democratic values: the dominant political and social values of western society, for example, freedom of speech and free elections.

Life chances: the chances that sections of society have of achieving the 'things' which are valued by their society.

Life expectancy: the age to which a person can be expected to live. Current UK figures are: male: 76.6; female: 81.

Lifestyle: the way in which members of a group use their resources. Lifestyle will reflect the attitudes and priorities of the group.

Longitudinal studies: studies that follow the same people over a long period of time.

M

Mainframe computer: large, room-sized early computers that stored data using reel-to-reel magnetic tape.

Malestream: a word occasionally used by feminists to mean 'mainstream', thereby drawing attention to the gender bias of much language.

Marketisation of education: changes to the education system in the late 1980s, so that it became more business-like.

Marriage: a legally recognised union of a man and a woman by religious or civil ceremony.

Marxist: someone who believes in the ideas of Karl Marx and sees the main divisions in society as being based on social class operating in a capitalist system.

Mass communication: reaching an audience of thousands or perhaps millions.

Mass culture: the transmission of cultural values through mass media of communication, for example, television.

Matrifocal: a family organised by and focused on the mother.

Means tested: income and savings assessed to find out if the total is less than a level set by the government.

Media amplification: blowing things out of proportion by over-reporting in the media.

Media imperialism: the idea that Western cultural values are imposed by a dominant media empire (swamping local cultures that lack the resources to match the volume of media output from countries like the US).

Media stereotype: simple media image based on prejudice.

Member of Parliament (MP): the person elected to represent a constituency in the House of Commons.

Meritocracy: a social system in which rewards are allocated justly on the basis of merit rather than factors such as class, gender, ethnicity.

Middle class: the section of society composed of people engaged in non-manual and professional work.

Mixed ability: pupils of all ability levels are taught as one group.

Modernity: relating to the modern world.

Monarchy: the political system that has a hereditary Head of State. Britain is a constitutional monarchy in which the monarch's powers are exercised by the Prime Minister.

Monogamy: the practice of being married to only one person at a time.

Moral panic: when media coverage of an issue leads to exaggerated public concern.

N

Nation state: an independent state whose inhabitants form a single national community.

National Census: a survey conducted on behalf of the government. Data that is collected from every household in the country provides detailed information about our way of life.

National Curriculum: subjects and subject content that must be studied by all children in state schools in an attempt to standardise educational provision.

Neo-conventional families: the new nuclear family headed by a married or cohabiting couple who are both working.

Neo-liberalism: a political approach based on the belief that governments should limit their activity to maintaining 'law and order'. In particular, governments should not interfere with market forces in the economy.

New media: computerised communications technology.

New social movement: an informal, loosely organised coalition of individuals or groups supporting an interest or cause.

New vocationalism: training aimed to equip the young with the skills and education required by a rapidly changing economy.

News value: the importance attached to a particular news item.

Non-indictable offences: less serious crimes such as parking offences.

Non-participant observation: researcher watches and records what is happening but is not involved in the group's activities.

Norm: an informal rule that guides our behaviour in a particular situation.

Norms and expectations: generally accepted and expected patterns of behaviour in a particular society.

Nuclear family: a family group consisting of the father, mother, and their dependent children.

O

Observation: researcher watches a group of people and records information, either as a participant or a non-participant and either overt or covert.

Ofcom: the independent regulator and competition authority for the UK communications industries.

Official crime statistics: the way crime is officially measured, based on statistics collected by the Home Office.

Official statistics: a set of statistics generated from data gathered by the government or other official organisations. Often used as secondary data in social research.

Ofsted (Office for Standards in Education): the government agency given the task of monitoring the quality of schools and teachers in the UK.

'Old' Labour: sees its main aim as protecting the interests of working people. Its approach to politics is based on working-class values such as solidarity.

Old media: print media and electronic communications developed during the mid-20th century or earlier.

Open question: requires a descriptive answer, not just 'yes' or 'no' for example.

Opportunistic sample: a technique that involves the researcher giving their questions to anyone who happens to be available. This means it is not a particularly representative type of sampling.

Opposition: the main party that is not in government.

Overt observation: the group being observed know why the researcher is there and what they are doing there.

P

Participant observation: researcher is actively involved in the group's activities as well as making a record of what they see.

Patriarchal: a situation where men dominate society and its institutions.

Patriarchy: the idea that men dominate society and its institutions.

Peer group pressure: a group of a person's own age who are important to them and often influence them to behave in a particular way.

Pilot study: a study on a small scale before the main research is done.

Pluralism: theories about the mass media that see variety and competition as healthy signs of a working democracy.

Police: agents of social control with the power to enforce the law.

Police caution: an alternative to prosecution. It is intended to act as an official warning to deter people from getting involved in further crime.

Political party: an organisation established to secure the election of its members or supporters into public office.

Political socialisation: the process by which people learn political skills, beliefs and values.

Polyandry: the accepted practice in some socities of a woman having more than one husband.

Polygamy: the accepted practice in some socities of having more than one spouse.

Polygyny: the accepted practice in some socities of a man having more than one wife.

Poverty: means being poor (but this can be defined in many different ways).

Poverty trap: the particular difficulties the poor may experience in, for example, finding a job that pays more than is received from benefits;

saving money by buying in bulk or by buying high quality goods; avoiding borrowing which adds interest payments to their spending.

Pressure group: a group, usually concerned with a single issue, that applies pressure to try to bring about change. (Some pressure groups protect sectional interests; others promote causes. Unlike political parties, pressure groups do not wish to form governments.)

Primary data: data collected for the first time by the researcher for a particular piece of research.

Primary schools (5–11 years): this is the first level of education in the UK. They are generally mixed sex, and usually located close to the child's home. Children tend to be with the same group throughout the day, and one teacher has responsibility for most of their work.

Prime Minister: the head of the government in Britain. He or she is the leader of the majority party in the House of Commons.

Probation: the suspension of a jail sentence. The person who has committed a crime is permitted to live in the community and follow certain conditions set by the court under the supervision of a probation officer.

Proletarianisation: the proposition that many non-manual jobs in a modern economy put their workers in situations very similar to that of the manual factory worker.

Propaganda: the selection and control of information usually for political ends.

Prosecution: conduct of legal proceedings against a defendant for criminal behaviour.

Q

Qualitative data: information in the form of text or images, that is rich in description and detail.

Quantitative data: information that is presented as numbers which can be analysed using statistical methods.

Questionnaire: a set of questions used to gather information.

Quota sample: controls for factors such as age, gender, ethnicity, social class. The researcher then sets about finding people to fit into these slots.

R

Racial discrimination: treating people unfairly because of their ethnicity.

Racism: attitudes to and beliefs about race which usually involve negative stereotypes of another race and lead to discrimination against people of that race (being prejudiced against people because of their race).

Random sample: a group selected from a sampling frame where everyone has an equal chance of being chosen.

Reconstituted family: a new family formed when two adults remarry or cohabit and live together with children from a previous relationship.

Recorded crime: crime that is recorded by the police. Not all reported crime is recorded.

Relative deprivation: felt when people compare their own situation to that of others whom they believe to be unfairly better off.

Relative poverty: a situation in which someone cannot afford to possess the kind of things and participate in the kind of activities considered by members of their society to be a normal part of life.

Reliability: data is reliable if it can be repeated and consistently come up with the same results.

Reported crime: crime that is reported to the police. Not all crime is reported.

Representative: your sample is not biased but the people are typical of those in the larger group.

Reprimand: a formal verbal warning given by a police officer to a young person who admits they are guilty of a minor first offence.

Respondent: someone who is providing the data for your research.

Role: patterns of behaviour expected of people in different situations.

S

Sample: the group of people who have been selected for your study.

Sampling frame: a complete list from which your sample is selected.

Sanction: agreed reward for positive actions or penalty for negative actions.

SATs (Standard Assessment Tests): assessment method used at the end of each key stage of schooling.

Secondary data: data that exists prior to and independent from the researcher's own research.

Secondary schools (11–16 years): most children transfer at the age of 11 to secondary school. Most cater for both sexes. Pupils are taught the National Curriculum subjects, normally by specialist teachers.

Segregated conjugal roles: husband and wife perform different tasks and have a number of separate interests and activities.

Self-fulfilling prophecy: people hear labels about themselves from people who are more powerful than they are. They come to believe the labels are true and then act as if they are true. Therefore, the labels become true.

Self-report surveys: surveys of the population which ask them to confess to crime they have committed but for which they have not been caught.

Serial monogamy: a pattern of divorce and monogamous remarriage.

Setting: a way of dividing pupils into groups for particular subjects based on their ability in those subjects.

Sexism: being prejudiced against people because of their gender.

Slavery: a form of stratification in which a section of the society has no rights. Individuals in this section of society are items of property which can be bought and sold.

Snowball sample: a small group of people that are probably not contained within a sampling frame, for example, single mums. Each person is then asked to pass on the researcher's questions to similar people. The snowball gets bigger as it rolls from one person to another.

Social class: people having the same social status measured by such things as occupation and income.

Social cohesion: 'sticking together'. It describes the integration of a society into a unified whole.

Social construct: patterns of behaviour that are based on society's norms and expectations, for example, masculinity and femininity.

Social control: the process by which people are persuaded to obey the rules and to conform.

Social convention: a generally expected form of social behaviour, for example, politeness and consideration of the needs of others (see Norms and expectations).

Social exclusion: when people are unable, or feel unable, to play a full part in society. This may be owing to lack of material resources, discrimination by others and/or a sense that the rest of society neither wants nor respects them.

Socialisation: the lifelong process of learning the skills, customs, attitudes, norms and values of your culture.

Socialists: wish to create a society based on equality.

Socially constructed: views of what is criminal or deviant behaviour are influenced by the values and norms of the society we live in.

Socially defined behaviour: thought of as natural but is actually the product of cultural expectations.

Social mobility: movement of individuals up or down a social scale.

Social networking site: virtual community that enables members to establish a user profile and communicate and share images and information.

Social policy: important decisions made by the government that aim to improve the conditions of people living in their society.

Social science: the systematic study of society and of human relationships within society.

Social stigma: branding something with negative feelings of shame and disgrace.

Social stratification: the way different groups in society are placed at different levels.

Social survey: a collection of information about members of a population. Can be carried out on the street, at home, in an organisation (school, workplace, etc.), by mail, by telephone, online.

Society: a group of people who have common interests and a distinctive culture.

SPAM: unwanted and unasked for bulk electronic messages accounting for much of the increased volume of e-mail traffic.

Spin: managing the message to influence the way in which events are reported.

Spouse: a marriage partner, husband or wife.

Status: the honour or prestige attached to a person's position in society.

Stereotype: a simple, fixed mental image (usually unfavourable) of a group of people generally based on the behaviour of a few individuals from within that group.

Stereotypical: oversimplified and sometimes exaggerated view.

Stigmatise: to mark a particular social group or individual as different, disapproved of and even dangerous to others.

Strata: bands or layers showing particular characteristics which are different from those above and below.

Stratified sample: mirrors the distribution of particular groups in a larger population.

Streaming: a way of dividing pupils according to their supposed ability. A pupil will normally remain in the same stream across all areas of the curriculum.

Sub-culture: a group with a set of values and ways of behaving which are distinctive from the generally accepted cultural values of society.

Subjective class: the class into which an individual places him or herself.

Substitute hearth: the idea that the television replaced the fireplace as the focus of the living room.

Surveillance: is the monitoring of the behaviour of people and objects within society.

Survey: a research tool, for example, a questionnaire or series of interviews.

Symmetrical family: family where responsibilities and tasks are equally shared between husband and wife.

Systematic sample: a sampling frame in which the researcher chooses, for example, every 10th or 15th person on a list.

T

Tabloid: popular newspapers generally published in a smaller format than the so called 'quality press'.

Technological change: the changing technology of communication, for example, the printing press and television.

Telesales: the selling of goods and services over the telephone.

Theoretical perspective: looking at a social issue through the eyes of one particular type of theorist.

Trade union: an organisation established by employees to protect their economic interests.

Transnational companies: companies, businesses which operate on a global scale, in many countries.

Triangulation: checking the accuracy of data collected through one method (for example, a questionnaire) by comparing it with data collected by using another method (for example, observation).

Tripartite system: three types of secondary school for different types of pupil based on an IQ (Intelligence Quotient) test at the age of 11.

U

UCAS: University and Colleges Admissions Service. The organisation responsible for the allocation and administration of university and college places.

Underclass: the group of people at the very bottom of the social structure who, either by their economic situation or culture, are cut off from the rest of society.

Unstructured interview: a relatively informal conversation where the respondent talks freely but the researcher keeps the conversation heading in the right direction.

V

Validity: data is valid if it gives a true picture of what is being studied.

Values: the beliefs held by a person or a social group that help to build a set of norms.

Victim surveys: surveys of the public which ask them to report any crimes they have experienced, whether or not they have reported them.

Vocational: describes a course or qualification designed to provide more of a 'hands-on' approach to learning. This encourages the application of knowledge and understanding of a subject in a practical way.

W

Wealth: the assets owned by an individual, for example, house, savings, a business.

Welfare scrounger: an individual who makes no contribution to society and exploits the benefits system, claiming as much as it is possible to get away with.

Welfare State: the government taking responsibility for the health and financial wellbeing of the population.

White collar: clerical, routine middle class.

White-collar crime: criminal acts committed by middle-class people in the course of their work.

Working class: the section of society composed of people engaged in manual work.

World information order: the idea that information is now available almost instantly in a global marketplace.

World view: a general view of the way that society works.

Index

A

absolute poverty 190
abuse of power 164, 165
academic freedom 150
achieved status 176
advertising 104, 126
Afro-Caribbeans 113, 136, 175, 198
ageism 182, 183
agency of social change 123
agent of social control 42, 106–7, 130
alienated 124
alienation 166
amplification of deviance 105
anomie 114
anonymity 33
anti-school sub-culture 50
arranged marriage 78
ASBO (Anti-Social Behaviour Order) 108
ascribed status 174, 175
assessing children 44–5
audience 37, 122, 124–5
authority 152

B

barriers to achievement 182–3
beanpole family 73, 90
behaviour 8–9, 20, 136
  anti-social 106–9
benefits 156, 172
bias 32, 128
bigamy 78
blogs 123, 140
breadwinner 54, 55, 70, 74
British Crime Survey (BCS) 14, 29, 99, 100, 116, 164
Brown, Gordon 129

C

Cameron, David 159, 192
canalisation 21

capitalism 13
capitalist society 104
caste 174, 175
CCTV (Closed circuit television) 106, 107
censorship 128
Census 29, 71, 169
cereal packet family 74, 75
charities 158–9
Child Support Agency 158
Children's Plan 61
chivalry thesis 110
chronic 88
citizen 150
civil liberties 151, 170
Civil Partnership Act 72
class alignment 154
class de-alignment 154
class rules 181
class societies 176
classification, socio-economic 17
cohabiting 72, 79
commune 86, 87
community 164, 165
community service 108
competition 49, 157
computers 133, 138
confidentiality 33
conflict 13
conformity 20, 21
conjugal bond 74
consensus 12, 13, 156–7
Conservatives 76, 154, 156, 188
constituency 148, 149
constraints 20, 21
counter-school group 15
crime 96, 97, 99, 100, 109
  and age 112, 117, 118
  and class 113–15
  and ethnicity 113
  explanations of 102–5
  fear of 26–7, 116
  and gender 110–11, 112

and location 111
  measuring 98–101
  statistics 29, 117
criminal offences 14, 96–7, 116, 117
criminal record 108
criminals 88, 102, 103, 118
crisis of masculinity 54, 55
cultural capital 53
culture 8, 9, 131, 132
culture of simulation 124, 125
cumulative effect 134
cycle of deprivation 194

D

dark figure of crime 99, 100
data presentation 14–15
decree absolute 80
deferential 162
democracy 148, 149, 150–2
dependent child 70
deprivation 57, 103, 118, 194
de-schooling 43
detention without charge 150
deviance 96, 120
deviancy amplification 136, 137
dictatorship 150, 151, 152
Diploma 44
direct action 160, 161
disabled people 47, 171, 182, 183, 184
  education 62–3
divorce 78, 80, 81, 93, 94
divorce petition 80
domestic division of labour 82, 83, 92

E

education 19, 23, 59
Education Action Zones (EAZs) 60
Education Acts 44, 58, 59
education boom 195

Education Maintenance
    Allowance (EMA) 60, 64, 65
education policies 58, 60
educational background 168, 169
educational success 54, 55
egalitarian 82, 83
elderly people 26, 85, 158
elections 148, 153
Eleven plus 58, 59
elite 126, 168, 169
embourgeoisement 188
empty nest family 73
empty shell marriage 80
environmental poverty 190, 191
equal opportunities 53, 184
ethical considerations 33
ethnic minority 136, 182
ethnicity 16, 56–7, 123
ethnocentric curriculum 56, 57
ethnography 37
exam tips 199
Excellence in Cities (EIC) 60
expectations 134, 135
experiments 64
exploitation 13, 189
extended family 70, 71
extremists 65, 149

F

faith schools 65, 66
family 19, 21, 70–2, 73, 74–5,
    77, 90
    alternatives to 72, 86
    breakdown 80
    diversity 70
    reconstituted 76, 81
    symmetrical 82, 83
fathers, types of 83
fear of crime 26–7, 116
female infanticide 78, 79
feminist 13
films 130, 131, 142, 181
financial dependency 90
"first past the post" system 148,
    149
formal curriculum 22, 48

formal education 42
free market society 178
freedom of speech 128
functionalism 104
functionalists 12, 42, 43, 74

G

gang culture 189
gatekeeper 33, 108, 128
GCSE (General Certificate in
    Secondary Education) 44
gender 16, 21, 135, 182
gender discrimination 49, 162,
    184
generation 70
generalisations 30
geographical proximity 90
glass ceiling 173, 184
Glitter, Gary 137
global capitalism 172–3
global culture 131
globalisation 162, 163
glossary 200–7
government 148
grid technologies 139
grounds for divorce 80

H

hidden curriculum 22, 48, 55
home background 53, 55, 57
household 70
housework 83, 84
hyperreality 124

I

identity theft 114, 115
image 128, 140, 155, 170
income 19, 186
indictable offences 14, 116, 117
industrial disputes 143
inequality 18, 176, 179
infant mortality rates 18
informal education 42
information overload 140
informed consent 33
injustice 112, 113

inner cities 111, 118, 136
institutional racism 112, 183,
    184
integrated conjugal roles 82, 83
interest groups 159
intergenerational 90
Internet 122, 123, 125, 138, 141
interviews 28, 34, 39, 64

J

jobs in Sociology 11
Joseph Rowntree Foundation 10,
    62, 190
journalism 10, 125
judiciary 23, 108
junk mail 140

K

kerboodle 5
kibbutz 86, 87
knives 136

L

labelling 50, 51, 104
Labour Party 76, 160, 188
ladettes 110, 111
lads' magazine 134
language 57, 194
law 8, 97, 164, 184
league tables 44, 59, 62
legislature 23
liberal democratic values 136
life chances 178, 180
life expectancy 84, 85
lifestyle 180
Lister, Ruth 89
lone parents 72, 73, 94
longitudinal studies 84

M

mainframe computer 138
malestream 162
market forces 187
marketisation of education 58,
    59
marriage 78, 80

Marxist   13, 66, 104, 126, 172–3
mass communication   122
mass culture   132
matrifocal   71
Meaningful Differences   194
means tested   158
media   22, 26, 27, 105, 145
media amplification   27
media imperialism   131
media stereotypes   134–7
mega-wealthy   186
Member of Parliament (MP)   148, 149, 168
meritocracy   42, 43
middle class   114, 180, 181
Middles   133
Miners' Strike   169
mixed ability   50
Mobley, Tony   102
modernity   143
monarchy   149, 150
Monbiot, George   126
monogamy   78
moral panic   27, 120, 137
Morecambe Bay   174
Murray, Charles   89, 91
Muslims   136, 183

N

nation state   162, 163
National Census   29, 71, 169
National Curriculum   44
National Health Service   156
nature/nurture debate   102
neo-conventional families   76
neo-liberalism   126, 156, 172
nepotism   177
New Labour   154
new media   138, 139
new social movement   162
new vocationalism   58, 59
news value   136, 137
non-indictable offences   116
norm   8, 120, 134, 135
nuclear family   70, 71, 72, 74–5, 77

O

observations   28, 34, 35, 36, 39, 64
Ofcom   132
offences   14, 116, 117
official crime statistics   98
official statistics   29, 98
Ofsted (Office for Standards in Education)   44, 59, 60
"Old" Labour   156, 157
old media   138, 139
Opposition   148, 149

P

parliamentary democracy   148
patriarchal   80
patriarchy   13, 164
peer group pressure   22, 104
pilot study   32
pluralism   126
police   23, 99, 108
political agendas   170
political parties   148, 149
political socialisation   152
polyandry   78, 79
polygamy   78
polygyny   78
poverty   24, 190, 191, 193, 197
   children in   24, 25, 196
poverty trap   192
power   164–5, 166, 167, 168
premenstrual tension (PMT)   103
pressure group   24, 152, 163, 171
primary data   28, 29, 62, 64
primary schools   46
Prime Minister   148, 149
prison   23, 112, 113
privacy   164
probation   23, 108
professionals   17, 173
proletarianism   188
propaganda   128
prosecution   108

Q

qualitative data   14, 34–5, 65
quantitative data   14, 28, 29, 40, 65
questionnaires   28, 29, 32, 34, 40, 64

R

racial discrimination   184, 185
racism   57, 174, 182, 183, 185
recession   150
reconstituted families   72, 76, 81
recorded crime   99
red tape   169, 184
relative deprivation   104, 190, 191
relative poverty   24, 190
reliability   32
reported crime   98, 99
representative   30
reprimand   108
research   34–5, 40
respondent   30
revision advice   198
robbery, armed   102
role   8
role models   55, 134, 176
roles in families   82–5

S

samples   30, 31
sampling frame   30
sanction   23
SATS (Standard Assessment Tests)   44, 45, 54, 59
scapegoats   120
school   22, 46, 47, 48
school gangs   167
secondary data   29, 62
secondary schools   46
segregated conjugal roles   82, 83
self-fulfilling prophecy   50, 53, 57, 104, 152
self-report surveys   98, 101, 118
serial monogamy   78

setting 50, 51, **58**, **59**
sexism 176, **182**, 183
slavery 174–5
smoking and class 178
social class 13, 16, 18, 50, 52, 123
social cohesion 42
social construct 134, 135
social control 20, 21, 23, 42, 49, 106–7
social convention 136
social exclusion 190
social mobility 42, 43, **176**, 195
social networking site 124, 125
social policy 10
social science 10
social services 156
social stigma 80
social stratification 16, 176, 194–5
social survey 14, 28, **29**
socialisation 12, **20**, **21**, 55, 110, 131
secondary 22, 42, 130, 146
socialists 156
socially constructed 102
socially defined behaviour 96, 99
society 8
socio-economic classification 17
sociologists 15, 25, 48
SPAM 140
spider diagrams 199
spin 125, **128**, **129**
spouse 78
statistics 62, 98, 170
status 16, 74

step family 72
stereotype 130, 131, 174
of women 134–5
stereotypical 75, 76
stigmatise 136
stop and search 113, 170
strata 16
streaming 50, 51, **58**, **59**
striking print workers 127
sub-culture 15, 104, 154, 181, 189
subjective class 180
substitute hearth 132
surveillance 106, 107, 140
surveillance society 170
survey 14, **28**, **29**, 123
British Crime (BCS) 14, 29, 99, 100, 116, 164
General Household 72, 73, 86
Northern Ireland Crime (NICS) 100–1
symmetrical family **82**, 83

T
tabloid **126**, 127
technological change 122, 123, 124, 140
telesales 140
television 132
terrorism 150, 151
Thatcher, Margaret 140, 156
theoretical perspective 12
tolerance 149
Toynbee, Polly 129, 183, 194, 195
trade union 162, 180, 181
transnational companies 162, 163

triangulation 33, 37
tripartite system 58

U
UCAS 54
underclass 88–9, **188**, **189**
unemployment 120, 150

V
validity (data) 32, 99
values 8, 9
victim surveys 98, 100, 101
vocational 46
voluntary organisations 158–9
voting 154–5

W
wages 13
wealth 186, 187
websites 5, 10, 77, 87, 99, 199
welfare scrounger 192
Welfare State 24, 156, 157
white collar 195
white collar crime 114–15
Willis, Paul 15, 37, 64
women, working 84, 92, 173, 184–5
women's movement 162
women's roles 80, 111
work 19, 22, 184–5
working class 180, 181
world information order 131
world view 126

Y
Youth Justice Board (YJB) 108, 112

Photo Acknowledgements

Copyright for 1.1A is shared by Nelson Thornes Ltd and Rupert Besley; **Advertising Archives:** 5.4B; **Alamy:** Tim Graham / 1.3F(3); Bubbles Photolibrary / 1.4B(1); Adams Picture Library / 1.4B(2); thislife pictures / 1.4B(3); Janine Wiedel / 2.3C; PCL / 3.1A; JUPITERIMAGES / 3.1B; Tetra Images / 3.2A(3); Image Source Pink / 3.4B; Bubbles Photolibrary / 3.4C; EPF / 3.6A; David J Green / 3.6B; D Hurst / 3.6C; ACE STOCK LIMITED / 3.6D; Phil Wills / 4.1B; Howard Barlow / 4.5D; fStop / 4.5E; ClassicStock / 5.3B; Old Visuals / 5.5A; Photofusion Picture Library / 7.4C; Janine Wiedel Photolibrary / 7.5B; Alex Segre / 7.5C(1); CountrySideCollection - Homer Sykes / 7.5C(2); **Cartoonstock.com:** 1.6A; Jerry King / 2.5B; **Corbis:** Heidi Benser/zefa / 3.4A; Jean Pierre Amet/BelOmbra / 5.2A; Reuters / 6.3A; Andy Rain/epa / 6.4A; **Fotolia:** 1.3G; 4.3A; 5.1A(3); 7.7B; Chapter banner

5; **Getty Images:** William F Campbell / 1.2B; Carl de Souza / 1.3F(1); Jeff J Mitchell / 1.3F(2); Robert Warren / 1.5A; Peter Dazeley / 1.5B; Kain Zernitsky / 3.3E; MENAHEM KAHANA/AFP / 3.5E; Christopher Furlong / 4.2B; Paula Bronstein / 5.3A; Scott Barbour / 6.6C; Andrew Winning / 6.7A; Christopher Furlong / 7.1A; Anwar Hussein / 7.1B; Keystone / 7.2B; John Waterman / 7.2C; P Broze / 7.3A; Steve Eason / 7.4A; **iStockphoto:** 1.1B; 1.6B; 4.3B; 4.4B; 5.1A(1); 5.1A(2); 5.1A(4); 5.2B; 5.6A; Chapter banners 1, 2, 3, 4; **Mary Nicholson (from The Australian):** Nicholsoncartoons.com.au: 2.4A; 2.5A; **PA Photos:** 1.4A; 5.2C; 5.5B; 6.1B; 6.1C; 6.1D; 6.2B; 6.3B; 6.4B; 6.5A; **Peter Dazeley:** 5.4C; **Rex Features:** 4.5B; **Rube Goldberg, Inc.:** 1.2A; **Simon Veit-Wilson:** 3.3F; **Terry Gilpin:** 3.2A(1); 3.2A(2); 3.3C

Text Acknowledgements

Crown Copyright materials reproduced with permission of the controller of the HMSO © Crown Copyright

1.1: Berger, P Invitation to Sociology; extract adapted from 'Sociology: The study of human societies and how they interact' staff, The Guardian, 1 May, 2008. Copyright © Guardian News & Media Ltd, 2008. Used with permission; 1.5: Oxfam quote, 2008, from http://www.oxfam.org.uk/resources/ukpoverty is reproduced with permission of Oxfam GB, Oxfam House, John Smith Drive, Cowley, Oxford OX4 2JY UK www.oxfam.org.uk, Oxfam GB does not necessarily endorse any text or activities that accompany the materials; 1.7: Foster, J Villains: crime and community in the inner city, Routledge (1990) Reprinted with permission of Taylor & Francis Books UK; 1.8: extracts adapted from 'Preschool learning boosts maths results' by James Randerson, The Guardian, 29 August, 2008. Copyright © Guardian News & Media Ltd, 2008. Used with permission; 2.2: SATs scores 'too generous for 1 in 3 pupils' The Times, August 5, 2008. copyright © NI Syndications 2005. Reprinted with permission; 2.3: extract adapted from 'Barriers to girls in 'male' jobs must go, says report', by Lucy Ward, The Guardian, 6 May, 2004. Copyright © Guardian News & Media Ltd 2004. Used with permission; 2.4: extract adapted from 'The mirage of meritocracy has sold our children short' by Jenni Russell, The Guardian, 5 June, 2008. Copyright © Guardian News & Media Ltd, 2008. Used with permission; extracts adapted from 'Young, gifted black' by Judith Judd, The Independent, 11 March, 1999. Reprinted with permission; 2.5: short extract from IDENTITY AND DIVERSITY: GENDER AND THE EXPERIENCE OF EDUCATION edited by Maud Blair, Janet Holland and Sue Sheldon, Multilingual Matters, 1995. Reprinted with permission; 2.6: extract from the Findings The education and employment of disabled young people published in 2005 by the Joseph Rowntree Foundation. Reproduced by permission of the Joseph Rowntree Foundation.; extract adapted from Hope, T, (2005) 'Building Success in Post-Compulsory Education: The Effectiveness of the Education Maintenance Allowance (EMA)' Social Science Teacher, Vol. 34. No 3, pp 6-9. Reprinted with kind permission of the author; 3.2: David Cameron MP, 11 July 2007.Reprinted with permission; 3.4: extracts from Norwich Union Media Centre 2002. Reprinted with permission; 3.5: short extract about Kibbutz life from The Jewish Virtual Library. Reprinted with permission; 3.6: Extract from UNDERCLASS +10, Charles Murray and the British Underclass 1990-2000, by Charles Murray, CIVITAS. Reprinted with permission of CIVITAS: Institute for the Study of Civil Society www.civitas.org.uk; Extract from CHARLES MURRAY AND THE UNDERCLASS: The Developing Debate, by Ruth Lister, CIVITAS. Reprinted with permission of CIVITAS: Institute for the Study of Civil Society www.civitas.org.uk; Extract adapted from 'Family Fortunes: The conventional nuclear family ..' by Madeleine Bunting, The Guardian, 25 September, 2004 Copyright © Guardian News and Media Ltd 2004. Used with permission; 3.7: graph adapted from 102 pg 239 'Introduction to Sociology 3rd edition' by Ken Browne, published by Polity Press. Reprinted with permission; Extract adapted from 'Divorce rate at its lowest for 26 years' by David Batty, The Guardian, 29 August, 2008. Copyright © Guardian News & Media Ltd, 2008. Used with permission; 4.5: Youth prison system in 'meltdown' by Elsa McLaren, from The Times, October 24 2006. Copyright © NI Syndications 2006. Reprinted with permission; Identity theft hits 135,000 a year' from The Times, October, 18, 2005. Copyright © NI Syndication 2005. Reprinted with permission; 4.6: extract adapted from 'Findings, Understanding and preventing youth crime' published in 1996 by the Joseph Rowntree Foundation. Reproduced with permission of the Joseph Rowntree Foundation; 4.7: table adapted from 'You don't know the half of it' Guardian Weekend, 24 February 2007. Table belongs to ICM Research. 5.1: extracts adapted from 'The survival of the book speaks volumes' staff, The Observer, 25 May, 2008. Copyright © Guardian News & Media Ltd 2008. Used with permission; 5.4: extracts adapted from 'Gary Glitter has served his time. So is it right that he can now be subjected to any degree of persecution?' by Alexander Chancellor, The Guardian, 22 August, 2008. Copyright © Guardian News & Media Ltd 2008. Used with permission; 5.5: extracts adapted from 'Coming soon: superfast internet' by Jonathan Leake, Science Editor, The Times, April 6, 2008. © Times Newspapers NI Syndications 2008. Reprinted with permission; 5.6: extracts from TELEVISION ETHNICITY AND CULTURAL CHANGE by Marie Gillespie, Routledge 1995. Reprinted with permission of Taylor & Francis Books UK;

6.1: extracts adapted from 'This is not the way I should be treated in a country I love' by Polly Curtis and Anthea Lipsett, The Guardian, 31 May, 2008. Copyright © Guardian News & Media Ltd 2008. Used with permission; 6.2: figures from MORI Observer, 2005. Reprinted with permission; 6.3: speech by David Cameron MP, 3 June 2008. Reprinted with permission; 6.4: extract from THE LABOUR GOVERNMENT1964-1970: A PERSONAL RECORD by Harold Wilson (Michael Joseph 1971) Copyright © 1971 by Harold Wilson. Reprinted with permission of Penguin Books UK and David Higham Associates ltd; extracts adapted from 'Pressure vessel: Stop Climate Chaos may have only seven staff members...'by John Vidal, The Guardian, 26 September, 2007. Copyright © Guardian News & Media Ltd 2007. Used with permission; 6.5: extracts adapted from 'Murder rate falls for fifth successive year, but concern over 'hidden' family' by Alan Travis, The Guardian, 1 February, 2008. Copyright © Guardian News & Media Ltd 2008. Used with permission; short extract and table from NEIGHBOURS FROM HELL by Frank Field, Methuen 2003. Reprinted with permission; extracts adapted from 'Schools told to take action on growing menace of gangs' by Polly Curtis, The Guardian, 22 May 2008. Copyright © Guardian News & Media Ltd 2008. Used with permission; 6.6: table adapted from pg 7 'Democracy in Britain' by Matt Cole, published by Edinburgh University Press. Reprinted with permission; 7.1: Short extract adapted from the Anti-Slavery website. www.antislavery.org. Reprinted with permission; short extract from 'Dalit Solidarity Network Report, July 2006. Reprinted with permission; 7.2: extracts adapted from 'The truth is some smokers are more equal than others' by Libby Brooks, The Guardian, 1 July, 2008. Copyright © Guardian News & Media Ltd 2008. Used with permission; extracts adapted from 'Class rules: As today's Guardian poll shows, Britain is still deeply divided by social status' by Decca Aitkenhead, The Guardian, 20 October, 2007. Copyright © Guardian News & Media Ltd 2007. Used with permission; 7.3: extracts adapted from 'Girlification is destroying the hope we felt in 1968' by Penny Toynbee, The Guardian, 15 April, 2008. Copyright © Guardian News & Media Ltd 2008. Used with permission; extracts adapted from 'Minister is dragged into police race row' by Mark Townsend, The Observer, 29 June, 2008. Copyright © Guardian News & Media Ltd, 2008. Used with permission; extract adapted from 'The baby blues: Study finds a third of mothers slip down career ladder' by Lucy Ward, The Guardian, 27 February, 2008. Copyright © Guardian News & Media Ltd 2008. Used with permission; table c, working women split between full-time and part-time employment, from ECONOMIC JOURNAL NES LFS. Reprinted with permission; short extract adapted from 'Poor boys are white victims too' by Trevor Phillips, The Guardian, 27th April 2008. Copyright © Trevor Phillips. Reprinted with permission of the author; 7.4: extracts from 'The tax-free lifestyle of Britain's new mega-wealthy is impoverishing us all' by Stewart Lansley, The Guardian, 1 April, 2006. © Stewart Lansley, 2006. Reprinted with kind permission of the author; short extract from 'Britain: Where gangs are the only family' by Iain Duncan Smith, Daily Mail Online, August 2007. Reprinted with permission of Solo Syndication Ltd; 7.5: from 'A minimum income standard for Britain: What people think' by Jonathan Bradshaw et al, published in 2008 by the Joseph Rowntree Foundation. Reproduced by permission of the Joseph Rowntree Foundation; extracts adapted from 'David Cameron tells the fat and the poor: take responsibility' The Times, July 8 2008 © The Times Newspapers , NI Syndication 2008. Reprinted with permission; Extracts adapted from 'Poverty in the UK: Case Study: The single mother 'It feels like I am not giving my children what I had' by Audrey Gillan, The Guardian, 11 June, 2008 Copyright © Guardian News & Media Ltd, 2008. Used with permission; 7.6: extracts adapted from 'We can break the vice of the great unmentionable' by Polly Toynbee, the Guardian, 2 January 2004. Copyright © Guardian News & Media Ltd 2004. Used with permission; extracts adapted from 'The education boom has proved a curse for the poor' by Polly Toynbee, The Guardian, 5 July, 2008. Copyright © Guardian News & Media Ltd, 2008. Used with permission; 7.7: extract adapted from Education: Case Study: The teachers just ignored him until he failed' by Staff, The Guardian, 5 September, 2008. Copyright © Guardian News & Media Ltd. 2008. Used with permission

The publishers have made every effort to contact copyright holders but apologise if any have been overlooked.